Quicksands...

Adolph Streckfuss

QUICKSANDS

FROM THE GERMAN OF
ADOLPH STRECKFUSS

BY
MRS. A. L. WISTER

TRANSLATOR OF "THE OLD MAMSELLE'S SECRET," "GOLD ELSIE," "ONLY
A GIRL," "A NOBLE NAME," "THE SECOND WIFE,"
"BANNED AND BLESSED," ETC.

PHILADELPHIA:
J. B. LIPPINCOTT COMPANY.
1897.

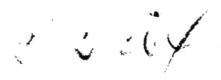

Copyright, 1884, by J. B. Lippincott & Co.

CONTENTS.

QUICKSANDS.

CHAPTER I.

AN EXCHANGE.

UPON the short, thick grass of a small, secluded opening in a magnificent forest of firs and beeches a young man lay, his hands clasped under his head, buried in waking dreams. He had chosen himself a charming retreat, where he was safe from all intrusion from wayfarers passing through the forest by any of the roads or paths that intersected it at a sufficient distance from this spot. The soft, grassy sod was a delightful couch, and the interlacing boughs of a huge beech-tree formed above the head of the dreamer a canopy that entirely protected him from the burning rays of the mid-day sun.

Profound quiet reigned in the forest, intensified, rather than disturbed, by the humming of insects; the very birds which had twittered and sung in the early morning seemed silenced by the heat; all creatures sought repose and refreshment at high noon on this glowing July day.

If the young fellow who lay thus luxuriously bedded were seeking mental as well as bodily repose, it was evident that he had not found it. He was not asleep; his dark eyes were wide open, gazing restlessly and discontentedly into the spaces of sky among the beech boughs until pained by their brilliancy. "How tiresome! how unutterably stupid!" he muttered, altering his comfortable position so as to rest his head upon his hand as he leaned upon his elbow. "That deadly-tiresome, monotonous stretch of brilliant blue sky is the very image of my own weary existence. Nothing but light and splendour; it is intolerable. If the sky were only covered with clouds,—if there could be a flash here and there of lightning, with thunder crashing and winds howling, one might have some satisfaction in sending a bullet through one's brains with the thunder for a dirge. But no, even that is not to be. I am to die as I have lived, surrounded by weary, soul-destroying sunshine. Ah, well, it is a fitting end to an insignificant and utterly useless life. Come, little friend, it is high time we were done with it."

He took from his breast-pocket a small, richly-inlaid revolver, and looked at it with a degree of affection. " You have helped me through many a long, weary hour. This moment would have come for me long ago but for you and my piano. It certainly was interesting to learn to shoot one spot after another out of the six of hearts. It was irritating not to succeed in hitting each with the same precision. A useless and silly enough aim in life, to be sure; still it was an aim, and now that it is attained it is just as tiresome as everything else. To-day you are to find my heart as surely as the hearts on the card. Or suppose we try the head; it would be easier; an involuntary quiver of a muscle, and the ball might miss the heart, but if this barrel lightly touch the temple the effect must be sure. Three or four balls in the brain must produce death instantaneously. It is the better plan."

He examined the revolver and made sure that it was loaded; his hand did not tremble, his look was clear and steadfast; there was even a smile of satisfaction on his lips as he contemplated the little weapon. "You will do your duty as you have always done it. You never were to blame if every spot on the card was not exactly hit, although the clumsy marksman would gladly have declared the fault yours. As soon as hand and aim were true, each heart was pierced precisely in the centre."

. He raised the pistol, and once more took in at a glance the scene around him, while his thoughts ran on: "Really, a lovely spot for my last act! Beneath these spreading boughs the body will lie comfortably on the soft grass,—for how long before it is found? For days, perhaps for weeks, the place is so secluded. I should like to know what they will say in Berlin when the newspapers announce, 'At last the body has been discovered of Egon von Ernau, who disappeared so many days or weeks ago,' etc., and there will, of course, follow a long description of the place where it was found, and of the condition and clothes of the corpse. The more there is to tell, the better for some poor devil of a reporter. I do not grudge it him. I can at least serve one man in the world by my death. And the news will fly like wildfire. It would be almost worth living for,—the hearing of all that heartless gossip. How busy all those empty heads will be with wondering what could have driven a fellow so favoured by fortune to suicide! 'An unfortunate love-affair,' the sentimentally disposed will declare. 'His father wished to force him into a marriage with a person of high rank, and in his despair he took his own life.' Of course they must invent some reason for a man's escaping from this wretched, wearisome existence. Fools! If life were worth living, why should I not comply with my respected parent's wishes? All women are alike. It is all the same tiresome sham."

He still held the revolver in his raised hand, when suddenly the hand sank by his side, and he sat up and listened.

A clear note broke upon the woodland quiet,—the sound of a man's tenor voice singing the hymn 'Rock of Ages' at no great distance from where Egon von Ernau lay.

He frowned angrily. "Confoundedly annoying!" he muttered. "If I shoot now, that stupid psalm-singer will hear it,—and then? Then all the delightful Berlin gossip will be spoiled, the body will be found immediately, and everything will be known to-morrow. No, no, those good people must puzzle their brains for a while to discover what has become of me. My Herr Papa must have some chance to show the world what a tender, anxious parent he is. We must choose a still more retired spot. But first let us see where the psalm-singer really is. He seems to have established himself in the forest here, for the sound continues to come from the same direction and from somewhere not very far off."

He uncocked his revolver, put the little weapon again into the breast-pocket of a very well made summer coat, and, rising to his feet, walked slowly through the wood in the direction whence came the sound of singing.

It was no easy task to make his way through the thick underbrush, particularly as he took great pains to make no noise. He wished to see the singer without being seen himself, and therefore he walked very slowly, and it was some minutes before he attained his purpose.

Still following the sound, he had reached the edge of the forest, and only a thick fringe of hazel-bushes obstructed his view beyond. Cautiously parting these he saw before him a landscape of extraordinary beauty. Beyond the velvet sward of a small meadow the land sloped down some eight or ten feet to a charming little lake, on the opposite shore of which green, smiling fields stretched far away to the mountain-slopes of the distant highlands.

The young man gave but a fleeting glance to this lovely picture; he was far more interested in the singer, whom he now saw at no great distance.

On the brink of the lake the psalm-singer was kneeling, his head held stiffly erect, his bony hands clasped and extended to the skies, while, quite unaware of his listener, he continued his hymn in loud, resonant tones. He was a young man hardly older than twenty-six, although the sallow, flabby features of his beardless face, showing no trace of youthful freshness, might well have caused him to be thought older than he really was. His face was turned to the heavens, and he was staring into the deep, cloudless blue with prominent, lacklustre eyes. The large, thick-lipped mouth was wide open as he shouted out the last verse of his hymn.

He certainly was not handsome, and he was made far more repulsive in appearance than he might have been by the ill-fitting, unsuitable black clothes that he wore. An old-fashioned dress-coat, the long pointed swallow-tail of which lay like a train behind him on the grass, hung in disorderly fashion about his bony frame; black, wrinkled trousers, a black waistcoat sufficiently open to display linen of doubtful cleanliness, a high, rusty, black silk cravat, from which projected the huge points of his shirt-collar on each side of his beardless chin, formed this extraordinary being's attire, which was, moreover, completed by a very tall and very shabby stove-pipe hat.

The hymn came to an end, but the singer did not change his attitude; he still held up his clasped hands to the skies. For a few moments he was silent; then, in a loud voice, he uttered an extemporaneous prayer.

"God of heaven," he cried, "a repentant wretch casts himself upon Thy mercy! Pardon my betrayal of my trust, my having again yielded to temptation. Pardon what I have done and what I am about to do. Receive me into Thy kingdom. Amen!"

With these words he suddenly sprang up; his clumsy black hat fell off upon the grass as he did so, but he paid it no attention. Clasping his hands above his head, he leaned forward, gazed for an instant into the deep green water of the lake, exclaimed, "God forgive me!" and plunged in head-foremost.

Thus far the listener had watched without stirring a limb or giving the slightest sign of his presence; but at this sudden termination of the prayer he broke through the thick underbrush, and in a moment had reached the spot whence the singer had taken the fatal plunge. Here he threw off his coat and hat, keenly scanning the while the lake where the man had disappeared, and where the water was still troubled and sending forth huge rippling circles, while a dark body was visible beneath the surface.

The young man looked about him for some piece of shelving shore where a swimmer could easily clamber upon land; scarcely ten steps to the left he saw what he desired, and in another moment the ripples of the lake broke over his head also.

He was an expert swimmer; when but a mere lad he had saved the life of a drowning comrade at the risk of his own, so tightly had the sinking boy clasped him in his despairing grasp. He remembered this as he now rose to the surface, and seeing a dark form directly before him he merely gave it a powerful push in the direction of the shelving shore, taking good care to avoid the grasp of the wildly struggling man. Keeping clear of this, he contrived to push him before him as he swam to the landing-place. As soon as he felt the ground beneath him, however, he seized the half-suffocated singer by the arm and dragged him ashore. The rescue had been easy, and had occupied but a very few moments of time.

For a while the rescued man lay gasping on the bank; then he started up and gazed wildly at his preserver, who stood quietly looking at him. The unfortunate man presented a still odder and uglier appearance than before; his long black hair hung in dripping locks over his pale face, and his wrinkled coat clinging to his spare figure was more ridiculous than ever.

"Why did you not let me die?" he cried, wringing his hands.

The young man half smiled. "You are right," he replied; "it was very stupid of me. It always is so when I act upon the impulse of the moment. Had I taken time to consider I should have said to myself, 'This gentleman is tired of life and voluntarily puts an end to it; you have no right to interfere with so reasonable a proceeding.' I should then have seated myself up there on the bank, and have looked on as you came two or three times to the surface gasping for breath.

2

sinking to rise again, and hastening your death, perhaps, by the frantic efforts you made to retain a detested existence.   Finally, you would have sunk to rise
no more, and at this moment you would be lying quiet
and comfortable, with only a slight quiver of the limbs,
at the bottom of the lake.   My impetuosity has deprived me of an interesting spectacle and prevented
your fulfilment of a sensible and laudable intention.   I
pray your pardon, and would suggest that you can
repair the wrong I have done.   We are but a few steps
away from the high bank whence you took your plunge
into the lake.   The spot was admirably selected, for
the water here is too shallow for your purpose.   I
promise you that you shall not be disturbed again; I
will look on with the greatest interest."

The young man's quiet words filled his hearer with
horror; his arms dropped by his sides, and his prominent
eyes opened wider and protruded still farther from his
head.   He shuddered at the description of his death-
agony; he looked in fear at his preserver, who could
talk so calmly of such horrors, and when the latter proposed that he should try another plunge into the lake
he was seized with a nameless dread.   Involuntarily he
recoiled a step, and with a gesture of abhorrence cried,
"No, no, I cannot!   It was too horrible!   When the
dark water closed over me, and I sank deeper and
deeper, the suffocation, the dreadful noises in my ears,
the throbbing in my temples—no, I cannot do it again!"

"Indeed?   True, death by drowning cannot be agreeable; I have heard so before from one of my acquaintances who very nearly lost his life in the water.   The
death-struggle is too long; it must be most unpleasant.
Now, a bullet through the head is instantaneous.   I
will make you another suggestion; I owe it to you

since I have interfered with your plans in so uncalled-for a manner. My coat lies on the bank yonder; in its breast-pocket there is a six-barrelled revolver. I was just putting it to my temple when I was arrested by your song. I only need two or three balls for my purpose. Come up on the bank with me, wait until my work is done, and my revolver is at your service. How people will wonder when the two bodies are found after a while lying peacefully side by side! What odd stories will be told of a duel without witnesses, or some such stupid nonsense! It is a pity one cannot be by to hear them. Come, we will soon make an end of the tiresome affair."

"I cannot! I cannot do it a second time! Good God! I can neither live nor die! Help me, I implore you! Shoot me down with your revolver; I cannot do it myself! Kill me! I will bless you with my dying breath!"

He flung himself upon his knees, wringing his hands, as he implored his preserver to kill him, but the young man shook his head decidedly, as he replied, "Very sorry, but the part of an executioner does not suit me; one must conclude such matters one's self, or let them alone. If you will not comply with my suggestion, there is nothing for you but to go on living. I wish you joy of it."

"Good God! what shall I do? I implore you to help me, to advise me!"

"How can I possibly advise you, when I have no knowledge of you or of the circumstances that have driven you to despair?"

"I will tell you about it. I am the most miserable man in the world! You have saved my life, and I will confide my wretchedness, my disgrace, to you."

The young man looked down thoughtfully for a moment before he said, " Very well, tell me. An hour more or less makes no difference. Let us sit down in the shade on the grass; you shall pour out your woes to me, and if I can give you help or counsel, I will do so."

" Will not the shade be rather too cool for us in our wet clothes? We might catch cold."

The young fellow laughed aloud at this strange mixture of despair and dread of taking cold.

" Well, then, sit in the sun," he said, still laughing. "I prefer the shade, since a cold is of no consequence to me. And now, since we find ourselves comrades after this odd fashion, here at our ease, you can initiate me in the dark mysteries of your life. I promise you an attentive listener."

He had thrown himself down beneath a huge beech-tree, while his companion was looking for a seat on some stone in the blazing sunshine.

" My wet clothes will soon dry here," said the singer. " When they are dried on the body they do not lose their shape." And as he spoke he looked down sadly at the long wet tails of his coat as they draggled dripping behind him. There was no trace to be seen in him of the contrition and despair which had possessed him a few moments since, his whole mind was given to the choosing of a spot in the sunshine. At last he found a fragment of rock which suited him, he sat down upon it, and leaning forward propped his elbows upon his knees and his chin upon his hands. In this attitude he looked, as his companion could not but inwardly observe, like a strange caricature of incredible ugliness. He paused a while to reflect, and then began, in a whining, lachrymose tone,—

"I have always been a child of misfortune. The Lord has punished me with the greatest severity for my sins, although I have tried to lead a pious, resigned life, however heavily His hand might be laid upon me. Wherefore, O Lord, shouldst Thou thus visit Thy most devoted servant——"

He could not go on, for his listener had stopped his ears, and exclaimed angrily, "Stop, stop! nothing in the world is quite so detestable and tiresome as circumlocution. If I am to listen, you must be brief, simple, and unaffected. Let us have no whining sentimentality. I hate it! Give me a clear, simple statement of facts."

"Out of the fulness of the heart the mouth speaketh," was the reply to this blunt interruption of the man's flow of eloquence. "I will command my emotion, if I can, out of regard for you, my preserver. I have always been unlucky; my very name was a misfortune,—not my first name, Gottlieb, which I received in holy baptism, but my surname, Pigglewitch. I always see a smile of derision upon the lips of those who hear it for the first time, when a boy I was always laughed at for my name, and this trial has never left me. But I will not murmur; it is the Lord's will that I inherit such a title, and His ways are always right. How can we, weak mortals that we are——"

"Hold, friend Pigglewitch! You are forgetting again. No preaching!"

"I have done," Gottlieb Pigglewitch replied, instantly subsiding into an ordinary narrative style. "My father was pastor of Wilhelmshagen. I scarcely remember him, he died when I was not quite six years old; my mother had died at my birth, and her brother now took me home, or rather kept me in my home, for he succeeded to my father's position. He said he befriended the orphan for the love of God, but he never showed me any affection, even as a little child I had to work hard for my daily food, he employed me to tend first his geese and afterwards his sheep. I was sent with the other village children to the village school, but as soon as I came home I had to work for my uncle, and the dread of a beating often made me perform tasks that were far beyond my strength. I was given many a blow, with very little to eat, and never a kind word; my uncle declared that I was a good-for-nothing, lazy young hypocrite and liar, who could not be treated too severely, I was fit for nothing but a stupid tiller of the ground. As such he meant to bring me up, but Herr Brandes, the Schulze of Wilhelmshagen, befriended me. He had been a friend of my father's, and would have taken me into his house and brought me up with his daughter Annemarie, who is two years younger than I, only he did not wish to interfere with my uncle.

"Nevertheless he stood my friend, and often when I was very hungry I got a good meal at his house; little Annemarie, too, would sometimes bring a piece of bread out to me in the fields and stay a while and play with me. Those were the only happy hours I can remember as a child. It was a time of sore trial, and I, unworthy sinful man——"

"Friend Pigglewitch!"

"Ah, to be sure! Well, the Schulze befriended me. 'After all, he is a pastor's son,' he said to my uncle, 'and every one is saying that he is being brought up like the son of a day-labourer.' My father had left me a small patrimony amounting to about a thousand thalers, and Herr Brandes told my uncle that he ought to demand a portion of this from the Guardians' Court, to be spent in sending me to town to school, where I might be suitably educated. At first my uncle refused to do this, he found me too useful on the farm, but he yielded at last to the Schulze's representations, seeing clearly that he should lose credit by refusing any longer to do so. So I was sent to town to board with one of the teachers of the public school. I nearly starved there, and I often wished myself back in Wilhelms-hagen, where I could always get something to eat at the Schulze's, for Annemarie was sure to put by a morsel for me. From the public school I went to college, and I have passed my examination as a Candidate for the ministry. The Lord was gracious to me. My mind moves slowly, and when I went up for examination I was conscious of ignorance with regard to various branches of secular knowledge. I was afraid of being plucked, but the Herr Director encouraged me. He told me to trust in the Lord, who would not forsake the most faithful of His servants. So I went up for ex-amination, and passed, although all my fellow-students predicted my failure. Immediately afterwards, through the influence of the Herr Director, I obtained a position as private teacher in Wilhelmshagen. I was delighted to receive my first employment in my old home. My uncle had left the place for a better parish in Wenners-dorf, in Silesia, and I was quite free. Never have I felt so happy as then. I never dreamed that the Lord was about to try me beyond my strength,—poor, sinful man that I am. I had hitherto lived with the great-est economy. I had never had a penny in my pocket. My comrades at the public school and in college cared nothing for me,—they called me a hypocrite, laughed at me when I failed in my lessons, and would have nothing to do with me. Now I suddenly found myself freed from all restraint. I had a position, and moreover, as I was of age, the rest of my patrimony amounting to five hundred thalers was paid over to me. I had money and friends. The sons of the wealthiest peasants made much of me; formerly they took no notice of me, now they felt it an honour to have me join them at the village inn and drink a glass or play a game of cards with them, which last I was only too glad to do. I never could resist the sight of a card. Often, when I returned home at night after having lost my money at play, I repented with tears and vowed never again to touch a card. I prayed to the Lord for strength to keep my vow, and resolved never to go near the inn again; but the next Saturday evening the temptation was sure to be too strong for me. I could not resist it.

"The Schulze had received me with great cordiality upon my return to Wilhelmshagen, and Annemarie had fallen upon my neck and given me an honest kiss. I was always welcome at the Schulzenhof. I loved my dear Annemarie, and she returned my love."

The young man, who lying stretched upon the grass had hitherto listened quietly, only interrupting the narrative now and then with a word of warning when Gottlieb Pigglewitch's discourse grew too unctional, started and sat upright when the speaker uttered the word love. He stared in amazement at the forlorn, bedraggled figure perched on the stone before him. Could it be? That caricature of humanity was talking of love, and there was a girl in the world who returned the affection of a Gottlieb Pigglewitch!

The young man's surprise was so evident that Gottlieb became embarrassed. "What is the matter?" he asked timidly.

"My worthy Pigglewitch, you have converted me to a belief in miracles. Seriously I begin to have faith in them. In fact is it not a miracle that I am actually interested in you and your history? I thought that nothing in this tedious world could entertain me; you have shown me that I was mistaken. Go on with your story. You had just come to where you loved and were loved in return."

"Yes, so it was. It was a brief period of bliss," Gottlieb Pigglewitch went on, with a deep-drawn sigh. "I trifled away my happiness by my own folly. The Schulze, who had received me so kindly, altered his treatment of me after a while. He remonstrated with me once or twice, telling me that it was not the thing for a teacher to sit until midnight of a Saturday drinking and playing cards with the young fellows of the village, such conduct was, at all events, quite beneath the son of a pastor, who, as such, ought to stand upon his dignity. I promised him then to shun the inn, but when Saturday came I could not withstand the burning desire for play. I dreamed of the cards and of the gains they might bring me, I had to go whether I would or not. Then, when I went the next evening to the Schulzenhof, Annemarie would receive me with tearful eyes, and her father with hard words. I was no longer welcome there, and I knew why. A hundred times I vowed improvement, but in vain. In short, I went on playing,—I could not help it,—and because I almost always lost, I drank too much in my despair. Several times my companions had to take me home drunk. I was most unfortunate. After living three years in Wilhelmshagen, I had to leave it. I had lost my entire patrimony at play, and with only twenty thalers in my pocket I had to look for another situation.

When I bade farewell to Annemarie, I thought I should have died, only the hope of seeing her again sustained me. I knew that the Herr Director in town would befriend me and procure me another situation. I told the Schulze this, and since I was on the subject of my hopes, I confessed my love for Annemarie, and declared my intention of returning to ask for her hand so soon as I had found another situation. I should not have had the courage to say this to him had I not just bidden good-by to my comrades in the inn parlor, where I had taken a glass more than was good for me. The Schulze did not let me finish my sentence, he called me a vagabond, a gambler, and a drunkard, who had squandered his patrimony, and who never should marry his child. If I ever became a respectable man once more, and could save up from my earnings the five hundred thalers I had lost, I might come to see them again, but not until then. And he thrust me from his door without even letting me give my Annemarie a farewell kiss. With despair in my heart I left Wilhelmshagen. My patron, the Herr Director, to whom I first applied, received me with a severe reproof; but when I had described with many tears my struggles, my agony, and my firm resolve to do better, he took pity upon me, and got me a situation in Berlin with a salary of twenty thalers a month."

"You could not possibly live in Berlin upon twenty thalers a month!" his hearer exclaimed.

"But I did do so. Of course I had to practise strict economy, and I could not lay by anything; but, as I had no acquaintances there to tempt me to drink or play, I got along. I had been more than a year in Berlin, when just three weeks ago to-day I received a letter from my patron, the Herr Director. He wrote me that he had heard with pleasure from my principal that I had become a respectable, industrious man. As there is more joy in heaven over one sinner——"

"Pigglewitch!"

"Well, the Herr Director wrote me that he had recommended me for a very advantageous situation to a Frau von Osternau, of Osternau, in Silesia, who had applied to him for a tutor for her son, a boy six years of age. I was to reside with the family and receive three hundred thalers yearly. I could enter upon my duties immediately. He enclosed a letter of introduction to Frau von Osternau, and another to my Principal requesting him to put no obstacle in the way of my good fortune, but to release me immediately from my engagement to him. I was supremely happy. Three hundred thalers and my board! I could save up two hundred thalers a year, and in two years and a half at the latest I should have my five hundred thalers again. I went instantly to my Principal, who, however, declared that he could not possibly spare me before the 3d of July. This I wrote to the Herr Director, and in a few days heard from him in reply that Frau von Osternau was willing to wait, and that she would expect me on the 6th of July."

"The 6th of July? Why, that is the day after to-morrow."

"Precisely. The day after to-morrow. I left my situation yesterday,—a day of misery which has ruined my life forever. So soon as I received from the Herr Director the letter which confirmed my hopes of the situation at Osternau I wrote to my Annemarie and told her of my good luck, in three years at the furthest, I wrote her, we should be married. I had written several letters to her during the year, and had received no reply from her; now I had an answer by return of mail. Her father had forbidden her, she told me, to reply before, but now that he had hopes of my becoming a respectable man once more, he had permitted her to write. She would be true to me, and surely wait the three years for me, but she was nevertheless afraid that we never should be man and wife, for she was forced to go with her father across the sea to America. They had been very unfortunate,—their farm-house had been burned down just after harvest, before the crops had been insured, and her father had therefore resolved to dispose of his farm and to try his fortune in America. Everything was prepared for their departure. Her father was to bring her to Berlin on the 1st of July, that he might receive the last payment of the purchase-money of his estate, and on the 3d they were to leave for Bremen, whence their passage to America was taken. I might expect them at the railway-station on the evening of the 1st, and we could at least spend a few hours together. It was a dear, good letter, as good and kind as my Annemarie herself. I wept as I read it, so transported was I with delight. She would be true to me. In three years I should have enough to follow her to America. Perhaps I could buy a small farm there with my five hundred thalers, and become a farmer. The world lies open to the man who has money, he can purchase every conceivable delight."

"Do you think so?" the listener drawled, contemptuously. "But go on; I beg pardon for interrupting you."

"On the evening of the 1st I received the Schulze and Annemarie at the railway-station, and went with them to the little inn where they were to lodge. Annemarie was unchanged, and the Schulze was as cordial to me as he had been formerly. He read my patron's letter carefully, as also the testimonial which my Principal had given me. He expressed his satisfaction with my plans for the future, and promised that he would give me Annemarie so soon as I could show him five hundred thalers of my own. His confidence in me was entirely restored, as was shown me the next day, when, after he had received all the purchase-money for his estate, he intrusted to me twelve hundred and seventy-two marks to hand over to my uncle in Wennersdorf. Many years ago my uncle had loaned this money upon interest to the Schulze, and had always objected to its repayment, but now, upon the eve of his departure for America, the Schulze as an honest man insisted upon returning it. On my way to Osternau in Silesia, it would be very easy for me to turn a little aside and visit my uncle Widman, at Wennersdorf. The Schulze impressed it upon me to get a receipt for the money and transmit it to him. I had a delightful day with my Annemarie and her father, and yesterday morning I accompanied them to the railway-station, where I took leave of them. At noon I was to leave for Wennersdorf, whence, after leaving the money with my uncle Widman, I could continue my journey to Osternau. Everything was ready for my departure.

"When Annemarie and her father had left me, and I turned away from the railway-station, my heart was so heavy that I could hardly bear it. I felt so weak, so forlorn, that I needed something to strengthen me, and I turned into a small restaurant to get a glass of beer. I seated myself at a table, and I had hardly done so before three men, who had entered the house just after me, took their places at my elbow. In the early morning we four were the only people in the room. The

men talked for a while, and then began to play cards,
—lansquenet,—taking no notice of me. I looked on,
not thinking of playing; but when I saw the thalers
passing from hand to hand, as the game grew more
absorbing, my interest grew keen, and the wretched
passion for play was again aroused within me. I was
seized with an uncontrollable desire to join the game.
The Evil One had me in his clutches once more——"

"Go on, Pigglewitch, go on!"

"Forgive me; I could not help it. I was, indeed,
possessed by a demon. I asked the gentlemen if I
might take part in the game, they assented, and in an
instant I had joined them. I had not played for more
than a year, but the passion for gambling had got hold
of me. I lost, doubled the stakes, lost again, and went
on increasing the stakes in hopes of winning back my
money. Still I went on losing, in my desperation I
drank glass after glass, everything reeled before my
eyes, and when at the end of an hour I had staked my
last piece of money, I suddenly became conscious that
I had gambled away my life. I was a thief condemned
to jail, for I had lost not only my own money, but the
sum intrusted to me for my uncle. I sat alone at the
table, the gentlemen had left me, finding I had nothing
more to lose, and I had not noticed their departure. The
last hour seemed to me like an evil dream. I laid my
head upon the table and wept. After a while a waiter
roused me and requested me to leave, my score had
been paid by my friends. I staggered out of the place.
How I reached my lodgings I do not know. I lay in a
feverish stupor all day long, in the evening I came to
myself. How terrible was my awaking! I now saw
clearly what I had done. I knew that I was lost.
My uncle would demand his money of me. I should be

handed over to the authorities as a thief. I should be sent to jail. I was lost,—lost past rescue. But I would die sooner than be sent to jail.

"Suddenly there arose in my memory the picture of the lake of Wandelitz. How often in my boyhood had I wandered away from Wilhelmshagen to this quiet lake in the forest, and, seated upon the bank yonder, passed hours in dreaming and gazing down into the green depths of water! The thought of it came to me like an inspiration. I gathered myself together. On the chair beside my bed lay my travelling-bag, I packed it early in the morning for my noon-day departure, and it contained, as I now remembered, ten silver thalers, every penny I possessed in the world. It was enough to purchase a ticket for Wilhelmshagen, whither I might go by the night train. I scarcely know what followed,—how I set out, how I arrived here. I only remember that I sang a hymn, and then —well, you know the rest. I am an unfortunate, miserable wretch!"

"You're a very queer fellow, friend Pigglewitch," the other declared, in answer to Gottlieb's last desperate exclamation. "You are a compound of contradictions. I do not understand you, and least of all can I comprehend how a fellow can be so overwhelmed by despair at losing a paltry twelve hundred marks at cards. Such a trifle!"

"I was horrified at the prison which awaited me," Pigglewitch declared. "Oh, I am lost,—lost beyond all hope!"

For a while his companion made no reply, but sat looking dreamily across the lake, while he mechanically plucked to pieces a tiny wild-flower. His face, rather handsome than otherwise; suddenly lost its habitual

expression of weary indifference, a smile played about
the lips, the dreamy eyes sparkled.

"Friend Pigglewitch," he said, scrutinizing keenly
the odd figure before him, "an idea has suddenly occurred to me,—an original, some sensible people might
call it an insane, idea! You, friend Pigglewitch, play
an important part in the development of this idea. You
please me, you interest me, and that is saying a great
deal, for I assure you that it is years since I have taken
any interest in anything, or any pleasure in a living
creature with the exception of my Bello, an abominable
mongrel pug, whose intense ugliness pleased me. But,
as I said, you too please me. It would be no end of a
pity if so magnificent a sample of humanity should be
early snatched from this world by despicable suicide.
I now rejoice that I pulled you out of the water.
You must live!"

"Why do you jeer at me?" Pigglewitch asked, in a
doleful tone of reproach. "I have done you no harm,
and have told you all my story."

"In return for which you shall have mine, with but
some trifling reservations. It is but reasonable that
you, in return for this recital of your life and its woes,
should listen to mine. It will be much shorter than
yours, for I really have had no experiences. My name
is—but why need you know my name? you cannot care
for it, and I am quite sure you will find it easier not to
mention it if you do not know it. Since from my earliest infancy Fortune has showered upon me her choicest
gifts, I will call myself Fritz Fortune. Yes, Fritz Fortune had from his birth everything that mankind con-
siders a means of happiness. His health was perfect,
they say he was a very handsome boy, he had quick
powers of mind, a lively intelligence which enabled

him to learn without trouble; he was the only son of an immensely wealthy father, his every desire was fulfilled before it was expressed. He had everything, everything, except one mere trifle of no real consequence in life,—affection. The stupid fellow, however, thought he wanted it. He loved his kind, and longed for love in return, but he did not find it. His mother had no time to bestow upon him. She was wonderfully lovely, and always surrounded by a crowd of adorers. There was not a moment of her day not given to society or to dressing for some grand entertainment, how could she possibly find a moment to devote to the boy, who was, besides, admirably cared for by a most expensive tutor and an excellent housekeeper? When Fritz Fortune was ten years old his mother died suddenly of disease of the heart. He did not miss her, for he scarcely knew her. His father was a model parent, he was willing to make any sacrifice for the child, upon whom he lavished enormous sums of money, save one,—the sacrifice of his time, which was devoted partly to business, but mostly to pleasure. Weeks passed continually without the boy's even seeing his father, but then no toy was too expensive to be purchased for him so soon as he expressed a wish for it to the housekeeper, there was no delicacy upon which he might not feed until it disgusted him. Everything, everything save affection was lavished upon him. Was he not the silliest of lads in that so far from being contented he sometimes shed bitter tears over his lot? He had soon done with tears, however. His tutor did just as the boy told him to, and the housekeeper and all the servants followed his example. Fritz Fortune's will was never gainsaid, if he had not chosen of his own accord to go to school, he never would have been sent there, but he was tired of his home, and hoped to be better entertained at school, consequently to school he went. There too luck pursued him. As he was clever enough and studied diligently, not from love of books but to beguile the time, he learned readily. He outstripped his school-fellows, and they consequently hated him, but as his pockets were always filled with money and school-boy dainties which he scattered with a lavish hand, the young rogues took care to conceal their dislike of him. They flattered the son of the wealthy banker, and for a short time the boy was really happy, for he thought himself beloved by his school-mates, for whom he had a sincere affection. Chance opened his eyes. He accidentally overheard a conversation between two boys whom he thought his best friends. Every word then spoken revealed their hatred, their mean envy of their comrade. It was enough. Fritz Fortune no longer lavished either gifts or affection upon his school-fellows, and they no longer concealed the true nature of their feelings towards him. They pursued him with falsehoods and calumny. There was a fresh battle to be fought at every recess, he was agile and strong, and declined none of them. Since he returned every blow with interest, and in addition had the teachers on his side, so that after a fight his opponents were the ones selected for punishment, he came out of all these contests victorious. He continued to be Fortune's favourite, but he was not happy, he was solitary and alone among his fellows.

"When only sixteen years old he passed a brilliant examination and entered the university, where he studied,—that is to say, he fluttered about from one science to another. There was no need of his pursuing any laborious course of study: he was wealthy in his own right by inheritance from his mother, and was, besides, the on y son of an immensely wealthy father, who gave him everything save affection. His career at the university was as successful as at school. Whatever he attempted was a success. He was a capital boxer, an untiring swimmer, a bold rider,—he was an object of admiration and envy.

"He had learned somewhat at school, his bitter experiences there had not been lost upon him. Again he scattered his money with a lavish hand, he was surrounded by flatterers and friends, but he now knew what they were worth. He despised the rabble of young men as he had despised their childish prototypes, but he was too wise to let this be seen. Solitude was too tedious. He wanted to enjoy life. To do this he needed jolly companions, his money bought him these. He drank deep of all these delights of student life, he was always surrounded by a merry throng of so-called good friends, but he was often wretchedly forlorn and unhappy.

"The wild, gay life that he led filled him with disgust, he forced himself to seem carelessly merry when he was constantly a prey to mortal *ennui.* Of course Fritz Fortune was a favourite with women. He had not in appearance fulfilled, it is true, the promise of his boyhood, but he was by no means an ugly fellow, and, what was far more to the point, he was rich, very rich. He was everywhere received with distinction,— the mothers flattered his vanity, the daughters met his advances far more than half-way. Once or twice, when a pair of blue eyes looked innocently into his own, when a rosy cheek blushed rosier still at his words, he thought the glance and the blush due to his real self, his heart beat high, hope dawned within him, but he was sure to be cruelly undeceived. Some skilled coquette behind a

mask of maidenly innocence had been speculating upon
his wealth, but Fortune still befriended him in that
he discovered in time the net in which he was to have
been caught.   He escaped, it is true, but every vestige
of his faith in mankind was left behind him in the toils
that had been spread for him.

"When he left the university he had not decided upon
a career.   Should he take part in his father's business?
He had no inclination to do so.   Why should he devote
himself to the accumulation of wealth?   The business
was in trustworthy, competent hands; his father, it
is true, was at the head of it, but he paid little attention to its details; more as a pastime than as a necessity he spent a couple of hours in his counting-room
every day, all the rest of his time was devoted to
pleasure.   He had no desire that his son should apply
himself to business.   He was so tender a father that he
gladly fulfilled his son's every wish, only asking in return that his son should not interfere with him or with
his little amusements.   Could a son ask more of a parent?   Certainly Fritz Fortune's was a most enviable
lot.   He was surrounded by young men of rank who
called themselves his devoted friends, and he was an
idol among women.   Wherever he went he was treated
with distinction, he drained every delight of the German capital to the dregs, there was no necessity for his
denying himself a single pleasure.   Whatever money
could procure might be his, for his father's cashier stood
ready to honour his drafts to any amount.   What could
he desire more?   And yet the foolish fellow was absolutely wretched; he had but one wish, and to fulfil it
money was of no avail,—he wished to be relieved from
the mortal tedium of an insufferable existence.   The
amusements of the capital disgusted him, society bored

him, he had no interest in any pursuit, he could not
decide to pursue any particular branch of study; even
music, which had formerly helped him to pass many a
lonely hour, no longer attracted him. In glowing physical health, his weary mind was 'sickening of a vague
disease,' his only wish being to close his eyes never to
open them again.

"It was some time before it occurred to him that it
was within his power to gratify this wish by a firm
resolve. He had become too indolent even to think, but
yesterday this brilliant idea occurred to him. It was
suggested by his reading in the morning's paper that
a young banker of his acquaintance had shot himself.
What in this case had been done in despair might also
be done to put an end to the tedium of existence. His
spirits improved on the instant, the mere thought that
he could rid himself of his burden dissipated his weariness for a while.

"He pondered upon what his numerous dear friends
would say if he should suddenly vanish from Berlin,
leaving no trace of his whereabouts. His fancy was
excited. He made all sorts of plans for best putting
an end to his wretched existence without causing an
immediate report of his death to be spread abroad
in Berlin.

"For the first time for years he was really entertained for a couple of hours, so great was his interest
in the different schemes thus contemplated. Forth-
with he proceeded to the carrying out of his resolve.
He drew from his father's bank a considerable sum of
money, that his friends might be led quite astray as to
his disappearance, called upon several acquaintances,
showed himself at the theatre, and left Berlin by the
night-train.

c

"Some years previously, in a summer excursion, he had noticed a charming forest in the neighbourhood of Wilhelmshagen. He remembered that one might wander there for hours and find no thoroughfare.

"In this forest he determined to search out a secluded spot, where his body might lie undiscovered for weeks. This plan he pursued. Was he not Fortune's favourite? He saw no one whom he knew at the railway-station. He made his journey entirely alone, in a first-class carriage, and, reaching Wilhelmshagen in the early morning, entered the forest without meeting a human being. Every trace of him was lost, no one could surmise what had become of him. For some hours he wandered about until he found a spot suitable for his purpose. Here he lay down upon the grass, and once more passed in mental review his entire wearisome, frustrated existence, it seemed to him so forlorn and pitiable that he was but confirmed in his resolution. He was about to carry it into effect, he had in fact raised his revolver for the purpose, when he heard a hymn sung near at hand. He dropped his hand, and—the rest you know. This is the history of Fritz Fortune. How do you like it, my worthy Pigglewitch?"

Gottlieb stared at the narrator with unutterable astonishment in his prominent eyes. "And is that all?" he asked, thinking it impossible that he had heard the end of the tale.

"Do you wish for more? As I told you, my story is brief, but edifying."

"Were you then going to shoot yourself out of mere *ennui*, Herr Fortune? It is inconceivable, impossible! I am almost always bored, especially when I am alone, but it never occurred to me to shoot myself upon that account. How can such an idea enter the head of any one who has money?"

A bitter smile hovered about Fortune's lips. "That is precisely the view of the mass of mankind," he said. "Whoever has money must be happy, and the silly fools rush after wealth, never perceiving that there is no greater misery than what they call happiness. If I were poor, if I had to strive and contrive for a pittance for my daily bread, if I had a single aim in life worth attaining, I too might perhaps endure existence. This thought occurred to me while you were telling your story, and I suddenly fancied that I should like to try whether existence under your circumstances could make the burden of life supportable. Should it prove as devoid of interest, as tiresome and insufferable as my former existence, I can always have recourse to my faithful revolver. I will make you an offer, friend Pigglewitch. If you accept it, it will help us both, you perhaps forever, myself at least for a while, but that is not your affair. The dearest wish of your heart at present is to be able to pay your uncle his money, and to gain as quickly as possible the five hundred thalers to enable you to follow your Annemarie to America. Are you willing to make a sacrifice to accomplish this end?"

"Any, every sacrifice!" Pigglewitch cried, eagerly. "Ask what you will of me, it shall be done."

"I will not ask much. You shall have the round sum of three thousand five hundred marks—just enough to pay your uncle, replace your patrimony, and take you to America—if you will give me, to dispose of as I may see fit, your beautiful name of Gottlieb Pigglewitch, with the necessary articles and documents thereto belonging,—to wit, your testimonials, credentials, letter of introduction to Osternau, etc., and, above all, your beautiful black suit, which fits you so admirably,—promising also to go direct from here to Wilhelmshagen, whence you can send your uncle his money, and whence you promise to take the next train, by way of Berlin, to Bremen, where you will embark in the first vessel bound for America, and all this without revealing to a living soul the occurrences of the last two days."

"You are making game of me, Herr Fortune," Pigglewitch said, in his most lachrymose tones; "but I must endure it, for you have saved my life."

"Don't mention it. That is a debit and credit affair. Had you not sung your hymn I should be lying in the forest with a bullet in my brains, and you would be reposing peacefully beneath the green, crystal waters of the lake. You certainly owe me nothing, and need think of nothing save your own advantage in deciding whether or not to accept the bargain I offer you, for I am not jesting. I make you the serious offer of three thousand five hundred marks cash, payable upon the receipt of your name, your credentials, your clothes, which you can exchange for mine,—and not a bad exchange either, it seems to me,—and lastly, of your express promise to emigrate immediately to America."

"Are you really not joking? Three thousand five hundred marks——"

"Cash. I pay *en amateur.* I like the beautiful name of Pigglewitch, and your black coat, with its long, pointed swallow-tail, enchants me. I am sure it will become me admirably."

Pigglewitch looked doubtfully at the young man, who spoke so calmly, but whom he was inclined to pronounce insane. "What do you want to do with my name and my credentials?" he said.

"I have lived a long time as Fortune, and for the sake of variety I should like to live and labour for a while as Pigglewitch. For how long? I do not know; and besides that is not the question between you and me. I shall go on living from day to day until the Pigglewitch existence also becomes intolerable to me. Come, decide, friend Pigglewitch; will you accept my proposal or not?"

Gottlieb reflected. Herr Fritz Fortune was evidently quite insane. Only a madman would kill himself from *ennui* when his pockets were full of money. His offer was a crazy one, but what business was that of Gottlieb Pigglewitch? The proposal was most tempting,—three thousand five hundred marks. He might well sell his credentials, which would be valueless in America, for such a sum. Why should he not in his need accept an offer which would lay the foundations of his fortune? It would be unpardonable folly not to seize with both hands so unexpected a piece of luck.

"If you are really in earnest," he said, with a suspicious look at Herr Fortune,—"I can hardly believe it, —but if your offer is made seriously, I will accept it."

"Bravo, friend Pigglewitch! you are a delightful fellow!" cried Fortune. "There's my hand, the bargain is concluded."

With some hesitation Pigglewitch took the offered hand. He was still in some doubt, but this vanished when Fortune sprang up and led him up the bank whence a short time previously each had thrown himself into the lake. Here upon the short grass lay Fortune's coat and hat, with Pigglewitch's tall beaver and travelling-bag. In the breast-pocket of his coat Fortune found a pocket-book, which he opened, taking from it a thick bundle of bank-notes of a thousand or

4

five hundred marks each, with here and there one for a hundred only. At this sight everything glimmered before the astonished eyes of Pigglewitch, who had never before seen so much money together. And the happy possessor of this wealth, which seemed quite 'beyond the dreams of avarice,' had very nearly killed himself voluntarily a short hour previously. Oh, the poor fellow was evidently mad, quite mad!

Meanwhile, Fortune selected three bank-notes of a thousand marks each, and ten hundred-mark notes. "Here, friend Pigglewitch," he said, "are four thousand marks; our bargain was for three thousand five hundred, but I add the rest and make the four thousand complete on condition that you make over to me your travelling-bag and its contents. I should like to begin my new life fully equipped as Pigglewitch. Do you agree?"

"Oh, certainly. You are most generous. I thank you from my soul, but——"

"But? Go on; why do you hesitate?"

"If you really wish to assume the life of a poor man like myself you must not carry about you so well filled a pocket-book."

Fortune looked up in surprise. "You are cleverer than I thought," he said; "you are right. It were best to throw the entire rubbish into the lake, where it can do no mischief."

"For God's sake, take care what you do, Herr Fortune!" Pigglewitch exclaimed, in dismay, seizing the young man by the arm as he was about to toss the pocket-book into the water. "It is a sin to destroy all that beautiful money. If you do not want it, give it to me."

Fortune's hand fell by his side, he reflected for a moment, and then said as he looked at Pigglewitch with a smile, "The appetite grows with eating. A moment ago four thousand marks seemed wealth to you, now you would like to have more. No, friend Pigglewitch, four thousand marks is enough. If you cannot begin life afresh with that sum, a larger one would assuredly plunge you into misery. But you were right, nevertheless, to prevent me from destroying this money, it would have been folly. I always act foolishly when I follow the impulse of the moment, and I thank you for hindering me. I will keep the pocket-book. There is no danger for me in the money, I know its worthlessness. Give me your travelling-bag. Is there a key to it? Yes? Thank you. I will deposit the pocket-book here in this bag, where it shall remain untouched. And now we will exchange clothes. I am longing to don your charming black suit as a bride longs to deck herself in her veil. We are about the same height, we shall have no difficulty in the matter."

He took off his cravat and waistcoat, and with a shake of the head Pigglewitch followed his example. In a few minutes the transformation was complete. Fritz Fortune in the wet black suit confronted its amazed former possessor; the clothes, 'a world too wide' for his slender, muscular figure, dangled and hung loosely about him, he clapped the tall black hat upon his head and exclaimed with a laugh as he looked at himself in a small pocket-mirror which he had taken from his own coat, "Horrible! ugly beyond belief! Indeed I am worthy of you, friend Pigglewitch. But my poor fellow, how you look! You have the worst of the bargain. My new summer coat suits you about as well as does a dress-coat a poodle. Look at yourself!"

He handed Pigglewitch the little mirror. Gottlieb

contemplated his image with much complacency. He thought he presented an aristocratic appearance in his elegant attire, and said so.

"Are you pleased? So much the better," said Fortune. "Then we are both satisfied. And now, friend Pigglewitch, let us take leave of each other, but first swear to me by all that you hold sacred, by the very salvation of your soul, that you never will reveal to a human being what has taken place between us, and that you will sail for America as soon as possible."

"I swear it, so help me God! Amen!" Pigglewitch rejoined, raising his hand towards the skies.

"Farewell, my worthy other self, then. Farewell until we meet in another world more pleasantly than we did in this. You are going towards Wilhelmshagen. My way lies in an opposite direction. Farewell."

He shook Pigglewitch cordially by the hand, took up the travelling-bag and hung it by the handle on the end of a stick, which he rested upon his shoulder. Then, with an elastic step, he started for the forest.

CHAPTER II.

OSTERNAU.

CASTLE OSTERNAU is situated in the midst of a country distinguished not for any conspicuous or unique beauty of natural scenery, but for luxuriance of cultivation. The undulating landscape forbids an extended view, it is only from the summit of some of the larger hills that the long range of the Riesengebirge can be discerned in the distance. All sight of this range is shut off from Castle Osternau itself by low hills.

Nevertheless, the country about the castle is by no means wanting in charm. The richly-cultured fields waving with golden grain, the luxuriant, flowery meadows, which lie like broad green ribbons among them, the dark forests which bound the horizon do not it is true combine to form a scene of majestic magnificence, but the landscape is full of a tender, benignant beauty, and in the eyes of Herr von Osternau, who was agriculturist to his very heart's core, there was in all Silesia no more beautiful spot than his dear Osternau. A field of wheat was far more lovely in his eyes than the most picturesque bare rocks. The steep mountains, available only for the cultivation of timber and inaccessible for the plough, where the peasant toiled laboriously to earn a scanty subsistence, were odious to him. An extensive, level, cultured plain was his ideal of beauty. It was hardly attained in the gently-undulating fields of Osternau, but, so far as luxuriance of cultivation was concerned, they left nothing to be desired.

All the lords of Osternau had been capable, practical agriculturists. The love of agriculture had descended for centuries from father to son with the entailed estate. Its proprietors had successively, from time immemorial, resided at Castle Osternau and personally superintended the management of its extensive lands, the younger sons only had devoted themselves to a diplomatic career, and, for the most part, not for long. So soon as they could lay claim to a pension from the government they had followed their natural bent, resigned their positions, and retired to Castle Osternau, where they had loyally assisted the elder brother in the management of his estates.

But few of these younger brothers had ever married, most of them had died bachelors. Thus the male descendants of the Osternau line had never been numerous. At present there were but three of them. The head of the house, Friedrich von Osternau, had but one son, a boy six years of age, and only one male relative, a cousin, Albrecht von Osternau by name, who had for a long time considered himself the heir-at-law, since the marriage of Friedrich von Osternau had been blessed for some years with a daughter only. When this daughter, however, had reached the age of eleven, the birth of a son had blasted the young man's hopes of succeeding to the estates.

Albrecht von Osternau was a young, pleasure-loving officer. As the future possessor of Osternau, he had cared very little for the fact that he had gambled away and squandered his patrimony in a few years. His credit was good, for it was supposed by the Berlin money-lenders that the present owner of Osternau was consumptive and could live but a few months longer at the furthest. But the victim of consumption lived not only months, but years, and just when his death was predicted with great certainty, he astonished the world with the news that a son and heir was born to him.

It was a fearful blow for Lieutenant Albrecht von Osternau when he suddenly learned, in a very kind letter from his cousin, that his expectations in life had crumbled to ruins. With his prospects of inheritance his credit also vanished. His creditors, hitherto most patient, besieged him, and in one case, where he had imprudently given his note of hand, he was threatened with a complaint to be lodged with his commanding officer. Until now the lieutenant had never found any difficulty in covering one debt with another; this was no longer possible. The money-lenders, who had formerly considered it an honour to accommodate the Herr Lieutenant, rudely refused compliance with his wishes.

In his great need, Albrecht von Osternau decided to apply to his only relative, the head of the house, although until now he had had but little intercourse with him. He paid a visit to Castle Osternau, where he was received with open arms. The good-natured Friedrich considered it a duty to indemnify his only relative, in some measure at least, for his shattered hopes. He recognized the severity of the law of entail which cuts off all the younger branches of a family from a share in the wealth which is lavished upon the heir, and he thought it quite natural that Albrecht should have heretofore ordered his life upon a scale commensurate with his expectations.

Since the state of his own health had prevented him from leading any but the simple life of a country gentleman, he was in the habit of yearly laying aside considerable sums, which were usually, however, expended in the improvement of the estates, wherefore his private property was not very large. Nevertheless, he gladly sacrificed a considerable amount of money in paying his cousin's debts.

Amply provided with means, Albrecht returned from Osternau to Berlin. He arrived there a day too late. His merciless creditor had already sent to the colonel of the regiment a notice of the note that was due. Upon the payment of his claim he would gladly have recalled it, but, since the colonel had received it, the latter was obliged to advise the young officer to send in his resignation from the service.

Albrecht's military career was ended. It must shortly have terminated at all events, for with his expensive tastes and habits he could not possibly have maintained his position as cavalry officer of the guards without loading himself with debt. What was he to do? At the age of twenty-four, in the very flower of his youth, he found himself without a future.

Once more he found a kind and ready friend in his cousin, to whom he confided his misfortune. Baron Friedrich invited him to come to Osternau, there to follow the traditions of the family in devoting himself to agriculture.

The luxurious young officer, accustomed to the delights of the capital, unused to work of any description, after living a careless life of pleasure among his wealthy comrades, was to bury himself in a lonely castle, where, in the society of an invalid cousin and his simple-hearted wife, he must spend his weary days in a pursuit that was odious to him. He who had been free as a bird of the air after the easy duties of his daily service were over, must now be his cousin's slave, condemned to constant occupation, obedient to command, assuming the part of an upper superintendent upon the very estates which he had been wont to consider as his own in the future. Could the munificent compensation offered him by his cousin atone to him for what he relinquished, for the delights he must resign? He felt no gratitude towards his generous relative; he hated him as he had always envied him. For years he had set all his hopes upon the death of the man whom he had believed a prey to consumption. These hopes were now annihilated, and he felt almost inclined to reproach his cousin for still living, and for being blessed with a direct heir. How could he be grateful to the hated relative whose subordinate, whose slave he was doomed to be? The thought was intolerable; and yet, hard as this lot was, no choice was left for the ruined officer.

Again and again he destroyed the letter in which he had tried to accept his cousin's offer with thanks. He ground his teeth as he wrote out the hollow expressions of his gratitude, but there was no help for it, he had to write them, and when the letter was finally finished he paced the floor of his room in a frenzy of envy and disgust.

In a few days he followed his letter to Castle Osternau, and from that time all the male members of the ancient family were united beneath its roof. Albrecht occupied some elegantly-furnished rooms in the third story of the castle; the windows of his sleeping-room looked out upon the court-yard, those of his other rooms upon the garden.

The head of the family himself occupied the second floor of the castle. He was so enthusiastic a farmer that he quite despised the lovely view of the castle gardens. His delight was in overlooking from the windows of his sitting-room the spacious court-yard, with its busy throng of servants and labourers. If the state of his health confined him to the house, he thus contrived still to maintain a supervision of his people. He would sit at these windows from early morning when the weather was bad, only leaving his post to repair to the dining-hall at dinner-time. From half-past two until half-past four was his only time for recreation or repose. If the weather were propitious he spent the entire remainder of the day out of doors, in the fields, on foot or on horseback, in the court-yard and stables. He took an interest in the smallest details of his extensive agricultural operations without relaxing in his strict general superintendence. The Osternau estates were regarded all through the country as a model of good management.

The castle court-yard was a huge quadrangle, one side of which was formed by the extensive structure of the castle itself. Its spacious barns were on the opposite side; to the right were long rows of stables for horses and cows, and to the left were those devoted to various breeds of sheep. In the midst of the large space thus enclosed was a pond for watering the cattle, and beside it stood a shed, beneath which was a fire-engine.

Perfect neatness and order reigned in the court-yard; the keen eye of the master of Osternau saw to it that these were always strictly maintained. He certainly was the gentlest and kindest of masters, but he could not endure the slightest disorder. Even the huge muck-heap before the cow-stables, the pride of its possessor and the ornament of the court-yard of an agricultural estate, was well kept, and gave no impression of uncleanliness; indeed, the neighboring landed proprietors regarded it with admiration when they drove past the court-yard on their way to pay a friendly visit to Herr von Osternau. They preferred to go round the narrower country road, past the court-yard, to gain the front entrance to the castle, rather than to approach it by the broader road leading directly from the highway.

CHAPTER III.

THE CASTLE'S LORD AND LADY.

HERR FRITZ VON OSTERNAU, the lord of the castle, was seated in his room at the open window looking discontentedly out upon the court-yard. In consequence of over-exertion he had suffered for some days from a violent attack of the spasmodic cough which many years previously ignorant physicians had pronounced consumption. These attacks of a chronic malady were not dangerous. The famous Mitterwurz, of Berlin, when consulted by Herr von Osternau, had assured him that with care he might regard his cough as a warrant for length of life, but care he must take. In stormy or very warm weather he must stay in the house, he must avoid violent exercise, and never ride far afield even in fair weather after an attack of coughing, as physical exertion might provoke a return of it. Since this verdict of the famous physician's, Frau von Osternau never had allowed her husband to indulge in his agricultural mania when he had coughed during the night. She would permit him to take a short walk, upon which she always accompanied him that he might not be induced to prolong it, and he was obliged to return to the castle after an hour at most of sauntering. He obeyed her at such times reluctantly, but still he obeyed, and thus he was sitting to-day at the open window instead of being where he longed to be, out in the fields superintending the harvesting. It was so tiresome to gaze out into the sunlit court-yard, where not a person was to be seen, every man and maid, as well as a host of day-labourers, being busy with the harvest.

Profound quiet reigned in the spacious quadrangle: even the poultry had retired to the barns out of the glowing sunshine and were silent. The court-yard was so lonely and deserted that its master grew tired of looking out of the window, and taking up a book he tried to read. But it would not do, his thoughts were with the harvesters, and the book did not interest him. He laid it down with a sigh of impatience.

"This sitting idly here is intolerable," he said to his wife, who was seated near him knitting diligently. "I detest laziness. Everybody is busy in the fields, and I sit here doing nothing. I cannot bear it any longer, Emma, I must go out, and besides there is no use in taking care of myself any longer, I have not coughed once for two hours."

Frau von Osternau dropped her knitting in her lap and looked at her husband with a smile. She was not beautiful, but her smile was wonderfully lovely and lent a charm to her face, revealing such simple kindness of heart that one forgot, in looking at it, its irregularity of feature, and in spite of her forty years she was still youthfully attractive. Her smile was really irresistible: it was sure to overcome any rebellion against her wishes upon her husband's part; when he would have obstinately resisted any severity of manner, he was powerless against his wife's smile.

"Dear Fritz, you forget your wretched night," she said, gently. "You coughed so terribly that neither of us slept an hour, and now you want to go out into the hot sun with the harvesters. For my sake, dear, stay quietly in your arm-chair. It will soon be noon, and the men will be back in the court-yard."

Herr von Osternau muttered some unintelligible words, but resigned himself to his fate with a sigh, and made another fruitless attempt to read.

"Emma," he said, after a pause, "do you know that to-day is the 6th of July?"

"I believe it is; but what makes you think of it?"

"You know we expected the tutor on the 6th."

"Then he will surely be here in the course of the day."

"I wish he would fail to keep his appointment. It would be a good reason for getting rid of him. I confess I cannot reconcile myself to your idea of having a tutor. We should have been wiser to engage a governess for Fritzchen. A cultivated, well-born young woman is a pleasant addition to one's household; she could easily have taught Fritzchen all he need learn for a couple of years, and it would have been well for our romp Lieschen to acknowledge a more strict control than yours."

"Do you imagine that Lieschen would have submitted to it? You know I thought at first of engaging a governess for Fritzchen, but our experiences with Lieschen's governesses were too terrible. I could not try that experiment again. If Liese drove her governess to desperation when she was a child of seven, it is hardly likely that she would be very docile as a girl of seventeen. She is too unaccustomed to control. No, no, it is better as it is. And I may as well tell you, Fritz, although I know how you will laugh at me, that when I wrote to Director Kramser I made it a stipulation that the young man whom he should send to us must be positively ugly. This I did in view of the position I wished him to occupy with regard to Liese, who is to take music-lessons of him."

"Oh, Emma, Emma! what an extraordinary idea!"
Herr von Osternau exclaimed, with a laugh.

"It is impossible to be too prudent," Frau von Osternau said, gravely. "Lieschen has an antipathy to everything ugly, there could be no danger for her in an
ugly, awkward man. Director Kramser is, as you
know, an old friend of mine, he used to be tutor to my
brother Karl——"

"I remember him," her husband interrupted her.
"I used to see him at your father's before we were
married. A very unattractive, awkward young man,
but in spite of that he has had a very successful career,
I believe."

"He certainly is rather awkward, but very good-
humoured, and as honest and good a man as ever lived.
I have great confidence in him. I told him so in my
letter, and frankly confessed to him the reason why I
wanted an ugly tutor. I did not wish that there should
be any danger for Liese in taking music-lessons of him,
and I am quite sure that Kramser will have had a
regard for my wishes in this respect."

"No doubt of it, so far as ugliness is concerned,"
her husband rejoined, with a laugh. "Speak of an
angel, and you hear the rustle of his wings; there comes
the tutor. Come to the window, Emma; there, I am
certain, comes your *protégé* across the court-yard.
Heavens! what a scarecrow!"

Frau von Osternau hastened to her husband's side
and looked out of the open window. His exclamation
had made her curious; she too had a slight shock, and
could not but admit that 'scarecrow' was not too
strong an expression, when she saw the young man
who had entered the court-yard by the gate between
the barns, and was now leisurely coming towards the

castle across the deserted quadrangle. He was still too
far off to allow of her distinguishing his features, but
his figure was certainly suggestive of a scarecrow.
With his clothes hanging loosely upon his long limbs
and the tails of his black coat dangling against his legs,
the man looked like a caricature. His tall, rusty hat, as
well as his coat, seemed the relic of a bygone age. With
a shabby old travelling-bag hung over his shoulder on
the end of a stick, he sauntered slowly along, casting
curious glances about him. Herr von Osternau continued to stare at the strange figure as it gradually
approached the castle. "Most certainly your friend
has obeyed your directions with regard to the ugliness, Emma. And we are to have this scarecrow
living beneath our roof and eating at our table?
Why my food will choke me with that thing before
my eyes!"

"He really does look almost too ugly," his wife replied, rather meekly; she began to feel that she had
laid too much stress upon ugliness in her letter to the
Herr Director.

As the man came nearer, and her keen eye could dis-
tinguish his features, she thought they did not quite
correspond to the impression made upon her by his
figure. He could hardly be called very handsome. The
nose was too large, the mouth, shaded by a large mous-
tache, not sufficiently well formed, and the face was too
pale to be pronounced very handsome; but surely the
large, dark eyes might be so considered, as they looked
observantly about the court-yard; and when, upon ad-
vancing sufficiently near the castle to perceive Herr
and Frau von Osternau at the window, the man lifted
his hat courteously, his manner of doing so was such a
contradiction of his appearance that Frau von Osternau

hardly knew what to think. The head from which the hat was lifted seemed by no means repulsive, the dark, expressive eyes lent it a certain interest.

Herr von Osternau's impressions with regard to the stranger were identical with his wife's. "A very odd person," he observed, as the man disappeared beneath the window. "I am really curious to see him." His wife said nothing, but looked eagerly towards the door of the sitting-room. She had not long to wait. In a moment Hildebrandt, Herr von Osternau's old personal attendant, appeared, to announce that a very odd-looking stranger had arrived with a travelling-bag; his name he said was Gottlieb Pigglewitch, and he asserted that he was the Herr Tutor whom madame expected.

Old Hildebrandt looked grave when his mistress desired him to show in the Herr Tutor immediately, and he ventured to observe that the man did not look like a respectable tutor, but like some tramp who had stolen his ill-fitting clothes; nevertheless he obeyed his mistress's reiterated order, and ushered Herr Gottlieb Pigglewitch into the sitting-room.

When the tutor appeared on the threshold of the door, which Hildebrandt held open for him, Frau von Osternau could not but be struck again by the contrast between the young man's exterior and his air and bearing. He held his shabby old hat in his hand with the careless grace of a gentleman paying a morning call, and the bow with which he greeted the mistress and master of the house was respectful but easy. As he bowed, the large, dark eyes rested keenly for an instant upon Frau von Osternau, and were then turned with the same observant glance upon her husband.

The shyness and the awkwardness which are wont

to attack young men unused to society upon first meeting persons of rank were evidently unknown to Herr
Gottlieb Pigglewitch. He approached Frau von Osternau, and bowing again slightly, said, "Madame, allow
me to introduce myself as the Candidate Gottlieb
Pigglewitch, whom Herr Director Kramser has recommended to you for a tutor. I beg to thank you for
your kindness in consenting to postpone my entering
upon the duties of the important post assigned me until
to-day, and to assure you that I am now ready to fulfil
them to the best of my ability. Yes, I confess that I
greatly desire to enter upon the honest performance of
them. I am eager to teach your little son what you
would have him learn."

It was an odd speech, and there was certainly no
trace to be found in it of the formal tone always
adopted upon every special occasion by the Herr Director Kramser in his youth. Everything about the
young man was different from what Frau von Osternau
had expected to find it. She was not easily embarrassed, in her gentle, kindly way she was used to be
equal to any emergency, but, oddly enough, she hardly
knew how to treat this tutor whom she had engaged,
this young man who was henceforth to occupy a superior position among the dependants of her household.
She had thought it but natural and right that she
should not be at all disturbed by his entrance, and
should calmly proceed with her knitting, but it was
laid aside, and she felt obliged to receive him as she
would have done a morning visitor of her own rank, as
in a few courteous words she expressed her pleasure in
seeing him and motioned him towards a seat.

Herr von Osternau's sensations were of a similar
kind. He too rose from his chair and left the win-

dow as the tutor entered, and when the latter took a chair near the sofa, in compliance with Frau von Oster- nau's invitation, her husband seated himself likewise, and felt himself impelled to continue the conversation his wife had begun.

"I am glad to find you so punctual, Herr Piggle- witch," he said, with a kindly nod. "I am quite sure, from the representations of Herr Director Kramser, who is an old friend of my wife's, that you will incul- cate fidelity to duty and punctuality in your teaching of my Fritz, but I must warn you upon one point. I prefer to undertake my son's training myself in all matters bearing upon religion. It is of importance to me that his views upon such subjects should agree with those of his parents."

At this explanation a smile hovered about the young man's lips. He inclined his head courteously towards the master of the house as he replied, "I thank you for relieving me of your son's religious instruction, since it is the department in which I feel myself least fitted to impart knowledge."

"That surprises me. I should have supposed the contrary from Herr Director Kramser's letter."

"Herr Director Kramser is probably disposed to judge too favourably of my capacity and acquirements. I frankly confess that I have had doubts whether I am capable of instructing and educating a boy, whether I am not wanting in conscientiousness in undertaking an office for which I may have no vocation. I decided to do so in a moment of excitement. Perhaps I should not have done so. Still, I may be able to overcome all difficulties, and accomplish my desire to do well and honestly what is required of me. I do not know whether I possess the patience, force, and talent required for the task, but I will hope so. I owe it to you to be frank with you, Herr von Osternau, and 1 pray you to permit a trial of my capacity,- a trial to which I concede your right to put an immediate stop provided I do not fulfil entirely to your satisfaction the duties required of me."

Herr and Frau von Osternau listened in increasing surprise to these words, which they could scarcely comprehend. They exchanged significant glances, and for a moment Herr von Osternau was doubtful whether it would not be best to dismiss Herr Gottlieb Pigglewitch at once. However, the young man's last sentence allayed his doubts. There could be no harm in making the trial of which he spoke. Therefore he replied, "I accept your proposal, although I confess myself surprised by your manner of making it. I really cannot understand how a Candidate, who has gone through the schools and passed his examination, should doubt his ability to instruct a boy of six."

"I have never been a private tutor."

"Indeed? You doubt then your success in imparting private instruction? That shows a laudable modesty. You certainly will have some difficulties to overcome. Fritzchen is an undisciplined little fellow. It will be hard to induce him to study, and as for Lieschen——"

"Lieschen? I beg your pardon. I thought my duties were confined to the instruction of a boy."

"True. But, since Herr Director Kramser wrote to my wife that you were very musical, we thought you might give some lessons weekly upon the piano to our daughter Lieschen. I am of course ready to make them an object of special remuneration."

"Not at all. You have relieved me from instruction in religion; instead I will gladly give lessons in music."

"You play the piano very well, as Herr Kramser informs me, and you have a fine voice," Frau von Osternau observed.

"So it is said, I believe."

"So Herr Director Kramser wrote me," the lady rejoined, in a tone sharper than it was her wont to use. She was aggrieved by the small degree of estimation shown in the young teacher's words for the Herr Director. "I shall be very sorry if your talent and capacity in this respect have been overrated by the Herr Director, for I laid special stress in my letter to him upon my desire that the tutor whom I engaged should be a good musician, not only because I wished that Lieschen should take lessons, but principally upon Fritzchen's account. I consider it of the first importance that a child should receive his primary instruction in music from a competent teacher."

"I cannot tell whether I shall be able to satisfy your desires in this respect, madame. I am but a *dilettante*, and have never given lessons in music. Here also I must pray you to make trial of me, as I will also try to adjust myself to my new duties. The future must show whether I can succeed in pleasing you and in satisfying myself. Will you allow me to give you some idea now of the amount of artistic skill I possess? the fine instrument yonder invites the test. You can at least judge whether my execution and touch are satisfactory, whether my voice pleases you. One does not like to purchase an article without first examining it; why should you engage a music-teacher without first hearing him? He can, unfortunately, give you no instant proof of his ability to impart instruction, but this is the case with every kind of teacher. I know from sad experience how large is the number of musicians, whom Heaven in its wrath has allowed to teach, who bring to their calling only the merest superficial facility, without the smallest vocation for teaching."

He arose as he spoke, and, without waiting for Frau von Osternau's permission, went towards the grand piano. It was open; Frau von Osternau, no mean performer herself, had been playing an hour or two before for her husband's entertainment, and had not closed it. Herr Pigglewitch looked at the notes upon the music-desk. "Beethoven," he said. "Is your daughter then so far advanced? It is refreshing nowadays to find such music open upon a piano. Young ladies whose execution is sufficiently brilliant to play the 'Moonlight Sonata' usually prefer to exhibit in what is called drawing-room music. Cultivated taste is but little thought of nowadays. The popular performers are those who can make most noise, and rattle off the greatest number of notes in a given time. I abhor such mere execution as I do the sentimental stuff so popular with the ladies of the present day."

Very admirable sentiments these, but in their ease and freedom of expression so very different from anything that Frau von Osternau had expected to hear from the tutor recommended by Director Kramser, that she looked in wide-eyed wonder at the singular person who, turning over the music and talking thus, appeared to have forgotten for the moment the purpose for which he had gone to the piano.

She believed herself exalted far above any aristocratic prejudice of rank; she prided herself upon the humanity and kindness of her treatment of inferiors, even of servants. The Inspectors of the estate and the various

governesses she had employed had been treated almost
like members of the family, she never had required of
them the servile respect customary among people employed in such capacities by many families of rank,
but the negligent ease of Gottlieb Pigglewitch's manner
and address seemed to her scarcely permissible. She
was tempted to recall him to a sense of his position,
but while she was pondering upon how this could best
be done, the young man had seated himself at the piano,
his fingers were wandering over the keys, and in another moment Frau von Osternau had completely forgotten that she had wished to reprove, so intense was
her enjoyment of the man's wonderful playing.

He had taken his place at the instrument to give
some proof of his musical ability, but no sooner did his
fingers touch the keys than this was quite forgotten.
He had not played for weeks, he had even felt a kind
of dislike of music, to the charm of which he had so
often yielded involuntarily. In the melancholy in which
he had been plunged life appeared to him so shallow
and wearisome that he could not spur himself to the
exertion of extricating himself from its cheerless misery.
But now, when the first tones of the piano responded
to his touch, they awakened within him memories of
hours in which he had lost himself and revelled in the
world of melody and harmony, music cast its spell
around him once more, life dawned upon him afresh,
and he gave expression in his playing to this feeling.
He improvised so wondrously that Frau von Osternau
was profoundly touched, and her husband forgot to look
out into the court-yard, where the men were returning
from the fields, he forgot all else save the music, to
which he listened with head bent and clasped hands.

The last chord died away, the player dropped his

hands from the keys upon which his gaze had rested dreamily, and turned to Frau von Osternau with a smile.

"Pardon me, madame," he said, "I forgot myself, and have given you my own wild fancies. I could not resist the impulse of the moment, it is my misfortune that I lack self-control. But I will try to improve, and will make an instant beginning by praying you to suggest something you would like to hear, only begging you not to ask to-day for what is mere technique. We will postpone that to another hour."

Frau von Osternau's eyes were moist as she replied,—

"You must play no more at present. I would not have the pleasure you have just given me disturbed by a single other note. You are an artist, a divinely-inspired artist, Herr——" She hesitated; she could not bear at the moment to pronounce the ridiculous name Pigglewitch, but it had to be done, nevertheless, and as she uttered it the spell that had held her was broken. The man's name recalled her to prosaic reality; again she was aware of the ugly, old-fashioned coat with its long pointed tails that hung down behind the music-stool and reached to the ground. There sat before her no longer the artist who had transported her to 'a purer ether,' but the Candidate Gottlieb Pigglewitch, awaiting her further commands.

"There is no need, Herr Pigglewitch," she continued, "that I should hear anything more to be sure that you are capable of giving my children instruction in music, the future must show whether to teach is your vocation in life. Let us make the trial, and discover whether you are fitted for the situation, and whether you can be comfortable in fulfilling its duties. I frankly confess to you that I have my misgivings. You do not at all answer to the idea I had formed of the tutor recom-

mended to me by the Herr Director Kramser, but
then reality seldom corresponds to the representations
of our imagination. With your consent, Fritz," she
added, turning to her husband, "I beg Herr Pigglewitch to consider himself from this time our children's
teacher."

"I give it with all my heart," Herr von Osternau
replied, with a nod, offering his hand to the young
man, who had left his seat and approached him.
"There's my hand, Herr Pigglewitch, we will all put
this matter honestly to the test. If we are unsuccessful, we can part friends, but I hope we shall succeed.
From this moment the castle is your home, and I pray
you to consider it such. My old Hildebrandt will show
you to the rooms that have been prepared for you, and
I will send Fritz to you that you may make acquaintance with your pupil. We dine at three, you can use
the time until then in establishing yourself in your new
quarters. At table and while coffee is being served we
can perhaps discuss some plan of instruction. We will
detain you no longer at present."

Pigglewitch, upon whom Herr von Osternau's kindly
manner made a most agreeable impression, thanked his
employers courteously, and when old Hildebrandt appeared in answer to a touch upon a silver bell on the
table beside his master, the young man followed him
after a graceful bow to the lord and lady of the castle.

Silence reigned for many minutes in the room he had
left. Frau von Osternau had taken up her knitting,
the needles clicked incessantly as they always did
when the lady was lost in thought. Her husband was
the first to speak. "Tell me frankly, Emma, how you
like your *protégé.*"

"I really do not know. I cannot make up my mind."

"Nor can I. A very strange fellow! He attracts and repels me. I called him a scarecrow when I saw him coming across the court-yard, but as he sat playing at the piano, and his dark eyes fairly shone, I thought him really handsome."

"So did I. What are we to think? But indeed since my good old friend Kramser has recommended him, we need be under no anxiety."

"It is odd though. I never should have imagined that so prosaic, commonplace a man as Kramser would have recommended so singular a person. How can the young fellow have been led to adopt teaching as a vocation? Will he, do you think, ever tame down the spirit that sparkles in those eyes to the dull routine of every-day life? If he does, we shall have cause for gratitude to your friend Kramser for many an hour of enjoyment. You were right when you called him a divinely-gifted artist."

CHAPTER IV.

A CATO IN GOLDEN CURLS.

"Beg pardon, Herr Candidate, I must request you to follow me."

Old Hildebrandt bowed as he spoke these words, and proceeded to conduct Herr Gottlieb Pigglewitch to his apartments. In a corner of the hall lay the ancient travelling-bag. Pigglewitch would have picked it up to carry it to his room himself, but this Hildebrandt would by no means allow. "I will call a servant," he said, taking the bag from the young man's hand, and in answer to his twice-repeated call of "Johann!" a footman appeared, who was taken to task for his dilatoriness and ordered instantly to carry the Herr Candidate's portmanteau to his room.

Johann scanned the figure of the stranger contemptuously, mentally comparing the threadbare coat of the latter with his own well-kept livery. It was really quite derogatory to his dignity to carry such a fellow's luggage up the stairs. "It's not my place to fetch and carry for *him!*" he was mentally ejaculating, when he suddenly encountered the glance of the stranger's eye, and what he saw there was in such contrast to his shabby exterior that he meekly took the bag and obeyed Hildebrandt's directions.

The old servant led the way up the broad staircase and along a wide corridor, at the end of which he threw open a door with "This is your sitting-room, Herr Candidate."

Pigglewitch was most agreeably surprised by the appearance of the apartment into which he was ushered, —a large, comfortably-furnished room, lighted by two broad windows. The low, chintz-covered sofa, with its large pillows, the big arm-chairs, the piano in one corner, the well-filled book-shelves, the study-table, all gave the place a refined air of comfort which gratified the young man's taste. He was especially pleased to find a piano here,—his dormant love of music had suddenly revived. Formerly his piano had been his best friend, he greeted it once more with joy.

He went to the window, which looked out upon a charming old-fashioned garden filled with bloom, and an extent of close-shaven lawn.

The old servant allowed the young man time to observe the prospect, and then remarked, "This door leads into your bedroom, Herr Candidate, where you will find your wardrobe and conveniences for washing, and where Johann has left your bag. The family dines at three o'clock punctually, and Herr von Osternau likes to have every one in the dining-hall as the clock begins to strike. It would be well if you would set your watch by the castle clock so as to be dressed by five minutes of three, when I shall with your permission show you the way to the dining-room. Madame likes to have every one dress for dinner; the Herr Lieutenant always does so, and when the Herr Inspectors are too busy to do so they dine in the Inspector's room and do not appear at table."

"You wish me to dress, then?" Pigglewitch asked, with a smile.

"If you please, Herr Candidate; I do not mean to presume, but you will like to know the custom of the household. Should you require anything further, you will be good enough to pull your bell three times in succession; the Herr Lieutenant rings twice and Herr von Osternau and madame once only. Johann will obey your summons immediately."

He bowed and left the room, leaving its occupant gazing thoughtfully out of the window. He looked across the blooming flower-beds, the velvet lawn, the luxuriant shrubbery, his eyes sought the distant horizon while his thoughts took shape in a half-muttered soliloquy: "The first step in the new life is taken, and everything differs utterly from my anticipations. Where is the haughty aristocrat, the scornful lady, whom I hoped to inspire with horror by my appearance? What has become of the struggle with arrogant self-assertion to which I looked forward? Positively my ill luck, the tiresome good fortune which has been lavished upon me ever since I was a child, pursues me here also, my irresponsible folly has introduced me to a household where any man save myself would be perfectly happy. Was it worth while to don Pigglewitch's ridiculous attire to be pursued here too by my fate? And, besides, how can I answer it to my conscience to deceive these worthy, unsuspicious people? If they were what I imagined them, arrogant, brutal, looking down with contempt upon the man whose services they had hired, there would have been some amusement in bringing their pride low in a contention with them. Such a struggle would have been worth a couple more weeks of existence. But now? Well, why not? I have something very different here from the eternal monotony of a fashionable society life. This one may be as tiresome, but variety will make it endurable for a time. I am already refreshed and enlivened by the idea of attempting to conform myself to new conditions of existence. But have I a right to play with these kindly people, to deceive them, for the gratification of a whim of the moment? Pshaw! It can do no harm to assume the *rôle* of a Candidate Pigglewitch for a few days. I have acknowledged frankly that this is but a trial, that I mistrusted my own qualifications for the position; what more could be desired? And, besides, if my *alter ego*, the real Pigglewitch, had come to them, would they have been any better off? They ought to thank me for ridding them of him. The farce is begun; it must be carried out until—until it grows too tiresome, and then the sham Pigglewitch can go the same way that the real Pigglewitch was so near going but lately."

He paused. His thoughts were diverted from their

course by the clear, joyous voice of a child in the garden below his windows.

A handsome little fellow, with fair close curls, broke forth from the shrubbery on the farther side of the lawn, and a few steps behind him came running, still faster, a girl hardly more than a child. She tried to catch the boy, he slipped from her but only for a moment. She caught him, lifted him in her arms, kissed him, and then putting him down with "Now catch me, Fritzchen!" she vanished again among the bushes. It was a charming picture. The graceful, girlish figure had glided like a fairy over the lawn, seeming to the spectator rather to fly than to run. With all her tender grace how strong and healthy she looked! Pigglewitch had but one fleeting glimpse of her face, when she lifted the boy and kissed him. It seemed to him wonderfully lovely, but the next instant she had disappeared in the shrubbery, and the boy followed her with a shout.

"Herr Fritzchen! Fräulein! Fräulein Lieschen!"

Old Hildebrandt was standing in the gravel-path that ran through the garden, calling in stentorian tones.

"Yes, yes!" came from the shrubbery, and immediately afterwards the brother and sister appeared, hand in hand, running swiftly. As they crossed the lawn, however, they slackened their pace, so that Pigglewitch could observe them at his ease. They were extremely alike, both handsome, but the maidenly charm of the young girl was indescribably attractive.

"What is it? Why are you calling us, Hildebrandt?" she asked, from a distance. The tone of her voice delighted the ear of the listener at the window. It was rich, clear, and melodious.

"Madame your mother sent me. The Herr Tutor

has come. Fritzchen is to go to him in his room immediately."

"The new tutor? Oh, I must see him too!" was Lieschen's reply, and hand in hand with her little brother she ran so swiftly towards the castle that her golden curls were blown backward by the wind.

Pigglewitch turned from the window and looked towards the door in expectation of the visit. That beautiful boy was to be his charge, that charming fairy his pupil in music. Here was another surprise. Would fortune never tire of showering her favours upon him? This time, however, her gifts did not strike him as tiresome. If he had ever hesitated as to whether he should carry out his mad scheme of remaining as tutor in Castle Osternau, all such hesitation was now at an end.

He waited but a few moments before light, tripping steps were heard in the corridor, then came a low, melodious laugh, and then a knock at his door.

"Come in!"

The door opened, and on the threshold there appeared, still hand in hand, the beautiful boy and the golden-haired fairy. The girl looked around the room with an air of arch curiosity, but no sooner did her eyes encounter Pigglewitch's figure than she burst into a laugh, which she vainly tried to suppress. She blushed, her efforts at self-control were evident, but they were of no use. One glance towards the new tutor was enough to provoke her merriment afresh. Thus, still laughing, she advanced into the room with Fritzchen, who looked in shy amazement at the stranger.

The young lady's unbridled mirth aroused in Pigglewitch, who guessed its cause, a very disagreeable sensation. On the day previous, and on this very morning, he had contemplated his image in his hand-glass with much complacency, congratulating himself upon the impression his slouching, bedraggled figure would make upon the aristocratic inmates of Castle Osternau. His expectations had been fulfilled, and were being fulfilled at this moment, but he was not enjoying himself. The prolonged laughter of the young girl vexed him, and as she sank into an arm-chair, and seemed entirely unable to regain her composure, he bit his lip and gave utterance to his annoyance by observing, sharply, "May I inquire the cause of your amiable merriment, Fräulein?"

The question only provoked a fresh burst of laughter, after which the girl controlled herself for a moment sufficiently to reply, "I am so sorry, but indeed I cannot help it when I look at you, you do look so utterly ridiculous!"

"Your pertinent reply bears testimony to taste in dress and to love of truth rather than to good breeding on your part, Fräulein."

Liesehen suddenly grew graver; she looked him fairly in the face for the first time. Hitherto her attention had been given to the queer black coat, with its long, pointed tails. She saw now that its wearer was offended, and she said, kindly and ruefully, "I am sorry to have vexed you, but indeed I could not help it. I mean no harm, but I must laugh when I look at you." Then, suddenly altering her tone, she went on, "But why should I excuse my conduct? Have you not just called my reply pertinent and a proof of good taste? consequently you must know yourself how utterly ridiculous that old-fashioned coat is, how ugly you look in it. If you come to Castle Osternau dressed like a scarecrow, you must not complain if you are laughed at. Hildebrandt told me how odd you looked. He prepared me, and yet I could not help laughing when I saw you. How can you wear such clothes? They do not suit your face at all, and Hildebrandt says you played the piano most delightfully."

She looked him full in the face as she thus lectured him, and shook her curls with a charming air of severity.

"A poor Candidate has no means wherewith to dress himself elegantly," Pigglewitch replied, colouring in spite of himself at the girl's reproof, the truth of which he could not deny, and taking refuge in prevarication.

"I do not believe you," Lieschen replied, adding after a short pause, during which she looked at him with grave reproof in her eyes, "It shows a want of respect for papa and mamma and for all of us. If you knew no better we could not help laughing at you although we should pity you, but your words betray your consciousness of the ridiculous appearance you present, and yet you come dressed thus to Castle Osternau. Papa always dresses for dinner, although he is an old man and the head of the house. And would you teach Fritzchen and me in that coat? Then do not ask us to be serious. Oh, I cannot help laughing when I look at you!"

She leaned back among the cushions of the arm-chair as her laughter burst forth again, while little Fritz, whom awe of the new tutor had hitherto kept quiet, was emboldened by his sister's example, and also laughed aloud.

The situation was by no means an agreeable one for Pigglewitch. If the girl's reproof had only not been so just! He cursed himself for his folly in exchanging clothes with the real Pigglewitch, but the deed was past recall, and he must bear the consequences.

"You ought not to ridicule poverty, Fräulein," he observed, merely for something to say.

Lieschen grew grave again; she was charming when she laughed, but still more attractive when she spoke with her little air of serious disapproval:

"I should be ashamed of laughing at a poor man because he could not dress in the fashion. I never should laugh at you for wearing a threadbare coat, although I cannot understand how a young man who has only himself to provide for should not be able to dress decently. You must have another suit of clothes. What is there in that old travelling-bag?"

She pointed to the bag which Johann had put just inside the open door of the next room. Her question embarrassed Pigglewitch. Had he told the truth he must have replied, "I don't know." He could not possibly say this, and again he had recourse to prevarication.

"Certainly nothing in the fashion," he replied. "Since, however, you lay such stress, Fräulein, upon my dress at table and during study hours, I will take care to provide myself as soon as possible with the best clothes that can be found here in the country. Until I have done so, I will beg madame your mother to dispense with my society at meals and to relieve me of my duties as instructor, for I cannot allow my pupils to laugh at me, even although one of them be a young lady."

Lieschen looked approval, she bethought herself a moment and then said, "I have a plan to propose, Herr Candidate. It would be a great pity that you should stay away from table for several days, for it will take the tailor fully that length of time to provide you with a new suit. Herr Storting will help you

He is just your size, and his clothes will at all events fit you better than that ugly, ridiculous coat."

"Who is Herr Storting?"

"Our second inspector. He is so obliging he will surely help you if I ask him to. He never refuses me anything, and I know he has a whole wardrobe full of suits. Do you consent? Indeed you must, you cannot reject my proposal, and in return I promise you that I will not even smile, either when you come to dinner or when you give me my first lesson on the piano. Herr Storting has just come in from the fields, I saw him ride into the court-yard a moment ago. I will go and ask him, and he will be here in five minutes and will offer to do anything for you. You need not say a word. Run quickly to the inspector's office, Fritzchen, and tell Herr Storting that I wish to speak to him immediately, and that I am waiting for him in the garden in the jessamine arbour. Adieu, Herr Candidate! We have had a little quarrel, but that is no matter, it can all be made up. We shall see each other again at dinner."

She did not wait for an answer: before Pigglewitch could either accept or reject her proposal she had tripped away, with Fritzchen running before her, eager to obey her orders.

"Egon, you have made an infernal fool of yourself," Pigglewitch muttered, when the young girl had left him. He felt really humiliated by the reproof uttered by those charming lips with so much girlish dignity. A mere child had ventured first to laugh at him, then to lecture him, and finally to act as it were as a kind of guardian over him. It was rather hard, especially as he could not but be conscious that Lieschen was right. Egon von Ernau, having taken upon himself Piggle-

witch's name and social standing, must submit to be
treated accordingly. He could withdraw from such
treatment, for he was not as yet bound even by any
promise. The idea occurred to him that he had best
leave Castle Osternau as quickly as possible, but it was
banished almost before it had taken shape. It would
be unpardonable weakness, actual cowardice, he said to
himself, to end the struggle for existence which he had
hardly begun, by a flight from the scene of action.
Was it the struggle only that interested him? Was
there not an attraction in the image of a charming
child, a fairy with golden curls, her dark-blue eyes now
dancing with laughter, now frankly reproachful? No,
he could not leave Castle Osternau at once, this child
must learn to respect him, and if he stayed it must not
be to afford the fairy occasion for mirth: he must lay
aside the ugly mask which he had purchased of the
real Pigglewitch. Perhaps the travelling-bag, as yet
unopened, would furnish more respectable apparel than
that which its owner had worn when travelling.

Egon had felt no antipathy to exchanging clothes
with Pigglewitch, but he was suddenly seized with
disgust for everything belonging to the man. He had
laughed when he had first looked at himself in the glass,
but as he now caught sight of his reflection he was
positively ashamed. "She called me a scarecrow," he
muttered, "and, by Jove! she was right. No scarecrow
could be a more ridiculous object than I am at this
minute."

He picked up the travelling-bag: it was locked and
there was no key, there was nothing for it but to force
the wretched lock with his pocket-knife. When it was
opened, the contents proved worse than he had imagined.
He found, to be sure, another suit of clothes rather better

than Pigglewitch's travelling attire, but it was made after precisely the same fashion, and when Egon put on the coat he thought he looked more like a scarecrow than before. The real Pigglewitch must have purchased his wardrobe in some old-clothes shop, with a special view to a certain bygone fashion. The newer coat being less shabby than the other could be less easily forgiven for its antique cut.

The linen which Egon discovered formed no contrast to the suit, it entirely disgusted him. What should he do until other clothes could be procured? and when could he procure these? Should he use the money in his pocket-book? He had determined not to touch it. It had been a chief part of his wild scheme to live for a while like a poor Candidate, with no other means than his salary as tutor. He had thought it interesting to try for once how life looked to a poor man, who must economize and contrive. Was he at the outset to be false to this scheme? No. Disagreeable as he might find it, he had resolved to taste, as Gottlieb Pigglewitch, the joys and sorrows of a poor Candidate, and he would carry out his intention. What would Gottlieb Pigglewitch do in his place? This was a question difficult to answer. He would hardly have been very sensitive beneath the laugh of the charming fairy. His usual dress had not been odious to him, and he would not probably have wished to exchange it for any other. In vain did Egon attempt to devise some way of procuring decent habiliments without having recourse to his pocket-book. He was pacing his room to and fro, in a very unenviable state of mind, when there was a knock at his door, and a fine-looking young man made his appearance. An involuntary smile played about his mouth at sight of Egon's peculiar attire, as, with a courteous inclination, he said, "Allow me to introduce myself to you, Herr Candidate. My name is Storting. Fräulein Lieschen sends me to you. You know the purpose of my coming, and I need not tell you how happy I shall be to serve you. My wardrobe is well supplied, and I can easily provide for you until you can make other arrangements."

The frank kindliness of the young man's offer embarrassed Egon afresh. He felt an eager desire to accept it, but was reluctant to place himself under such obligations to a stranger. Herr Storting's tall, well-made figure was like his own. Fräulein Lieschen had truly guessed that the young inspector's coat would fit him, but—— " I really do not see how I can accept your exceedingly kind offer, for which I thank you most cordially," he said, with hesitation.

"But indeed you must accept it," Storting replied, with a laugh. " It is Fräulein Lieschen's wish, and, as you will acknowledge before you have passed many days in Castle Osternau, this is a sufficient reason with every one of its inmates, from Herr von Osternau to the gardener's boy, with the exception perhaps of the Herr Lieutenant, for turning the world upside down. It is Fräulein Lieschen's wish, and to this wish you must bend. Pray come with me to my room. We shall soon be able to equip you suitably. To be honest with you, the young lady's wish is perfectly justifiable. You must not take my frankness amiss, I cannot help telling you that it would never do to appear at dinner in that coat. You would expose yourself to the derision of the servants, and compromise your position in the castle."

" I understand, but——"

"Do not hesitate to accept my offer. What harm

D 7

can it do to wear a coat which I do not need myself, for a couple of days, until you have fitted yourself out?"

"Until I have fitted myself out? But when shall I be able to do this?"

"Ah! yes, I understand you. You are for the moment in some pecuniary embarrassment."

"And supposing this to be the case?"

"That can easily be arranged. We will both ask for leave of absence for to-morrow forenoon. Mirbach Station is only a quarter of a mile from the castle. We can take the first train thence to-morrow, and be in Breslau by eight o'clock. I will take you to my tailor there, who will give you credit upon my recommendation, if you will promise to make quarterly payments on account when you receive your salary. He has a large establishment of ready-made clothing, and is not too dear. For fifty thalers you can easily procure a summer outfit, and I shall be happy to be of service to you in your selection, since you are probably not familiar with the prevailing fashions. We will take with us to Breslau the suit which you have on and that other lying on the chair, and dispose of them to the best advantage, for really they are not suitable to be worn at Castle Osternau. Do you agree?"

"Assuredly, and with a thousand thanks for your courtesy," Egon replied. He might, he thought, accept this proposal, and he quite enjoyed the idea of needing a sponsor to procure him a credit of fifty thalers, and of selling the wardrobe of the worthy Pigglewitch to an old-clothes dealer. Certainly there was variety here for Egon von Ernau.

He immediately followed Herr Storting to his room, where the wardrobes were found almost too well stocked, as the young inspector remarked, for their owner's means. "But better too many clothes than too few," he added. "It is specially needful to be always well dressed in the country, where there is so much temptation to be negligent, and where one's authority among the peasants and labourers depends more than would be believed upon a certain distinction of dress. Wherefore I am grateful to Herr von Oster-nau for strictly requiring that we should dress for dinner. It confirms us in good habits, as you, Herr Candidate, will admit when you have been a few weeks here."

Egon made no reply to this exordium. He merely expressed his thanks again, as Herr Storting selected from a wardrobe and placed at his disposal a plain but well-made summer suit, and it was with a positive sense of relief that he stripped off Pigglewitch's habiliments. As he did so Storting observed with surprise in his tone, "You are a riddle to me, Herr Candidate. Your linen is of the finest, and of the latest and most expensive fashion, while the remainder of your attire is so inconceivably forlorn. I cannot understand it. But my coat, you see, fits you as if it were made for you. You look a different man without that swallow-tailed abomination."

The pleasure with which Egon now contemplated himself in the looking-glass was an entirely new sensation. Involuntarily he wondered whether Fräulein Lieschen would again liken him to a scarecrow.

CHAPTER V.

DINNER AND DESSERT.

HERR VON OSTERNAU had no fancy for aristocratic conventionalities. He lived the life of a plain country gentleman, was on the best of terms with his servants and peasants, and treated his inspectors quite as if they belonged to his family, gave them a place at his table, and frequently invited them to join the family circle in the evenings. Nevertheless he observed certain forms. When his inspectors appeared at dinner or at tea in the drawing-room they were expected to do so in simple evening dress. No orders were given to this effect, but they knew what Herr and Frau von Osternau desired, and conformed to their wishes.

As the clock struck three, dinner was announced: the most exact punctuality was observed. The lord of the castle always betook himself half an hour before the time to the large dining-hall, at one end of which the table was set. Here he paced the long room to and fro, and it pleased him to have the members of his family bear him company here. During this half-hour before dinner he liked to talk with his children. He would often pace to and fro with Lieschen hanging on his right arm and Fritz holding his left hand. Frau von Osternau would sit by with her constant knitting, and at times Cousin Albrecht, the Lieutenant, would join the small party.

After dinner coffee was served in the adjoining billiard-room, whither the inspectors followed the family only on holidays or when there was comparatively little to be done out of doors. They usually took their leave, to return to their duties of superintendence, so soon as Herr von Osternau rose from table. The only exception to this rule was the superintendent, Lieutenant von Osternau, who belonged to the family, and who was, besides, not very strict in the discharge of his duties, although he drew with great punctuality when quarter-day came round the very considerable sum which he received as salary. As he himself was wont to say, his office as superintendent of the entire estate did not require him to oversee the smaller details of its management, and he could therefore always find time for a game of billiards with his cousin and Lieschen, as well as for visits to the neighbouring estates, with frequent hunting expeditions. He could do this the more readily since Herr von Osternau himself always exercised a general supervision of all agricultural operations and kindly allowed his young cousin every possible liberty.

On the day upon which the Candidate Gottlieb Pigglewitch arrived at the castle, Lieutenant Albrecht von Osternau appeared in the dining-hall somewhat before half-past two. The third inspector, Herr von Wangen, was overseeing the harvesters in the Oster meadow and had excused himself from appearing at table, and Herr Storting was busy with the reception of the first instalments of hay. Therefore the superintendent had seen no necessity for exerting himself in the hot sun, but had taken a siesta from twelve to two, and was now awaiting his cousin in the cool, airy dining-hall.

He had not long to wait. Punctual as ever, Herr and Frau von Osternau entered. A minute later, Fritz

rushed in, and Lieschen came to take her father's arm
and accompany him in his daily promenade. Cousin
Albrecht accosted her, but she slipped past him with
an arch glance and the half-contemptuous inquiry,
"Are you up again, cousin? I hope you enjoyed your
nap."

"What makes you think I have been sleeping?"
Albrecht asked, crossly, annoyed that Lieschen should
betray him. Kind and courteous as was the castle's
lord, he could hardly be pleased to learn that his
superintendent had spent the precious time in a nap
before dinner.

"Can you deny it, cousin?" Lieschen rejoined, with
a laugh. "You had better not try that. So loud and
sonorous a sound came from your room as I passed
your door a while ago, that I stopped for a moment to
wonder what it was. It was wonderful music. You
say you are not very musical, but no one who has heard
you snore will believe you."

"What were you doing at my room door? What
did you want of me?"

Lieschen looked round scornfully at her cousin, who
was following a few steps behind her father and herself.
"You do not suppose, do you, that I was going to pay
you a visit? No, Cousin Albrecht, I was on my way
to one more worthy of such an honour, our new Candidate. Why do you look surprised? Oh, I understand, you do not know yet that we have a new inmate.
You have been sleeping sweetly and snoring most
musically while the Candidate was being installed in
his rooms, which are just beyond yours. You cannot
deny now that you have been asleep."

Albrecht was at a loss for a reply, and was relieved
by Herr von Osternau's turning to Lieschen with the

ınquiry, "Did you pay the Candidate a visit in his room?"

"Of course, papa. I was frightfully curious to see him."

"And how did you like him?" asked her father.

"Do you know, papa, I have been thinking that over for an hour, and I cannot make up my mind?"

"Why, you laughed at him terribly, Lieschen, and told him he looked like a scarecrow," little Fritz interposed.

Her father and mother exchanged a glance of intelligence, and Herr von Osternau said, "The same comparison occurred to me as I saw him crossing the court-yard, so the resemblance must have been striking. But, Lieschen, you ought not to have used such a word to him: you are too old, my child, to let your tongue so run away with you. We ought not to say everything that we think, and, besides, it is impossible to judge a man by his exterior. The Candidate himself is a proof of this. At first sight he seems only an awkward, uncouth man, but no one can look into his eyes and not see intelligence sparkling there."

"I saw no sparks," interposed Fritz again.

"But I did," Lieschen said, thoughtfully, "and that was precisely why I told you just now, papa, that I could not make up my mind."

Again Herr von Osternau exchanged a glance of intelligence with his wife. They had each used almost the same words which Lieschen had just uttered to express their own inability to pronounce judgment upon the stranger.

"This sparkling-eyed Candidate must be an extraordinary man," Albrecht remarked. "What is his name? You have not mentioned his name, cousin."

"Pigglewitch."

The name produced an instant effect. Albrecht burst into a laugh, in which Lieschen and Fritz joined, while even Frau von Osternau could not suppress a smile.

"Pigglewitch! A charming name! I am really curious to make his acquaintance."

"You will stop laughing, and never bestow a thought upon either his ridiculous name or his odd appearance, when you see him at the piano and hear the wondrous charm of his music," Herr von Osternau replied to Albrecht's remark. "There's magic in his playing. It positively bewitched me. I scarcely ventured to breathe while the melody lasted, and when the tones had died away on the air the echo still rang on in my heart."

"He'll not bewitch me," Albrecht declared, still laughing. "The name of Pigglewitch will act as a counter-charm to provoke laughter in spite of all the melody imaginable."

Lieschen agreed with her cousin, and Fritz seemed quite of the same opinion, inasmuch as he repeated the name several times, and always with fresh merriment. Frau von Osternau had some difficulty in subduing the young people's mirthfulness, in which she was half tempted to join, strictly forbidding Fritz to offend the Herr Candidate by any show of amusement at his odd name. It would be best that, until he became used to its sound, he should address his tutor as Herr Candidate, "and Lieschen and Cousin Albrecht," she added, with a glance towards the pair, "would do well to observe the same rule." Whereupon Cousin Albrecht declared that he could not promise to do so, that ridiculous people existed in order that others might have the pleasure of chaffing them, and that if the Candidate's name was Pigglewitch he must expect to have it laughed at. Besides, there was no fear of offending the man, that sort of people ought to feel it an honour to be noticed at all, he would doubtless be flattered by their laughter.

Herr von Osternau objected to this remark of his cousin's, but Albrecht maintained that he was right, and there ensued a sharp war of words, in which Albrecht showed himself a thorough conservative aristocrat, despising all, even the most cultivated, of the *bourgeoisie*, and quite unable to conceive how a Candidate could prefer any claim to be received in what he called society, while the elder cousin with much greater persistence expressed his liberal views and declared that he required that the Herr Lieutenant should treat their new inmate with the courtesy due to every man of culture, whatever might be his social standing.

Herr von Osternau was always extremely forbearing in his treatment of Cousin Albrecht, for whose disappointment with regard to his inheritance he felt great compassion, but to-day he showed some irritation in the warmth of his defence of the Candidate's rights. He declared that he would not suffer any slight or want of courtesy to be shown in his house to a young man to whom he had confided the instruction of his children.

Albrecht rejoined that he would have no rules laid down for his conduct towards a man who was too much his inferior to be worthy of notice; he could not possibly treat the Candidate as a social equal; such people could not but be conscious that they were merely tolerated.

The dispute between the cousins threatened to become warmer still, and the gentle words of Frau von Osternau

f

failed of their usual soothing effect, when fortunately
the bell of the castle clock tolled three, and before it
had finished the folding doors of the dining-hall were
opened, and Herr Storting and the Candidate Pigglewitch appeared, followed by Johann bearing the souptureen.

But was this really the Candidate Pigglewitch? Herr
and Frau von Osternau could scarcely believe their eyes,
so complete was the transformation. There was no
longer a trace to be seen of the awkwardness of gait
or carriage that had seemed a part of his antique,
dangling habiliments. So easy and unconstrained were
his movements in the simple summer coat with which
Herr Storting had provided him that there was hardly
anything about him by which to recognize Pigglewitch.
His first glance as he entered the room was for Lieschen,
his first bow of course for her mother, whom he approached with respectful courtesy, while he was quite
conscious of the roguish sparkle in the fairy's eyes, by
which she showed her satisfaction in the metamorphosis
her power had effected.

In consequence of the interrupted dispute the lord
of the castle received the Candidate with extreme
kindliness, offering him his hand as he said, " Welcome
to our small circle, Herr Pigglewitch. Most of its
members you are already acquainted with, my children
have introduced themselves to you, and Herr Storting
has become known to you as I see by your coming into
the room together ; my cousin, then, is the only stranger
to you here. Herr Candidate Pigglewitch, Herr Lieutenant Albrecht von Osternau."

At this formal introduction Egon was about to bow
courteously, but, observing that the lieutenant held
himself haughtily erect with the faintest acknowledg-

ment of his cousin's introduction, he only slightly inclined his head, with a half-smile at the scowl with
which Albrecht noted his behaviour. Not a word was
exchanged between the young men, but each felt in-
stinctively that they were foes.

"The soup is upon the table," said Herr von Osternau, who had observed this little scene with some displeasure and was in a hurry to cut it short. "Let us
be seated. Your place is here between Lieschen and
Fritz, Herr Pigglewitch."

Herr von Osternau was wont during dinner to discuss
with his inspectors the various agricultural interests of
the estate. Of course it would have been natural that
he should apply first in such matters to his superintendent, Cousin Albrecht, but he knew that he should
receive unsatisfactory replies from that quarter, and
accordingly he conversed upon these subjects directly
with Herr Storting and the third inspector, Herr von
Wangen. As, however, the latter had excused himself
from dining with the family to-day, being too much occupied with the harvesting, Herr von Osternau directed
his inquiries and remarks to Herr Storting only.

These farming disquisitions, questions as to the yield
of hay to be expected from this or that meadow, as to
the excellence of the crop, etc., matters of vivid interest to the landed proprietor, were utterly devoid of such
for Egon. He knew perfectly well that hay was dried
grass and was used for fodder for horses and cattle,
but he had no idea of the importance of the labour
which was necessary to gather in and duly store this
precious product of the fields. He really could not
follow the conversation which was carried on almost
entirely between Herr von Osternau and Storting, with
here and there a remark thrown in by Cousin Albrecht

by way of asserting his dignity as superintendent, and he would have been very much bored had his attention not been entirely absorbed by his neighbour on his right.

As he took his place beside her Lieschen had given him a charming little nod, and when her father began his agricultural talk with Herr Storting, she turned to Egon and said, in a low tone,—

"I thank you, Herr Piggle——" She paused; "Herr Candidate," she added.

"Why do you interrupt yourself, Fräulein Lieschen?"

"I promised not to laugh at you at table, and I do not wish to break my word. You must not take it amiss, but indeed your name is too comical, I should laugh if I said it, and that would mortify you."

"Not in the least. I resign my ridiculous name with pleasure to your tender mercies. Laugh if you like, and I will join your laughter at 'Pigglewitch.' The owner of such a name must make up his mind to have it laughed at, so it is his best policy to laugh too."

Lieschen looked at him in surprise.

"That I cannot understand," she said. "How can any one laugh at his own name, however ridiculous it may be? For him who bears it a name must be something sacred, to be revered as a memento of parents and grandparents who have borne it."

"If you think thus, Fräulein Lieschen, you ought not to laugh at a ridiculous name."

"You are right, Herr Pigglewitch. I will call you by your name, and I promise you that not a muscle of my face shall stir as I do so."

"No, no, Fräulein Lieschen, I was not in such grave earnest. You will not mortify me, on the contrary it will please me if the name of Pigglewitch excite your merriment, and I am convinced that all the Pigglewitches now with God would take no offence at a smile upon such charming lips."

"Now you are laughing at your ancestors. I do not like to have you do that. Some things are too sacred to be trifled with. I do not know what to think of you. You really pleased me just now when you reproved me, but your sneer at what every man should hold sacred spoils it all. I am afraid you are not a good man, Herr Pigglewitch."

"I do not think I am, and yet I am not as bad as I might be," Egon replied. "I pray you, Fräulein Lieschen, take me for what I am; besides, I am capable of improvement, as I have proved to you. Have I not sacrificed to you my beautiful coat with its charming long tails, and consented to appear no longer in the part of scarecrow, but as an ordinary human being in Herr Storting's clothes?"

"I have already thanked you for that."

"Quite unnecessarily. I deserve no thanks. You read me a charming homily, and I deserved it. I knew you were right, and the result you have before you. I have even arranged with Herr Storting, who has been extremely kind to me, to go early to-morrow to Breslau, where my beautiful black coat is to find its grave in the shop of some humane old-clothes dealer until some needy wretch effects its resurrection. I shall return from Breslau stripped of the borrowed plumes which at present adorn me, but in attire, I trust, which will allow me to appear before you without being considered a ridiculously ugly scarecrow."

"You have not forgotten my thoughtless word," Lieschen said, with a blush.

"No, I do not mean to forget it, it was just, and made a deep impression upon me. You see I am capable of being instructed. Perhaps you may be induced to be kind enough to occupy yourself somewhat with my neglected education."

Lieschen opened her eyes in wonder. "It would seem to be really necessary," she said, gravely. "I know you are laughing at me when you ask an inexperienced girl of seventeen and your future pupil to attend to your education, but indeed you might learn one thing from me,—frankness. Papa blamed me a little while ago for always speaking out my thoughts, but indeed I cannot help it, and I tell you plainly that I think your way odious of ridiculing everything, even yourself, your name, your parents and ancestors, and— me for venturing to declare your old clothes ugly. Your ridicule wounds and offends me. We shall never be good friends if you talk so to me."

The girl's sharp reproof surprised Egon so much that he was at a loss for a reply. He was used in society to meet with the greatest complaisance from any young lady upon whom he bestowed attention. It is true he understood the reason for this, he knew why the belles of the capital lent so ready an ear to him, manifesting the greatest interest in everything that he said, and from this knowledge he had acquired the habit— now become to him second nature—of treating them with an easy air of superiority. He was consequently greatly surprised to find a girl scarcely more than a child administering to him for the second time to-day a rebuke which he could not but be conscious was well merited. He was really in some embarrassment as to how he should reply to her, when he was fortunately relieved of the necessity for doing so.

The discussion of the important agricultural matters which had claimed Herr von Osternau's entire attention, and had been listened to with such interest by his wife that she had paid no heed to the conversation between the Candidate and her daughter, came to an end after Herr von Osternau had arranged operations for the next day, and he now turned to Egon, saying kindly, "You must have been somewhat bored, Herr Pigglewitch: you can hardly take any great interest in agricultural pursuits, but if you are to live at Castle Osternau I trust you will find some in what concerns us here so nearly. It will come, I think, on a closer acquaintance with the subject. The management of an extensive landed estate, the pursuit of agriculture, always seems to one town-bred as an inferior, unintellectual occupation. To him the ordinary peasant is stupidity personified,—a man who follows his plough like some soulless machine,—and the landed proprietor is but slightly the superior of his peasants. Among our titled official circles, if a son is too dull for diplomacy they make a soldier of him, and if there are fears as to his passing his examination as an officer he is thought at all events clever enough for agriculture. They buy him an estate, and should he find a clever, well-taught superintendent, the machinery of his farms works well, and the opinion that the dullest fellow is not too dull for an agricultural career receives confirmation. The poor development of our agricultural resources in many parts of our country is owing to this wretched prejudice. The larger number of landed proprietors have no idea of the significance of their vocation, they farm after the fashions which have been handed down to them through long generations, without a thought of the study which should be devoted to the agriculture of to-day. For the enlightened management of a large farming interest a constant and keen observation of nature's methods is required, and an understanding that must be well directed by a cultivated intellect. It is so easy to tread the well-worn paths that our forefathers have trod, and in doing so one wins approval as a practical farmer from those who are always ready to point out the mistakes of others whom they regard as given over to theories, never suspecting how study might enable them to treble the produce of their fields and meadows. The intelligent farmer makes science his servant, by whom he wrings nature's secrets from her and turns them to the best advantage. The smallest agricultural details are of importance to him, for through exactitude in these the whole vast machinery of a large estate is kept in order, and small results will be reached by those who despise them. But I hardly meant, Herr Pigglewitch, to deliver you a lecture upon agriculture. I only wish to prove to you that an interest in the details of a large farming establishment is not so tiresome and belittling as you may have hitherto believed. When you have been here some time you will begin to perceive the complicated wheel-work of the vast machine, and will perhaps take some pleasure in our daily discussion of agricultural matters."

Egon listened attentively to this long explanation, and as he did so a new sphere of ideas lay revealed before him. He himself possessed an extensive estate in Western Prussia, Plagnitz, which he had inherited from his mother, but he had never concerned himself in the slightest degree with its management; indeed, he had never visited it but once, when, after a stay of somewhat less than a week, he had left it with the

determination never to see it again, so flat, stale, and
unprofitable did life seem to him in a country where the
scenery was not particularly fine, in an old manor-house
that might have been a mediæval castle. His administrator, who bore the reputation of a good, practical
agriculturist, was interested in nothing save rye and
wheat, cows and sheep. Upon no other subject could
a word be exchanged either with him or with his wife,
who was an admirable housekeeper. He had conducted
his young master through stalls and stables, and would,
if allowed, have told him the history and pedigree of
every horse and ox. He knew just how much milk
every cow gave daily, and the number of calves born
on the estate in a year, all which details he was desirous
of giving to his master. The sheep were passed in
review before their lord, and the administrator grew
enthusiastic over the merits of Negrettis and Merinos.
Egon hardly understood a word of his explanation, and
was simply bored. Then horses were brought, and the
two men rode over the entire estate. Egon was called
upon to admire the crops, when he really did not know
the difference between wheat, oats, and rye. Everything that the administrator admired tired his master.
Egon was delighted to leave Plagnitz at the end of
four days; he made up his mind that nothing was more
stupid or conducive to intellectual torpor than the pursuit of agriculture. Since this visit he had not even
read his administrator's letters; he gave them to some
one of his father's clerks to answer, and drew from his
father's bank the income from the estate, heedless
whether it was as large as it ought to be or not. Such
details were too insignificant to occupy his attention.
He had more money than he knew how to spend. He
really had not thought of his West Prussian estate for

a long time, when it suddenly occurred to him during Herr von Osternau's discourse. With the remembrance of it came, however, the memory of the intolerable tedium of his visit there. Could it have been his own ignorance that made the management of his estate so utterly devoid of interest for him? Was his administrator one of the practical farmers spoken of by Herr von Osternau? Was it possible to introduce more enlightened methods at Plagnitz,—methods with a scientific basis, which might make of it a model for the cultivation of the surrounding estates? He would consider this when he returned to Berlin. But should he ever return to Berlin? Had he then quite relinquished the purpose for which he had left the capital? His present existence was to have been only a short episode before the close of a useless career, and here he was thinking of the future and of something to be done after a while. It was folly. He must live in the present, there was no future for him.

For a moment he lost himself in memory and reflection. He was recalled to the present by a sneering remark of the Lieutenant's: "You are preaching to deaf ears, my dear cousin. Herr Pigglewitch does not find your admonitions worth listening to."

"You are mistaken, Herr Lieutenant," Egon rejoined, hastily, "I have not only been listening attentively, but have been drawing conclusions from what Herr von Osternau has been saying which may prove of advantage to me, and for which I thank him. I frankly confess that I have hitherto had no idea that the cultivation of the soil required any amount of intellectual capacity, and I cannot tell whether I shall ever feel any real interest in agriculture. At present I am so absolutely ignorant upon the subject that the meaning of various words and phrases that fell upon my ear during your discussion, as, for instance, four-course rotation, naked fallow, extirpator, is unknown to me."

Herr von Osternau laughed at the young man's frank confession of ignorance, at which Frau von Osternau was much surprised.

"You amaze me, Herr Pigglewitch," she said. "Director Kramser wrote me that you were the son of a country clergyman and had been brought up in the country."

"Again I have made a blunder," thought Egon. "Impudence, befriend me!" and, without seeming at all confused, he turned to the lady of the house. "I confess, to my shame, madame," he replied, "that as a boy I had a great dislike for every sort of occupation not connected with my books. And then the small farm attached to a country parsonage is a very insignificant affair. I took no kind of interest in it then, nor did my tastes change with years. A teacher who is not content with inferiority in his training has very little time for any occupation save what is connected with his future vocation."

"Ah! with such incessant study you must have become wonderfully learned," the Lieutenant observed.

Egon took no notice of the remark: he was only too glad that he had been able to satisfy the mistress of the house without telling a direct falsehood. He saw that he had come off conqueror when Frau von Osternau gave him a kindly nod and said, "You have turned your time to good account, Herr Pigglewitch, your wonderful music to-day was proof of that. I can understand how long and how diligent has been the practice which has given you so brilliant an execution. The expression, the feeling in your playing cannot be taught or learned, it is a God-given inspiration possessed by comparatively few of us. I shall be too happy if you are able to call forth only a hint of it in my children."

"Herr Pigglewitch is then an artist as well as a scholar," the Lieutenant observed. "Really, I begin to stand in awe of him, and to consider Fritz most fortunate in having such a light to illumine the path of wisdom for him. 'Tis a pity that for the present Fritz must confine himself to the A B C of learning, or Herr Pigglewitch could regale him with chemistry, physics, mathematics, Latin, Greek, French, English,—in short, with everything worth knowing."

"Add Italian, and your list of the subjects upon which I ought to be competent to teach will be complete," Egon rejoined, quietly, as if unconscious of any irony in the Lieutenant's words.

"What! you understand five languages besides your own?" Herr von Osternau asked in amazement that a Candidate should be thus accomplished. "I thought that modern languages were rather neglected in our first-class schools."

"I did not learn them at school," Egon said, smiling. "I was always ambitious to learn something more than was prescribed by the school curriculum, and I have a natural gift for languages. I like to read great poets in the original, translations are apt to be but weak transcriptions, therefore I studied English to read Shakespeare, and Italian for the sake of Dante. Every educated man understands French of course, and Greek and Latin form part of the usual classical education."

Frau von Osternau was indeed surprised. Were these quietly-uttered words true, or was Herr Pigglewitch boasting of accomplishments which he did not possess, in the belief that no one at Castle Osternau could put his knowledge to the test? If this last were the case he was mistaken. True, she herself had no knowledge of Greek, Latin, or Italian, but she spoke both French and English quite well. She addressed him in English, expressing her pleasure at his proficiency in languages; he answered her in the same tongue with an accent and with fluency superior to her own. French he spoke with equal purity and facility. She could not, after a short conversation in both tongues, forbear an expression of her admiration of his ability, and was a little embarrassed when he rejoined, in German, "I have then been undergoing a slight examination. Perhaps Lieutenant von Osternau will have the kindness to continue it, and to test my qualifications in Latin and Greek, mathematics, chemistry, and physics. I gladly place myself at his disposal."

"I have never had anything to do with school examinations, and feel no desire to begin to-day," the Lieutenant replied, giving the insufferable Pigglewitch a look that was meant to be crushing, but which was only furious.

"You are right there, Cousin Albrecht," Lieschen interposed; "you would come to grief if you attempted the part of an examiner."

The Lieutenant had no chance to reply to his young cousin, for Herr von Osternau rose from table and every one followed his example.

On week-days the inspectors always took their leave, returning to their duties, but to-day Herr Storting lingered and asked for leave of absence for the next morning. Herr von Osternau seemed surprised. "Is your business in Breslau so very pressing?" he asked. "You know every hour is precious during the harvesting."

"Yes, papa, Herr Storting has very urgent business in Breslau," Lieschen replied in the young man's stead. "He and Herr Pigglewitch must both pay a visit there to-morrow morning. Please, papa, do not ask why now, I will tell you by and by."

"And why not now?"

"Because Cousin Albrecht stands there pricking his ears most curiously, and the matter is no affair of his. I am sure, papa dear, you will allow Herr Storting and the Herr Candidate to go to-morrow without asking any questions. They will both be back by noon."

"Of course we must all do as you please, you witch," her father replied, stroking back the golden curls from his darling's forehead. "I will ask no questions. Certainly they should both have gone without your interference. I am sure Herr Storting has good reasons for wishing to spend any time away from Osternau during the hay-harvest."

Storting looked a little confused. "Indeed you are most kind, Herr von Osternau. I was perhaps in a trifle too much haste, I might postpone——"

"Do not believe him, papa, he cannot possibly postpone, and I'll tell you in your ear why,—you will allow me, Herr Pigglewitch?"

"No, Fräulein Lieschen, I beg you, on the contrary, to withdraw your request," Egon replied. "I cannot suffer Herr Storting to leave his duty here to do me a favour. The matter in question is a favour to me, Herr von Osternau, and I really cannot see why it should be kept secret. I could not appear at dinner in the only clothes which I possessed. Herr Storting therefore very kindly lent me one of his own suits, and offered to go with me to-morrow to Breslau and help me in the

choice of attire suitable for a residence in Castle Osternau. This is the entire mystery."

"A ridiculous trifle!" exclaimed the Lieutenant.
"And Herr Storting was to go to Breslau during
harvest for this? An extraordinary idea!"

"Which never occurred to me," replied Egon. "Herr
Storting offered to accompany me, and I accepted his
proposal, not imagining that his short absence could
be any disadvantage in the farming operations, which
are carried on under the distinguished auspices of
Herr Lieutenant von Osternau. Since, however, I am
now better informed, I beg to decline his kind offer,
and will, with Herr von Osternau's permission, go to
Breslau alone."

"For Heaven's sake, do not let him, papa!" Lieschen
whispered to her father. "Think of that black coat!
No, you must not go alone, Herr Storting must go with
you and advise you."

Herr von Osternau laughed at his daughter's zeal,
nevertheless the remembrance of the black coat outweighed any objection he might have had to dispensing
with Storting's services. The Herr Candidate might
be a very accomplished and cultivated man, but he certainly had no idea of how to dress himself. Storting
must look after him in this respect. He did not indeed give this as a reason for his ready acquiescence
in his daughter's wishes, but cut short a remonstrance
on the part of the Lieutenant by declaring that the
matter was settled, Herr Storting and Herr Pigglewitch would start on the morrow for Breslau, and if
they found their business required more time than was
anticipated, they need be in no hurry to return, but
could spend the entire day there. When the Lieutenant
here ventured to remark that Herr von Wangen would

find it difficult to superintend the harvesters alone, his cousin replied, with some asperity, "Then perhaps you, Cousin Albrecht, will have the kindness to take Herr Storting's place, since he is certainly going to Breslau. And now no more of this. We will take our coffee in the billiard-room. Do you play billiards, Herr Pigglewitch? Yes? So much the better, you can take part in our game. There are usually but three of us, Cousin Albrecht, Lieschen, and myself. Four players make the game much more entertaining. We usually spend an hour every day in billiards. When I am kept within-doors, as to-day, it is my only exercise. You must prepare yourself for a hard contest, Herr Pigglewitch, for Albrecht is a master of the game. Fortunately, we play for glory only, and Lieschen and I are always forced to yield this to the Lieutenant."

"Herr Pigglewitch will probably dispute this glory with me: he is, no doubt, also a master of the game," rejoined the Lieutenant.

Albrecht certainly was an extremely good billiard-player, he had had an admirable opportunity to become so during the hours spent at his military club, and he was inclined to resent the idea that he should find an actual antagonist in a man who could not possibly be a proficient in a game requiring for its mastery both time and money. Chance gave him precedence of Egon in the present game, and he made sure of soon establishing the Candidate's insignificance and his own supremacy as a player. But he was much mistaken; he could not but see very shortly that he had found his master. At Egon's first successful stroke Albrecht muttered something about "luck" and "beginners," but when the course of the game did but further reveal the Candidate's skill and brilliant play, the Lieutenant grew furious. He tried to preserve an appearance of equanimity, but when the game was at an end he refused to take part in another, declaring that he must ride out to the harvest-field. It did not improve his temper, when his cousin repeated his request to him to stay for one more round, for Lieschen to say, with a laugh, "Do not tease him, papa dear. How can you ask him to play on after his discomfiture? He must calm himself down with a ride,—

"'He scarcely breathes within these walls,
Forth to the meadows nature calls!'"

"Your school-girl quotation fails of its mark," the Lieutenant said, crossly; "I am not at all discomfited, and it would not in the least affect me if this gentleman, who appears to have used his time for study to such good purpose, really played a better game of billiards than I. My calling is not that of a billiard-player, and I have never attempted to acquire the artistic skill which I grant is possessed by Herr Pigglewitch. I leave that to professional gamblers."

He uttered the last words with an expression of great contempt, looking full at Egon, who had hitherto listened in silence, but who now turned with flashing eyes and addressed the Lieutenant in a voice which he forced to sound calm: "You have made use of a word, Herr Lieutenant, which I require you instantly to retract. Out of regard for the ladies and Herr von Osternau, I have hitherto taken no notice of your offensive expressions; your last remark touches my honour, and you will either retract it or give me satisfaction."

"The fellow is insane. He presumes to take me to task and to demand satisfaction of me!"

"Which you will give the gentleman, Cousin Al-

E   *g*   9

brecht," Herr von Osternau said, sharply, before Egon
could reply to this fresh insult. "You will give it immediately by apologizing to him. Take care, cousin!
I would advise you to reflect before uttering words that
may be irrevocable. I told you an hour ago that I
would not suffer the man to whom I have intrusted my
children's instruction to be treated beneath my roof
otherwise than as a gentleman. You have insulted Herr
Pigglewitch without provocation; this I will not permit. I give you your choice: either you retract your
offensive expressions, or you leave Castle Osternau this
very day. I am not jesting, Cousin Albrecht, my word
is immovable. You have insulted *me* in insulting Herr
Pigglewitch. I require an apology not only for his
sake, but for my own."

Was this the easy, good-natured man who had not
spoken a harsh word for years to the cousin whom he
had received into his household? His figure, usually
slightly bent, stood erect, his keen glance scanned Albrecht's features, in which surprise was evident, as he
spoke in a manner that admitted of no contradiction.

"You are very kind in thus espousing my cause,
Herr von Osternau," Egon interposed. "I cannot think
of causing any dispute between yourself and your relative by my presence beneath your roof. I thank you
sincerely for your generous words, which make all the
more clear to me the necessity for ending this contest
by my departure from Castle Osternau. I see clearly
that 1 am not fit for the position of tutor. I never
should have undertaken to accept it. I shall know how
to obtain satisfaction hereafter from Lieutenant von
Osternau, and it only remains for me, my dear sir, to
bid you a grateful farewell."

"Not at all! Not a word of that!" the old man replied.

"You have made a contract which cannot be cancelled save by the consent of both parties. You will, as you have promised to do, attempt the duties of my children's tutor. Until that attempt has been made I shall not release you from your promise. And as you have just heard, I demand an apology, not only for you but for myself. This Cousin Albrecht will make, and immediately, or leave Castle Osternau forever. Forever, Albrecht! Reflect what you are doing!"

The Lieutenant could not meet his cousin's flashing eyes, before which he cast down his own. The fire of his anger had quickly died out, but from his very soul he hated this insolent plebeian Candidate who had thus humiliated him. And he must apologize to him,—he must, he could not refuse to do so. He knew how stern was his cousin's resolve when once made known, how implacable his resentment when once it had found a lodgement in his kindly nature. There was no choice left him. What was he to do if his generous relative refused to shelter him? He thought of the future with horror. He had lost at play during his occasional visits to Berlin the entire large sum of this year's salary received for his unimportant services at Osternau, and had contracted debts for which he was continually dunned, although his creditors knew that they would be paid, as had so frequently been the case before, by his magnanimous cousin. How should he satisfy them if he were banished from Castle Osternau?

"Well, Cousin Albrecht, I await your decision."

The Lieutenant bit his lip; he could no longer hesitate; he must submit to the humiliation, but he registered a mental vow that he would avenge it upon the man who had been the cause of it. His task now was to make this humiliation as little apparent as possible: so, although the blood tingled in his veins, he forced himself to appear calm, as he replied to his cousin, "There really was no need of harsh words from you, Cousin Fritz, to induce me to recall a thoughtless expression, which I regretted as soon as 1 perceived that it had been misunderstood. I had no idea of styling Herr Pigglewitch a professional gambler, and I should have told him this, and asked to be excused for my misunderstood expression, had he not demanded with such an air of menace the satisfaction which the difference in our rank makes it impossible that I should give him. This declaration, to which I add that I had no intention to offend, and that I gladly retract any expression that could be considered insulting, will, I hope, entirely accord with your wishes."

"Entirely, and I think Herr Pigglewitch too will be quite satisfied," said Herr von Osternau, kindly, offering Albrecht his hand.

Egon bowed. He was not satisfied, but the Candidate Pigglewitch was forced to be so since Herr von Osternau was. Egon von Ernau would have rejected the apology and demanded again the satisfaction that had been denied him, finding in the reference to a difference of rank a fresh insult, but in the Candidate Pigglewitch such conduct would be unjustifiable, he must submit to seem content. He was even forced to admit that his adversary had gone farther to conciliate him than was absolutely necessary when, upon leaving the room to ride out to the harvest-fields, the haughty Lieutenant von Osternau offered him his hand in token of amity.

CHAPTER VI.

SOLIMAN'S TRICKS

It is no easy matter to be a tutor! This was the sum of Egon von Ernau's reflections as he sat at the study-table in his sitting-room an hour after the late scene with the Lieutenant, awaiting his little pupil. When Albrecht left the billiard-room, Herr and Frau von Osternau had a conversation with their new tutor concerning the course they wished him to pursue with their son. Frau von Osternau was desirous that the child should not be kept too long at his books. She thought that with two hours of daily instruction he could soon learn to read, write, and cipher, which was all that need be thought of at present. If, in addition, Herr Pigglewitch would give him a music-lesson every day, Fritz would be sufficiently occupied, at least for the first few months. Any excess of application was sure to be a physical disadvantage to the child, and his physical health and strength were the first considerations.

These views certainly differed widely from any that Egon had found in the teachers who had conducted his own education; nevertheless they seemed reasonable, and he undertook, by Frau von Osternau's desire, to give Fritz his first hour of instruction on the same afternoon.

For the first hour, which was to begin at five o'clock, he was now preparing himself. It had suddenly occurred to him upon his return to his room that he

9*

really had no conception of how to teach a boy to read
and write. He had but the faintest remembrance of
how he had been taught himself, and there was besides
a dim idea in his mind of having heard somewhere that
the old methods were no longer in use, that children
were not taught first to read and then to write, but
that there was a way by which both arts could be
acquired at the same time, and with surprising rapidity.
What could it be?

He opened one of the various books for the instruction of the young with which his table had been provided by the careful mother of his pupil, and tried to
imagine himself a perfectly ignorant child,—a very difficult task.

It is no easy matter, after all, to be a tutor! How
had Egon looked down hitherto upon this calling, and
here he sat racking his brains over the problem of
how to teach a child his A B C! Half an hour passed
like a moment, when a timid knock was heard at the
door, and Fritz entered shyly. Positively Egon felt
his heart beat quicker. Never, even when about to
pass the most difficult examination, had he felt such
trepidation, such a sense of the utter inadequacy of
his knowledge as at this moment. He could not but
smile at his cowardice, he could not understand himself. How had he come to take thus seriously the wild
jest that had been prompted by the whim of the moment?

'Some things are too sacred to be trifled with!'
A charming child had said these words to him a few
hours before, and they had sunk into his heart. He
had intended to play a madcap prank, but the jest had
come to be earnest. He was really undertaking the
duty of a teacher, and this duty took grand and sacred

proportions in his eyes as he looked at the handsome boy gazing with a smile, but with some shyness, into his face.

In fact, the teacher was more embarrassed than the pupil, but he collected himself, and drew the little fellow towards him, stroked his curls, and said, kindly,—

"Well, Fritz, are you going to please mamma, and study like a good lad?"

"Yes, I have promised mamma, and I promised Lieschen that I will not laugh when I call you Herr Pigglewitch."

"That's right, my boy. Well, here is a primer, and I see you have brought a slate and pencil. We'll begin at once."

And the first hour of Egon's tutorship began. It went better and easier than he had imagined. He contrived to interest his little pupil upon the spot, and the boy's cleverness and capacity interested him in turn. Egon could hardly believe that an hour had really passed when, upon the last stroke of six, Lieschen made her appearance as her mother's ambassador to carry off Fritz.

"We are to go to the meadows by the Oster," Lieschen said, to appease her brother's discontent at being forced to leave his new and delightful occupation. "It will be so pleasant there; even all the maids are busy raking the hay. Can anything be more charming than harvest in such glorious weather? If you will come with us, Herr Pigglewitch, I can perhaps fulfil the wish you expressed to-day in derision, and do something in aid of your neglected education. You may be very learned, and speak Greek and Latin, as well as English and French, but every peasant-lad here in the country will laugh at you if you know nothing of the simplest farming work; there an ignorant country-girl like myself can instruct you."

"You will find me an attentive and grateful pupil, Fräulein Lieschen."

"Then come with us in our walk, that I may enter immediately upon my new office."

"Are we going to walk?" Fritz asked. "No, Lieschen, let us ride. We have had no ride to-day. You would rather ride, Herr Pigglewitch, would you not?"

"I like to ride, but since I have no horse——"

"Do you know how to ride?" Lieschen interrupted him. "Is riding taught at the schools? Oh, if you like to ride you can easily have a horse; but no, now I think of it, I must not offer you papa's riding-horse, he does not like to have Cousin Albrecht or the inspectors ride it, and Herr Storting and Herr von Wangen are both using their horses to-day. There is Cousin Albrecht's second horse, but I don't know whether he would allow——"

"And even if he would I should not take advantage of his permission."

"But Soliman is in his stall," Fritz interposed.

"We must not offer Herr Pigglewitch Soliman, he is too wild and uncontrollable. No one can ride him except Cousin Albrecht, and he has, as you know, Fritz, been thrown twice."

"I do not think Soliman would throw me," Egon said.

"Oh, you do not know how tricky he is," was Lieschen's grave reply. "Even Cousin Albrecht, who is a very skilful horseman, has as much as he can do to control Soliman; he advised papa to sell the beautiful creature at any price, for he never can be cured of his tricks."

"You make me really anxious to try my fortune with Soliman. There is no pleasure in riding a quiet horse. The pleasure in riding comes from the necessity of straining every muscle and exercising all one's will to keep one's horse well in hand."

"But indeed Soliman is too dangerous, I cannot have him saddled for you," said Lieschen.

"If there were any real danger it would but make the temptation to ride him greater. Surely one ought eagerly to seek occasion for investing our commonplace existence with interest by means of physical and mental exertion. One might perhaps find life attractive if one had to struggle for it, it would then cease to be such an intolerable bore."

"I do not understand you, Herr Pigglewitch," Lieschen replied, staring at Egon in wide-eyed wonder. "What wicked nonsense are you talking? I cannot comprehend your meaning perfectly, but I can see that you are wrong in speaking thus before Fritz."

Here was another deserved reproof! But it did not offend Egon. The youthful moralist, with her dark, reproachful eyes raised to his, was so very charming. She was a lovely fairy when she laughed, but an angel when she spoke so gravely.

"I will try to improve, and to set a watch upon my tongue," Egon rejoined, humbly. "If you had not spoken of danger, Fraulein Lieschen, I should not have exposed myself to your censure. There is really no danger for me in riding an unruly horse. I assure you that I can control him."

Lieschen was hard to convince, but the certainty of power shown in Egon's continued persuasions to be permitted to ride Soliman had its effect at last. Fritz was sent to order Soliman, with his sister's mare and his own Shetland pony, to be brought round, and Lieschen ran off to put on her habit, assuring Herr Pigglewitch that she would meet him at the side-entrance from the court-yard in five minutes.

Fritz fulfilled his commission with delight, but old Wenzel, the groom, shook his head dubiously when he heard that Soliman was to be saddled for the Herr Candidate. No good would come of it, he said; but since Fräulein Lieschen had ordered it, it must be done. He was just leading the restless, dancing animal from his stall when the Lieutenant, on his return from the meadow, rode into the court-yard.

"Halloo, Wenzel! what are you about?" he called out. "Are you saddling Soliman? Who is going to ride the brute? I hope my cousin has no idea of such a thing?"

"No, Herr Lieutenant, the master is not well enough to ride at all to-day. The Herr Candidate is to ride Soliman."

"What! he? Nonsense! Who ordered him saddled?"

"Fräulein Lieschen sent Master Fritz to tell me to saddle him."

"Another of her crazy notions. She probably supposes that the Herr Candidate has six necks and will not mind breaking one. Soliman will throw him before he is fairly in the saddle."

"So I think, Herr Lieutenant. It will never do. But I have Fräulein Lieschen's orders."

"You're right, old fellow, there's no gainsaying them. Go on, saddle Soliman for the Candidate; it will be a very interesting sight. What is it to me," Albrecht muttered to himself, "if the insolent scoundrel breaks a leg or an arm? it will teach him to know his place."

He rode across the court-yard to the side-entrance,

where Egon and Lieschen were already waiting, Lieschen looking wonderfully lovely in her close-fitting habit and little round hat set jauntily upon her golden curls.

"I am glad you have come, Cousin Albrecht," she called out to the Lieutenant. "Herr Pigglewitch has taken it into his head to ride Soliman, because there is no other riding-horse in the stables except yours. I have allowed myself to be persuaded to have him saddled, but I knew I was wrong. Now you can relieve my mind, cousin, by offering Herr Pigglewitch your other horse."

"I would do so with pleasure," the Lieutenant replied, "were I not convinced that Herr Pigglewitch rides as admirably as he plays billiards. It would be an insult to him to dissuade him from riding Soliman, who is fiery, to be sure, but much better than his reputation. If, however, Herr Pigglewitch is afraid——"

"No need to discuss my state of mind, Herr Lieutenant," Egon said, sharply.

"Beg pardon, I meant no offence, but only to offer you my lamb-like riding-horse, should Soliman be too fiery for you."

"Thanks, I prefer to ride Soliman."

"Good luck to your preference! It will afford you pleasure. You have no spurs, I see; take my riding-whip. A good cut at the right moment will inspire Soliman with respect."

"Your manner to Herr Pigglewitch is odious, cousin," Lieschen interposed. Her anxiety lest the Candidate should meet with an accident increased every minute. She reproached herself for the consent she had given, which could not now be withdrawn, and her fears were confirmed by the malice in the smile with which her cousin listened to the Candidate's declaration that he should ride Soliman.

There was nothing to be done, however. Old Wenzel was leading up Soliman, keeping a sharp watch upon the spirited creature lest he should break loose from him.

"The brute is perfectly wild to-day, he would not bear even the Herr Lieutenant," the old man muttered, intentionally loud enough for Lieschen to hear, while his glance towards her seemed to say, "If any accident should happen it will be all your fault."

"I do most earnestly entreat you, Herr Pigglewitch," Lieschen exclaimed, her anxiety reaching its height, "to give up riding Soliman! Let us walk, I pray you. Do, for my sake!"

"Against such words I am defenceless," said Egon, who had approached the beautiful animal and was gently stroking its back, but who now retired.

"You're right; very wise and prudent," said the Lieutenant. "Lead Soliman up and down a little, Wenzel, you need not take off his saddle, I will ride him after a while to show Herr Pigglewitch that the horse is not so wicked after all. But you are quite right, Herr Pigglewitch, to accede to Lieschen's request. Soliman might be dangerous for a tyro in horsemanship. You shall take my Iduna here for your ride with Lieschen, she is as quiet as a lamb and will not throw you, I'll engage."

Egon bit his lip; his eyes sparkled with irritation and the colour rose to his cheek.

"Do you still persist in your request, Fräulein Lieschen?" he said to the girl, in a low voice. "Do you wish me to be thus derided and accused of cowardice? I will keep my word if you insist upon it, but put yourself in my place, and I think you will not desire it."

"No, I do not," Lieschen rejoined, with an angry glance at her cousin. "It will be your fault, Cousin Albrecht, if there is any accident, and I never will forgive you for it as long as I live."

A smile of victorious malice was the Lieutenant's only reply, but it faded from his face the next moment to give place to an expression of sheer amazement. Without the aid of the stirrups the despised Candidate had swung himself into the saddle, and caught up in a firm hand the bridle which old Wenzel dropped. Soliman reared, but his rider kept his seat as quietly as if he were upon the meekest of horses, smiling down at Lieschen, who was pale with terror.

"Have no fear, Fräulein Lieschen," he called down to her. "Soliman will know in a few minutes that he has found his master."

"Wait until he tries some of his tricks," the Lieutenant muttered between his teeth.

And Soliman proceeded to do so; he was not yet conquered. He tried the same tricks that had twice unseated the Lieutenant and thrown him in the dirt,— the same tricks that had forced his former possessor to sell the magnificent creature for a mere song. He reared again and again, then, standing on his hind legs, turned round and round quickly, and finished by leaping and plunging wildly.

Twice when this last point was reached the Lieutenant had been thrown over Soliman's head; the two following times he had mounted the horse, however, he had succeeded in keeping his seat, although gasping and exhausted, since when Soliman had not attempted his tricks when ridden by the Lieutenant. He now

10

tried them again with his new rider, but without any
result. Egon sat as quietly firm in the saddle as if he
were part of the animal, holding the bridle in a hand
of iron, and so compressing the horse's flanks with his
knees that, after a few more unsuccessful plunges, the
creature stood still, with dilated nostrils and foaming
at the bit. His rider, however, showed no signs of
physical exertion; he nodded with a smile to the Lieutenant, whose last muttered words he had heard and
understood. "You are right, Herr Lieutenant," he
said, "Soliman is rather too fiery for a tyro in horsemanship, but only a tyro would ever be unseated by
his tricks. He will not try them again; he knows
his master now, and will soon know him better. He
certainly is a magnificent animal."

He stroked the panting creature's neck caressingly,
and then, after giving him a moment's rest, shortened
his bridle, and with a degree of ease and skill which
seemed to the Lieutenant little short of miraculous in a
Candidate, put the horse through all his paces, guiding
him in a wide circle around the court-yard. Soliman
attempted no further rebellion, and when Egon halted
at the side-entrance again he could confidently assure
Lieschen that their ride would have no disturbance
from Soliman's tricks.

Lieschen had followed the rider's movements with
genuine admiration. When the horse first tried his
'tricks' she grew ashy pale, but the next instant her
anxiety vanished, there was no danger. Her cousin
Albrecht was a bold and skilful horseman, the best
she had known hitherto, but his glory faded when she
compared him with this rider. How could she ever
have thought that proud, graceful man ugly? How
easy was his bearing! The control of his spirited

steed seemed to cost him no exertion. He could smile whilst all who were watching him were trembling with dread.

Upon his return Lieschen received him with a beaming face, Fritz clapped his hands and shouted, and old Wenzel grinned as he said, "He knows how to ride, Herr Lieutenant. He'll teach Soliman to have done with his capers."

The Lieutenant made no reply. He looked darkly at the daring horseman, whom he could not but admire, but whom he hated all the more bitterly. He had been outdone, outdone in the very art upon which he most prided himself. He had exulted in being the best rider in the country, and here was this wretched Candidate disputing his honours with him.

Lieschen invited him to join them in their ride to the Oster meadows, but he crossly declined to accept her invitation, and when the detested stranger sprang from the saddle, throwing the bridle to old Wenzel, in order to put Lieschen on her mare, he muttered a curse, turned his horse, and rode out of the court-yard in a direction opposite to that in which lay the Oster meadows. Lieschen, however, rode out into the fields between Egon and Fritz, laughing and talking, and throwing kisses to her father, who was standing at his window. She was gayer and happier than words could tell.

CHAPTER VII.

THE HARVEST-FIELD.

As Egon rode by Lieschen's side along the road leading through the fields to the Oster meadows he was more
light of heart than he could remember ever being before.
She pointed out to him the various villages and farms
in the neighbourhood of the castle, and his eyes, it is
true, followed the direction of her extended riding-whip,
but his attention was not given to the rather commonplace landscape; his interest was all for his charming
companion. How pure and clear was the look in the
dark-blue eyes raised so confidingly to his own! Her
smile was frank and free, as she made no attempt to
conceal her admiration of his courage and strength in
subduing Soliman. She told him how delighted she
was with his success, and how her heart had seemed
fairly to stand still with terror when she saw him in
such peril and by her fault.

Her *naïve* frankness, her open avowal of whatever
filled her mind, enchanted Egon. He seemed to have
entered a new world. The compliments and admiration
which he had received from other girls as to his music,
his singing, or some other of his accomplishments had
always aroused the suspicion in his mind that such
words were for the wealthy Egon von Ernau, uttered to
flatter his vanity, to entrap him. But as he listened to
Lieschen's artless talk he paid homage to the sincerity
of this girlish nature, and was refreshed and cheered
even by her words of reproof. His sensations were a

surprise to himself: he thought he was indifferent alike to praise and blame, but here he was positively exulting in the admiration of a mere child.

"There are the Oster meadows!" Fritz called out from the summit of a low hill, which he had gained in advance of his companions.

Egon sighed; they had nearly reached the goal of their ride, and he would gladly have ridden thus through the lovely fields for hours.

"Is not the prospect from here charming?" Lieschen asked, when she with Egon had reached the eminence.

He had to answer her, and that he might do so he looked around him, although he would far rather have continued to gaze into his companion's lovely face. As if awaking from a dream, he saw before him a picturesque landscape,—a green extensive valley, through which wound the Oster, a small river, which, making its way among low, distant hills, was lost in the mighty chain of the Riesengebirge.

The rich meadows that bordered the Oster on either side presented an animated scene. On one hand the mowers were wielding their scythes, on another women, girls, and children were turning the hay with long rakes, while from some of the fields the piled hay-wagons, each drawn by four stout horses, were beginning their slow journey to the barns of Castle Osternau. All who were able to work were busy gathering in the plentiful hay-crop of the year, for there had been warning clouds in the west at sunset for two or three days, although hitherto they had fled before the dawn. They were massing now about the descending sun. The harvesters would occasionally cast an anxious glance towards the west, and then proceed with their labour with renewed zeal.

"Is not the prospect from here charming?" Lieschen had asked, and Egon replied, "Most charming!" giving utterance to his sincere conviction. At the moment the broad, smiling valley, with the silver river winding through it, seemed to him inexpressibly attractive; but the words had scarcely left his lips before he was aware that they were at variance with all his previous ideas and sentiments. He had never found anything to admire in peaceful, smiling valleys, they had always impressed him as the ideal of tedious, commonplace rusticity; he had turned for enjoyment to the wild grandeur of rocky mountain fastnesses, to the splendour of glacier and torrent. The more savage the aspect of nature the more beautiful it had seemed to him. When he had been caught in a mountain storm, the crashing of the thunder among the giant peaks and the vivid play of the lightning had quickened his pulses. What could make this simple landscape at which he was gazing with Lieschen seem so charming in his eyes? Had he undergone a transformation in the last few hours? Could it be that a warm, sunny ray from heaven had pierced his soul and made it sensitive to the charm of a simple scene from which he would but yesterday have turned in weary disgust? He had a sense of disgrace in the consciousness that he was so hopelessly given over to the influence of the moment. Yes, he was ashamed of thus belying all his former tastes just because——yes, because a pair of sparkling, girlish eyes were beholding with rapture the petty, commonplace scene before them,—yes, it suddenly grew to be commonplace and petty, the charm that had transfigured it was broken, the ray that had penetrated his soul was extinguished.

A horseman came galloping up the hill from the

meadow. It was Herr Storting; he waved a greeting to Lieschen as he drew near, but as he drew up his horse beside Egon he exclaimed, in surprise, "Can it be possible, Herr Pigglewitch, that you are riding Soliman?"

"As you see," Egon replied, curtly, his good humour all gone.

"I see, but I do not understand. Why, even the Lieutenant does not venture to take that horse any distance from the castle, he only rides it in the fields just beyond the garden. Pardon my saying so, Fräulein Lieschen, but you have been wrong in exposing Herr Pigglewitch to a danger the extent of which he cannot understand, since he does not know Soliman's tricks and temper."

Before Lieschen could reply, Egon interposed, "Your reproof is administered to the wrong person, Herr Storting. I insisted on riding Soliman precisely because of his tricks and his temper. And now we know each other, Soliman and I, and he is afraid of me, not I of him. You need have no anxiety on my account."

Egon's words by no means satisfied Storting. "You must be a capital rider to have kept your seat upon Soliman until now, but the danger will not be over until the horse is back in his stall. I beg you to return at once, and at all events do not attempt to ride him down into the meadows. The brute shies terribly, when people are about he grows restless, and the least sudden movement, the lifting of a rake, the flutter of one of the women's white kerchiefs, or the merest trifle, will suffice to make him mad with terror. At such times no rider can control him or keep his seat."

But Egon only smiled. "Are you really so unruly, my poor Soliman?" he said, leaning forward and patting the beautiful creature's slender neck. "I could wish you would try your worst, that I might have the opportunity to convince you of a will stronger than your own."

"Foolhardy words," Storting said, sternly. "Again let me beg you to turn back. If you ride down to the meadows you run the risk of having Soliman plunge with you into the Oster. Such a ride would be suicidal."

"Your ugly word does not terrify me," Egon said. "I surely have a right over my own body, my own life. I need take counsel with none, if I choose to end the drama with a bullet in my heart or a wild ride. Come, Soliman, let us measure our strength together, and if you come off conqueror I shall not care; let the waters of the Oster do their worst."

A smart stroke of his riding-whip accompanied his last words. It had a fearful effect upon the fiery animal, who had scarcely yet been brought under his rider's perfect control. Soliman put back his ears and tore down the hill to the Oster meadows.

"My God! what madness!" Storting exclaimed, horror-struck. The colour faded from his sunburned cheek as he gazed after the rider, who was being carried directly towards the spot where the river was deepest and the current strongest. To the inspector the man's fate was sealed. How could the Candidate have dreamed of riding Soliman? It was a miracle that the fellow still kept his seat.

He not only kept his seat, but on the very brink of the river, when Storting was convinced that his doom was certain, the horse was pulled up on his haunches, his rider had mastered him. Storting could hardly believe his eyes. Was that wonderful rider sitting easily and as if unconscious of danger upon the fiery brute, now stamping the soft meadow soil with impatient hoofs, but held in rein by a hand of iron, the same ridiculous, awkward tutor whom he, Storting, had transformed to the likeness of humanity with a suit of his own clothes?

Lieschen too had been terrified for a moment, when Egon had driven Soliman wild by the stroke of his whip, but she did not share in Storting's forebodings; she had seen Soliman obey Egon's strength and skill, and she had entire confidence in them. Still there was a cloud upon her brow, and the gaze with which she followed the daring rider was scarcely one of approval. When she saw that the horse was stayed at the river's brink, she simply said, "Let us follow," and without another word rode quietly down into the meadows after Fritz, who had started off to overtake his admired tutor.

Egon awaited their approach. The swift gallop, the struggle with the furious horse, which again called into play all his force and skill, had quickly dispelled his sudden ill humour. He called out to Storting, "You see, Herr Storting, there really is no danger in my riding Soliman. The horse is far better than his reputation. He needs only to be kept firmly in rein, and then he obeys every pressure of the knee. The magnificent creature knows me now, and I will answer for it will not shy or run so long as he feels my hand upon his bridle. You see that your reproof was quite undeserved by Fräulein Lieschen. If the horse is really timid I will engage to cure him of it. Shall we not ride towards those people who are working so busily over there? Fräulein von Osternau has promised to be my teacher, and to instruct me in some of the elementary principles of agriculture, and I am eager to prove myself a docile, intelligent pupil. Make friends with me again, Herr

Storting, you will not remain provoked with me for answering your kindly warning by a furious run of a moment or two?"

He held out his hand as he spoke to the inspector, who could not any longer maintain a show of irritation, although he was not quite satisfied, nor was Lieschen. Storting, however, took pains to conceal the remnant of his displeasure, and succeeded in doing so, but Lieschen made no attempt to hide the fact that she was seriously displeased with Herr Pigglewitch. She took her place again, it is true, beside him, but she answered his questions in monosyllables, and left it to Storting to give him any information with regard to the harvesting. His desire to receive the promised instruction from her was evident as they rode around the meadows, but when he turned to her with an inquiry she only replied, "Herr Storting will explain it to you." She could not be easy and friendly with him, for the last words he had spoken on the hill still resounded in her ears, and they had shocked her profoundly.

Lieschen's taciturnity had its effect upon Egon's recovered gayety; he ceased to ask questions, and scarcely bestowed a glance upon the harvesters. He forced himself to listen with an appearance of interest to Herr Storting's explanations, out of regard for the inspector, but the merry songs of the girls raking the hay struck harshly on his ears, he was tired of it all, and he was relieved when at the end of half an hour Lieschen announced that it was time to return home.

Herr Storting could not yet leave the harvest-field, Fritz galloped ahead to the castle, and thus Egon being left alone with Lieschen had an opportunity to ask her the cause of her sudden reserve; was she displeased, and why? he had not, he thought, given her cause to be so.

She looked gravely up at him, and said in surprise,—

"Do you not know why I am displeased? Have you no suspicion of how your wicked words shocked me? Yes, I am displeased. I cannot forgive you for sneering at what is most sacred. I told you so before to-day. You are not a good man, Herr Pigglewitch. You almost frighten me."

"What have I done or said to provoke such a reproof from you?" Egon asked, in dismay.

"You do not know? So much the worse. You do not even admit that what you said was wicked. Do you not remember what you said here upon the hill, yes, upon this very spot, just before you gave Soliman that stroke with your whip? You said you should not care if Soliman drowned you! yes, you declared that you had a right to take your own life!"

"And was that what displeased you? Have I not the right to end my miserable existence if it becomes too heavy a burden to be borne?"

"No, you have *no* right to do so, and it is a sin even to think of it!" Lieschen replied, her beautiful eyes lifted to Egon's in stern reproach. "Your words shocked me deeply. Is there any courage in putting an end by the act of an instant to an intolerable existence? It is cowardice, miserable cowardice, to turn and flee from the battle of life. I have heard pity bestowed upon those wretched men who in despair have taken their own lives; for my part I cannot help despising them, and I cannot understand how a man can find a word to say in defence of such cowardice."

What Lieschen said was neither novel nor clever, and yet her simple words made a deep impression upon

Egon. He had lately read a learned essay upon the right of self-destruction, in which every conceivable argument was brought forward to prove that nothing save insanity could excuse the act, but the sapient disquisition had only provoked a smile as he read, while these few simple words of the young girl's staggered him in the views he had hitherto held. Involuntarily the image of the real Pigglewitch arose in his mind, he saw the ridiculous figure kneeling singing upon the green bank, then suddenly start up and leap into the water. He saw the wretched creature standing dripping before him, wringing his hands and entreating to have his miserable life ended for him, he was afraid to do it himself. Did it really require more courage to endure a sad existence than to end it with a pistol-bullet? Was it cowardice to flee from a blank, weary world? Lieschen felt contempt, not compassion, for a suicide. She did not know how her words fitted Egon's case. He could not look into her clear eyes, he was forced to cast down his own.

It was Egon's nature to be easily swayed by the impulse of the moment; thus it was with him now, as he said, after a short pause,—

"You judge harshly, very harshly, but perhaps justly. You can have no idea of how nearly your words touch me. I promise to reflect upon what you have said, and now I beg you not to be angry with me any longer. I cannot bear to have you look so gravely and disapprovingly at me. I will try never to shock you again by thoughtless words which may seem to you like a sneer at sacred things, but I beg you to have patience with me. You promised to be my teacher, and a teacher ought not to be impatient."

"Now you are making game of me again."

"No, I declare to you I am not jesting. What I said half in jest to you at dinner I now repeat in earnest. I am conscious to-day for the first time that the experience of my life has made me morbid. Regard me as a sick man, and when some word of mine shocks you, do not be angry, but tell me of it frankly, without reserve. Blame me, take me to task, and I shall be your debtor."

Lieschen looked at him rather dubiously. "I do not know what to think of you, Herr Pigglewitch," she replied, shaking her pretty head thoughtfully. "You change with every moment. When a little while ago you talked so wickedly and urged Soliman towards the river, I was afraid of you, and now you suddenly speak so sadly and gently that I almost have faith in you. But since you only ask that I should tell you what I think, without reserve, I can easily grant your request, I should do so whether or not, because I cannot help it."

CHAPTER VIII.

NEWS FROM BERLIN.

WHILST Egon, with Lieschen and Fritz, was taking his ride to the Oster meadows, Herr von Osternau was pacing his room slowly to and fro.

From his window he had observed old Wenzel saddling Soliman, but he had naturally supposed that Albrecht had ordered the horse, and it never entered his mind that the fiery animal had been saddled for the Candidate, or he would have instantly put a stop to it.

He was not aware of the true state of the case until

the moment when Egon swung himself lightly into
the saddle, and then remonstrance was useless. Involuntarily he had uttered an exclamation of dismay,
which called Frau von Osternau to his side, and together they had looked on while Egon reduced Soliman
to submission. Their horror was speedily transformed
to admiration as they saw how firm was the rider's seat,
how powerless were Soliman's leaps and plunges to do
him any injury.

Not a word was exchanged between them until the
riding-party had left the court-yard, when Herr von
Osternau first gave utterance to his amazement:

"This surpasses belief. If I had not seen it with my
own eyes I never could have believed that a mere Candidate, who one would have supposed had never been
on horseback before, could ride Soliman, and ride him
in such a fashion! The man is a riddle. If we were
not sure from your old friend Kramser's letter that he
is a Candidate, I should think it impossible. He is com-
pounded of contradictions, he is never the same for a
moment. When I saw him coming across the court-
yard this morning I was fairly frightened by his ugliness, I called him a scarecrow, and so did Lieschen
when she first saw him, he looked so inconceivably
ridiculous and uncouth, but ten minutes had not passed
before I changed my mind. As he sat there at the
piano, playing in that inspired way, he seemed to me a
divinely-gifted artist. He cannot be a mere ordinary
Candidate. His carriage and air are those of one used
to refined society, and the conventional habits of such
society are acquired only by association. Remember
his manner to Albrecht in the billiard-room. He demanded satisfaction just as any well-bred gentleman
would have done, and received Albrecht's apology in

the same way. He speaks English and French with an accent so admirable that he must have had the best instruction in those languages. It requires capital teachers and years of practice to attain such proficiency as he possesses in music, he plays billiards so well as almost to justify Albrecht's sneer about the professional gambler, and, finally, he has just shown himself a first-class horseman. No riding-master could have put Soliman more finely through his paces. The man is a perfect puzzle."

Herr von Osternau had begun to pace the room to and fro as he spoke. He paused and looked inquiringly at his wife. She nodded assent to what he said, and he went on: "The more I think of it the more incomprehensible it is to me that Kramser should have recommended to us just this sort of man, one who in no single particular corresponds to the description contained in Kramser's letter."

"I am quite as much puzzled as yourself," Frau von Osternau said, meekly.

"Go and get Kramser's letter; let us read it once more, and see if it can give us any explanation."

Frau von Osternau brought the letter from her desk and read it aloud to her husband:

"MOST RESPECTED LADY,—It has been to me an exceeding great joy that, after the lapse of so many years since the happy season of childhood, you still remember me, and honour me with the great confidence shown in your esteemed epistle. My heart swells with gratitude at the thought of having it in my power to be of service in any way to so highly honoured a lady.

"I have bestowed the gravest reflection upon the choice among my numerous scholars of one possessing the qualifications which you desire for the tutor of your amiable son.

"You ask for a young man possessing the education requisite to give primary instruction to a boy of six, and sufficiently proficient in music to be able to give lessons to your daughter of seventeen. You require, finally, that the young man shall be in no wise distinguished by beauty of person. Nay, you would on the contrary have him ungainly in outward appearance, that the Fräulein your daughter may find no attraction in the person of her preceptor.

"I sympathize fully with your maternal anxieties, and I have therefore, in this connection, carefully stricken from my list of pupils all those possessing goodly exteriors; of those who remain, all are indeed qualified as scholars to teach the rudiments of learning to a boy of six, but few, alas! are sufficiently proficient in music to give lessons on the piano to a lady. At last I have found one, formerly my favourite pupil, whom I can recommend to you, respected madam, in full confidence that he will prove a faithful servant to you, and a capable tutor for your son.

"The Candidate Gottlieb Pigglewitch possesses in the highest degree all the desired qualifications. He is of an ungainly exterior, but in his uncouth form there dwells a soul of great piety, strong in faith in the Lord. There are, indeed, deficiencies in his worldly attainments, but he knows quite enough for the instruction of a boy of six, and his musical capacity far excels that of any of my other pupils. He plays very well upon the piano, and the Lord has bestowed upon him the gift of song, his voice is clear and pleasing.

"Pigglewitch has been an usher in schools for three years, the last of which he has passed in a boys' school in Berlin, where, as I am assured by the principal, he has discharged his duties with diligence and zeal. Of all my pupils he, respected madam, is the one whom I can most earnestly recommend.

"I have written to Gottlieb Pigglewitch; he is only too glad to accept the honourable position offered him, upon the terms you propose, but he cannot enter upon its duties before the 6th of July, since he is not released from his present situation until July 3d. Should this arrangement meet your approval, respected madam, I beg you to write me to that effect, and the Candidate Gottlieb Pigglewitch will appear at Castle Osternau punctually upon the 6th of July.

"With grateful and respectful regard, yours to command,
                                        "KRAMSER."

"Is there an imaginable contrast greater than that between your friend's recommendation and the reality?" asked Herr von Osternau when his wife had finished reading the letter. "His worldly knowledge ought to be deficient, but sufficient for the instruction of a child of six, yet he speaks French and English fluently. He ought to be awkward and ungainly, and nothing can be more easy and graceful than his air and carriage. And then his ugliness! Uncouth enough he was in that queer coat, but since he threw that aside he has become another being. I cannot understand your friend Kramser."

Frau von Osternau agreed with her husband. "You are right," she said, thoughtfully. "Neither can I understand him. When that young fellow's eyes flashed to-day as he confronted Albrecht, I thought him actually handsome, and I could not but admire him again just now as he rode out of the court-yard, keeping

11*

Soliman so perfectly in rein. It makes me very anxious.
It would be terrible to have Lieschen admire him too.
He offered to leave Castle Osternau rather than be a
cause of dissension in our family. Suppose you——"

"Not a word more, Emma," her husband interrupted
her. "After his dispute with Albrecht, in which he
conducted himself with such absolute propriety, it
would be a crying injustice to dismiss him. Did I not
declare that he must remain until we had made trial
of his capacity as Fritzchen's tutor?"

"But Lieschen? I have heard you say you should
be glad to have Lieschen marry Albrecht. What if
she should take a fancy to the Candidate?"

"No fear of that. The little witch has no idea of
taking a fancy to any one, and as for the wish I may
have expressed to you some time ago, I confess that I
no longer cherish it. It arose from my desire to indemnify our cousin for the loss of the estate, but Lieschen's happiness is my first consideration, and I do not
think Albrecht is the man to make a woman happy.
He is wanting in force of character, he cannot forget
his gay life in the capital, indeed I am afraid that he
has continued it in his frequent visits to Berlin, and
that he is in debt again. But why should we puzzle
our brains with what the future has in store for us? I
cannot deny that it is a disagreeable sensation, the not
knowing what to think of this strange man, I wish
we had some one else, even although much more awkward and uninstructed, for Fritz's tutor, but since we
have him and have undertaken certain obligations with
regard to him, they must be fulfilled. We must show
him all the respect we would have Fritz feel for him,
we must receive him into our domestic circle that he
may feel at home here, but in the mean time we must

observe him closely, and should he neglect his duty, or prove to be unfitted for his situation, we can, as we agreed to, part with him."

"But Lieschen——?"

"Will take piano-lessons from him. Do not worry yourself unnecessarily; you can always superintend the girl's music-lessons if it will make you less anxious to do so, and can soon convince yourself that there is no danger for the child in Herr Pigglewitch."

Frau von Osternau was not so easy in her mind, but she did not contradict her husband, she only resolved to watch her daughter and the Candidate closely, not only during the music-lessons, but at all times when they were together. The idea of her child's entertaining any warmer feeling for Herr Pigglewitch than that which a pupil should have for a teacher was extremely distasteful to her. She was not reassured when, soon after the above conversation, she saw the riders return from their visit to the harvesters, and observed the gentle, happy smile with which Lieschen thanked the Candidate for the ready, easy aid which he lent her in dismounting. The mother imagined that she perceived a change in her unconscious child.

Fritz, who had preceded his sister and her cavalier, and had been seeing that his favourite pony was properly attended to, rushed into the room. He had a long story to tell his father and mother, first about the charms of his new tutor during the study-hour, and then of his wonderful riding. "Even Herr Storting grew pale when he saw Soliman tearing down to the Oster, but Herr Pigglewitch didn't care, he only laughed; ah, he knows how to ride! why, he rides better than even Cousin Albrecht!"

Fritz poured out his raptures over his new tutor,

much to his father's delight, while Frau von Osternau's maternal anxiety was sensibly increased. She was hardly pleased when her husband sent old Hildebrandt to invite the Candidate to take tea with the family at eight o'clock, in the sitting-room; it seemed to her that it was too speedy a welcome to the domestic circle.

But her fears were appeased when Lieschen, having taken off her habit, made her appearance, and talked without reserve or embarrassment of her ride. The very fact of her expressing with perfect frankness her admiration for the fearless rider and his courage reassured her mother, and when the girl went on to give a faithful account of her conversation with the Candidate, and the rebuke she had administered to him for entertaining such wicked ideas with regard to suicide, her parents exchanged glances of entire satisfaction.

"Was I not right?" Herr von Osternau asked his wife, with a smile, and she nodded a pleased assent. Lieschen's freedom from all reserve had quite reassured her, although, as she repeated to herself, her fears had not been altogether groundless, since the girl's interest in the stranger was evident from her manner of speaking of him. Even when she blamed him there was an unwonted seriousness in her voice and manner, she really seemed to have suddenly grown older.

Egon appeared punctually at eight o'clock in accordance with his invitation, and immediately afterwards Albrecht arrived, not by any means pleased to find the Candidate installed as a member of the circle. His humour was not improved by hearing Herr von Osternau request the tutor to consider himself henceforth as one of the family, joining them at tea whenever he felt so inclined, without further invitation, a privilege hitherto enjoyed by the Lieutenant alone. The two other inspectors never appeared at the tea-table without being specially invited to do so.

In fact, Lieutenant von Osternau did not at all enjoy himself on this particular evening. Until now he had been the enlivening element of the little circle, he had, as it were, formed the centre of conversational interest, but he suddenly found himself superseded by the Candidate, who conducted himself with an easy assurance inconceivable in a man of his station, receiving Herr von Osternau's gracious advances as if they were a matter of course, and taking part in the conversation as though perfectly accustomed to intercourse with people of rank.

And yet, as the Lieutenant could not but admit to himself, the Candidate never thrust himself forward, never attempted to lead in the conversation. When it naturally turned upon his mastery of Soliman, he made no claim to any special bravery or skill, but smilingly put by all the compliments addressed to him, and skilfully changed the subject by remarking upon the interest he had felt in the harvesting, which had been to him so novel a spectacle. He thus gave Herr von Osternau an opportunity to expatiate upon his favourite theme.

When the lord of the castle was once fairly launched upon this subject he usually held forth at great length, but to-day, when Herr Pigglewitch mentioned the singing of the girls and men as they raked the hay, Herr von Osternau called to mind the praise given by Herr Kramser to Herr Pigglewitch's pleasing voice, and he suddenly closed his discourse by a request that the Candidate would gratify him with a song.

With ready amiability Egon went instantly to the piano, where he sang to his own accompaniment, and in a full, rich baritone, a simple Folksong:

i

> "In Oden forest stands a tree
>   With branches fresh and green,
> Beneath its shade a thousand times
>   I with my love have been."

The Lieutenant observed, with positive rage in his heart, the effect which this song produced upon every member of the family. Frau von Osternau, who was busy at her tea-table, dropped her hands in her lap at the first notes, and listened intently, with eyes fixed upon the singer. Her husband sat leaning back in his arm-chair, scarcely daring to move, for fear of losing one delicious tone, while Lieschen bent forward in rapt delight with sparkling eyes and parted lips, and when the last sounds had died away, and Egon arose to take his place again beside her at the tea-table, she looked up at him with a dreamy, far-away expression in her dark eyes, which told how great had been her enjoyment, although she said not a word.

"Charming! Delicious!" Herr von Osternau exclaimed. "Thank you! thank you! I never heard that song so exquisitely sung. Every note came from the heart, and, of course, went straight to the heart. You understand, Herr Candidate, how to render our 'folk-songs' with the simplicity that belongs to them, without any of our modern frippery hung about them."

Egon bowed slightly. Herr von Osternau's cordial enthusiasm was gratifying, but Lieschen's eyes, as she looked up at him, filled him with a delicious intoxication, which, however, quickly evaporated when the Lieutenant, feeling forced to repress his irritation, uttered a few commendatory phrases in order to display his appreciation of music. His praise sobered Egon at once. He would willingly have disclaimed it in a few sharp words, but he suppressed them out of regard for

the master and mistress of the house. He was glad to
have further discussion of his song interrupted by old
Hildebrandt's entrance with the post-bag, which had
just arrived from Station Mirbach.

"A letter for you already, Herr Pigglewitch," Herr
von Osternau said, handing Egon an envelope.

Egon hesitated for a moment to take the letter which
could not possibly be for him, but there was no help for
it, and he laid it on the table before him.

"Read your letter, Herr Pigglewitch, you need not
stand upon ceremony," Herr von Osternau continued,
kindly. "Here in the country the advent of letters is
quite another matter than the receiving them in town.
We live here so secluded from the world that letters
are all we have to connect us with it, and of course
we wish to open our envelopes as soon as they are
brought to us. The post-bag comes in at this time
every evening, and each of us instantly opens and reads
whatever it brings him or her,—the contents often give
us matter for discussion and conversation. So pray
read your letter, I will set you an example by opening
mine, whilst my wife, Lieschen, and Cousin Albrecht
look through the papers and journals."

He broke the seal of his letter as he spoke, and
became instantly so absorbed in its contents that he did
not observe that Egon thrust the one addressed to
Herr Pigglewitch into his breast-pocket without opening it.

Herr von Osternau's letter was very long, and it took
him some time to read it through. Meanwhile there
was a pause in the conversation around the tea-table.
Frau von Osternau and the Lieutenant were busy with
the newspapers, and Lieschen turned over the leaves
of a journal, without, however, reading a word; she

could not fix her attention, the melody of the song she
had just heard so rang in her ears.

"A very odd, disagreeable letter from your uncle
Sastrow," Herr von Osternau said, after a long pause,
turning to his wife. "He wishes us to invite Bertha
von Massenburg to pay a long visit at Castle Osternau,
and I cannot very well see how we can help complying
with his wish."

Egon, who had been reflecting for the last few minutes upon what was to be done with Gottlieb Pigglewitch's letter, started from his revery as the name of
Bertha von Massenburg struck upon his ear. He
turned, with an interest he could hardly conceal, to
Herr von Osternau, who went on:

"Very unpleasant things have been happening in
Berlin, things that concern us, although not very nearly:
still we are distantly related to the Massenburgs, and
Sastrow reckons upon the relationship. Bertha should
be withdrawn from public attention and the gossip of
the capital for a considerable time, your uncle says, and
he thinks her best asylum would be with us; wherefore
he begs me to send her an invitation at his house as
soon as possible."

"What has happened?" asked his wife.

"Oh, 'tis a very ugly kind of story. I had better
read you Sastrow's letter: 'My dear Fritz——' "

Egon rose as Herr von Osternau began reading the
letter aloud. However great his curiosity might be, he
could not but remind Herr von Osternau that there was
a stranger present who had no right to a knowledge of
private family affairs. He was about to withdraw, but
Herr von Osternau kindly signed to him to sit down
again.

"I appreciate your delicacy, Herr Pigglewitch, but

I pray you to remain. This letter does, to be sure, contain a very unpleasant bit of family scandal, but it is unfortunately no secret. At the present time, when distance is annihilated, Berlin gossip spreads far and wide in an incredibly short space of time. If Bertha von Massenburg comes to us, the scandal of which she is the innocent subject will follow her very shortly; all our neighbours will know everything about Bertha and her unfortunate betrothal, and it will be hard to separate truth from falsehood. So it is better that you should know the truth from a trustworthy source, especially as she stands in a certain relationship to our family. You can then aid to the best of your ability in putting a stop to idle gossip; therefore I would rather you should hear the letter.

"MY DEAR FRITZ,—There must, of course, be some important reason for my sitting here in the middle of the night writing you a lengthy epistle which must be sent to the post at dawn, that you may receive it to-morrow evening. This reason consists in my great desire to avert as far as is possible the consequences of a most unpleasant family affair. I will be as brief as possible; of course our cousin Werner von Massenburg is at the bottom of it; who other of the family could provoke a scandal?

"You have lost money enough by the man to know him well, although perhaps not so thoroughly as I know him. Of course he is always in pecuniary difficulties, but even I, poor as is my opinion of him, should not have suspected him of attempting to relieve himself of his debts by selling his daughter,—the expression is not too strong,—and this is just what he has done.

"About two weeks ago Werner came to me and in-

formed me that he was about to betroth Bertha to a
distinguished young fellow, Egon von Ernau, the son of
the Privy Councillor von Ernau. The affair had been
concluded with the young man's father, who declared
that his son was nothing loath. All that remained to
be done was to bring the young people together that
the betrothal might take place in the usual way, since
it could not very well be announced before they had
even seen each other. He therefore begged me to invite
Bertha to pay us a visit; he would introduce young
Ernau to us, and everything could be speedily arranged.

"When I expressed my great disapproval of a marriage thus contracted, he went on to explain that it
was a matter of life and death to him. His old friend
the Privy Councillor Ernau had promised to liquidate
all his debts in case the recent patent of nobility of
the Ernaus should receive the aristocratic veneer which
would be given it by a union with the old knightly line
of the Massenburgs. He was so persistent in his entreaties that at last I consented, although sorely against
my better judgment, and wrote to Königsberg, inviting
Bertha to exchange for a while her aunt Massenburg's
home in Königsberg for our house in Berlin. By return
of post I received a charming letter from Bertha accepting my invitation, and she arrived here yesterday.

"After writing to Bertha, I thought it my duty to
inform myself with regard to our future connections
the Ernaus. What I learned of them was by no means
reassuring. Privy Councillor von Ernau is, it is true,
immensely wealthy, the head of an extensive banking
business, his reputation for honesty and business capacity has never been even breathed upon, but he is
the most insufferably self-important, conceited fellow,
who never loses an opportunity of seeing his name in

the papers, so great is his love of notoriety. He keeps open house, and poses as a patron of art and science without having a conception of either. He keeps a racing stud, although he is no horseman; and he contributes vast sums for political purposes, without the faintest real interest in politics. Only let his name appear in the papers and he is content, no sacrifice is too great to make to his vanity.

"What I could gather concerning the son is scarcely any better. It is generally conceded that Herr Egon von Ernau is a very talented young fellow, but that he abuses most frivolously the brilliant gifts bestowed upon him by nature. He studied and passed brilliant examinations, without turning his knowledge to any account. He has inherited from his father—with whom, moreover, he is on terms of no intimacy, father and son sometimes not meeting for weeks—an enormous stock of vanity, which, however, he shows after an entirely different fashion. It is his pleasure to pay no heed whatever to the opinion of the world, to appear alike indifferent to praise and to blame, to attach no importance to worldly honours. He has drained to the dregs every pleasure, every delight that wealth can give, and he is to the last degree *blasé*. In the assurance of his own superiority he despises all other men and treats them accordingly. He is a man of talent but of no character, and he utterly lacks balance and self-control.

"It is easy to see that such a man is not calculated to make a wife happy; therefore I thought it my duty, before the affair was finally decided, to talk seriously to Massenburg, but it was too late; he could not withdraw, even had he desired to do so. He had made binding promises to Councillor Ernau; the betrothal, if not actually announced, was known everywhere. The

Councillor had informed his friends on 'Change that the betrothal of his son Egon to the noble Fräulein Bertha von Massenburg was shortly to be celebrated by a grand entertainment, and Werner himself had been so imprudent as to admit this when questioned upon the subject. The betrothal was already an open secret, much discussed among the aristocracy of money as well as of blood. There was pity expressed for the poor girl who was to be sacrificed to a vain, heartless *roué*. There were various remarks made at the club in Werner's hearing with regard to the burnishing of an aristocratic scutcheon with money gained in trade, but he was firm in his resolve. The effect of all this gossip was to induce him to hurry as much as possible the public announcement of the betrothal. It was arranged by the two fathers that Herr Egon von Ernau should pay his first visit here yesterday and should be invited by me to an evening party. So soon as the young people had fairly met, there was to be a large garden-party at the Councillor's villa, and the betrothal was to be formally announced.

"It was very distasteful to me, of course, to lend myself to what was to bring about a connection which I considered so undesirable, but I was forced to consent to what was asked of me. I did so, however, only upon condition that I should be allowed immediately after Bertha's arrival to lay before her the true state of affairs. Should she decline then to accede to her father's schemes, I declared that no force should be put upon her beneath my roof. I would then refuse to receive young Ernau.

"Early yesterday morning (the express train from Königsberg arrives in Berlin at six o'clock) I went to the railway-station to meet Bertha. I did not recognize her when she first stepped out on the platform. I had not seen her for several years, and she had grown from a pretty little school-girl into an elegant young lady. She, however, instantly recognized me, rushed into my arms, calling me 'dearest cousin,' and was so charming and amiable that she won my heart at once. All the more did I hold it to be my duty to warn her against the wretched scheme.

"I did so as we drove home from the station. We were alone, and I had plenty of time to explain matters thoroughly.

"To my exceeding surprise, I found that she showed no distaste whatever for the union forced upon her, she had without hesitation written to her father that she was quite ready to bestow her hand upon Herr von Ernau. Even my unflattering portrait of the young man did not make her waver in her resolve. With a degree of cool equanimity which seemed unnatural in so young a girl, she explained that the faults which I attributed to Herr von Ernau were common to all wealthy young men who had lived fast, and that she was not at all shocked by them. Certainly, from all she could hear, she judged young Ernau to be a man of honour, very clever, and withal extremely rich, wherefore she was quite willing to forgive him some small faults of which he would probably be cured in the course of time. She had lived a life of weary dependence with her aunt Massenburg and longed for freedom. She should not have refused to marry even a less distinguished suitor than Herr von Ernau, to be relieved from the cheerless existence she had been leading.

"After the cordiality and affection with which Bertha had greeted me, I was entirely unprepared to find her so coolly calculating. I told her so, and she replied with a smile that she was too old—she is just nineteen —to be deceived by any illusions as to 'love's young dream,' that the place to seek such was in popular romances; in real life a poor girl of rank must learn to be practical and to take reason for her guide. No better match could be found than the one her father had provided for her, and since she had no fancy for being an old maid, she certainly should not commit the folly of rejecting such good fortune.

"Much disappointed, I dropped the subject; the girl no longer appeared so charming to me. Her wonderful self-possession, her cool calculation, made a very disagreeable impression upon me, but this vanished when I spoke to her of her father. She was so frankly rejoiced to relieve him from his embarrassments, to restore to him the possession of his ancestral estate, and she expressed her joy so warmly and with so much love for her father, that I was quite reconciled to her again. And it was just so with my wife. Bertha took her heart by storm. During breakfast, when the Ernaus were discussed, she was as displeased as I had been by Bertha's cynicism, but her displeasure was only transitory. The girl soon conquered her again by her amiability.

"I really dreaded Egon von Ernau's visit. Werner had informed me that the young man would make his appearance about twelve, but he did not come. Hours passed, and at four o'clock Werner appeared in his stead. Bertha rushed into his arms, she was bewitching in her delight at seeing her father again; indeed, she was like some artless, lovely child in her tender, caressing ways with her father.

"You know Werner, he neither deserves nor appreciates such affection. I really think he cares more for a fine race-horse than for his charming daughter, whose caresses evidently annoyed him. He endured without returning them, only bestowing a cold kiss upon Bertha's cheek, and immediately desiring to see me in private.

"As soon as we were alone in my library the tempest, the signs of which I had already seen in his face, burst forth, he raged and swore, talked of putting a bullet through his brains; and some time elapsed before he was sufficiently calm to explain to me the cause of his anger.

"His affairs certainly looked black enough. The son-in-law of his desires had disappeared, thus destroying the scheme upon which all Werner's hopes had been based.

"The Privy Councillor von Ernau had risen, according to his wont, at eight in the morning, and, not at all according to his wont, had been desirous of breakfasting with his son, that he might consult him with regard to the arrangements for the celebration of his betrothal. He therefore sent to desire his son to come to him. The servant sent returned in a few minutes with Egon's man, who explained that his master had not returned home at all on the previous night, his bed was untouched, and upon his writing-table a letter had been found, addressed to his father, in his handwriting. This letter was handed to the Privy Councillor. He broke the seal, as he himself stated, with a trembling hand, but this last is doubtful. The letter contained only the words 'Farewell! E. von E.'

"'He has destroyed himself!' was the father's exclamation, as he hastened to Egon's rooms in company with the servant, and searched them through in hopes of finding some scrap of writing that might allay his apprehensions, but in vain. His first words seemed the only true explanation of his son's disappearance.

"Egon could not have left town for a journey, his

servant had received no directions to prepare for a trip,
and the young man's clothes were undisturbed, none
were missing save those which he wore when last seen.
A costly revolver, a favourite weapon of Egon's, was
not to be found. Everything strengthened the Privy
Councillor in the belief that his son had committed
suicide. He had hitherto taken but a languid interest in
his son, he had often indeed passed weeks without seeing
him, although the same roof sheltered both; now the
Privy Councillor suddenly assumed the part of a tender,
agonized parent. He burst into loud lamentations over
the terrible fate of his beloved son, he reproached himself for having driven him to put an end to himself.
Nothing but despair at being forced to marry a girl
whom he did not love could have driven Egon to such
a horrible deed.

"These lamentations were publicly made, and by them
Herr von Ernau attained a vast notoriety. He was
quite given over to the *rôle* of tender, agonized parent.
He played it before his servants at home and the clerks
in his counting-room. In vain they all tried to soothe
him, to represent that there was as yet no proof that
his terrible suspicion was correct; in vain did his cashier
declare that if Herr Egon had contemplated suicide he
would not have drawn, as he had done the day before,
twenty thousand marks from the bank. The Privy
Councillor insisted that his son had shot himself, the
drawing of the twenty thousand marks was an additional proof of the deed. Egon had wished to pay everything that he owed before his death, and had drawn the
money for this purpose.

"Werner von Massenburg believed that the Councillor's loud lamentations were all dictated by his vanity,
which was always urging him to seek notoriety at any

price. At nine o'clock he had ordered his carriage and was driving about among all his intimate friends and acquaintances enacting the same scene over and over again, and declaring that the wretched proposed betrothal had driven Egon to despair. By noon the universal topic on 'Change was young Ernau's suicide and its cause, and the story flew like wildfire all through the town. An hour previously it had reached Werner, and he had hurried to the Councillor, with whom he had gone through a terrible scene. The Councillor, in his false, theatrical fashion, had cursed the unfortunate projected betrothal, and had heaped reproaches upon Werner, who, of course, was not slow in retaliating, until at last Ernau vowed angrily that if the faint hope that still existed should prove a certainty, and Egon be found to be alive, the hated betrothal should never take place.

"This was the sum of Werner's incoherent narrative. He cursed the Ernaus, father and son, and in his utter selfishness even found fault with Bertha for bringing him into this frightful difficulty by a too ready acquiescence in his plans. She must be completely compromised by the scandal, which was now known all over the town, and in a few days society would cast scorn upon the names of Massenburg and Ernau, and the wildest exaggerations of the story of Egon's suicide would be told everywhere.

"I tried to soothe Werner, but with small success. He left me at last with the task upon my hands of informing Bertha of what had occurred.

"This was unpleasant enough, but the girl made it as easy for me as possible. She listened to my account with great composure, only expressing her sorrow that her poor father should be disappointed in his dearest hopes. When my wife spoke indignantly of young Ernau, she shrugged her shoulders. 'I am sorry for him,' she said, in a tone expressive of quite as much scorn as pity; 'he is evidently one of those unfortunate men who, bred in the lap of luxury, have lost all force of character, all capacity to shape their destiny. He is certainly more to be pitied than blamed for shuffling off his life like a coward instead of opposing his father's schemes like a man.'

"I was glad that she so easily acquiesced in the inevitable, and I hoped that Werner's fear lest her reputation should suffer from what had occurred would prove groundless. To-day has, unfortunately, convinced me of the contrary.

"The scandal is full-blown. The whole story is talked of everywhere, and one of the morning papers tells it in detail, with all sorts of additions. It is hinted that Herr Egon von Ernau is the victim of a low money speculation on the part of a family of rank. Fräulein Bertha von Massenburg knew that he was in love with a girl of the middle class, but would not withdraw her pretensions because she did not choose to lose a wealthy *parti*. The young man had been led, by his love for his father, into giving his consent to the betrothal, in hopes that Fräulein von Massenburg would reject his hand when she learned that he loved another. Disappointed in this hope, he had recourse to his revolver.

"Although everybody knows how perfectly untrustworthy are these romantic tales conceived in the brain of some newspaper reporter, everybody believes them, as I have, alas! seen only too clearly during the past day. In the course of it my wife has had more visits than she has received for weeks from friends and acquaintances of every degree of intimacy, and she is in despair over the expressions of commiseration and the curious inquiries concerning private family affairs to which she has been compelled to listen. These visits have so unnerved her that I have been forced to forbid the admission of visitors to the house for some days to come.

"This is only the beginning of the annoyance. The newspapers will all shortly have their various versions of the affair. Instead of pitying the poor girl, as people would have done a few days ago for being sacrificed to a *roué,* all now condemn her, and lavish their compassion on the poor fellow who was tormented into putting an end to a life so full of promise.

"Under these circumstances Bertha cannot remain in Berlin. Her stay here would be intolerable, both for her and for my poor wife. Neither can her aunt Massenburg recall her to Königsberg, where gossip would inevitably pursue her and be more rife in the provincial town than in the capital. Moreover, Aunt Massenburg is, as you know, a person of such very strict ideas that it is doubtful whether she will ever again receive beneath her roof a girl so talked about.

"In our need we have thought of you, dear Fritz. You are, through your wife, related to poor Bertha, and you must give her an asylum in your house until the storm has blown over. After a few weeks, at most after a few months, no one will remember that there ever was an Egon von Ernau. We live quickly, and forget as quickly, at the present day.

"So I entreat you to invite Bertha to pay a long visit to Castle Osternau. I know that I ask you to make a sacrifice in granting my request. Malicious gossip may follow Bertha even to the depths of the country and cause you annoyance, but I know you

well enough to be sure that you will not on that
account hesitate to do such a kindness. Nothing can
so surely tend to re-establish Bertha's reputation in
public opinion as the knowledge that she is the guest
of a family so highly esteemed as your own.

"And now farewell. My warm regards to your excellent wife. Do not let her be vexed with her old
uncle for asking so great a service at your hands.
Write soon to yours faithfully,

"Sastrow."

A long silence followed upon the reading of this
lengthy epistle. Herr von Osternau waited in vain for
some expression of opinion from his wife. "Well,
Emma," he asked, at last, "what do you think of this
unfortunate story?"

"I pity the poor girl," Frau von Osternau replied.
"The punishment of her folly is almost too hard."

"I cannot even see in what her folly has consisted,"
observed the Lieutenant. "What has she done to deserve such a reproach? She obeyed her father, consented to make a brilliant match, and did it gladly.
She could not possibly foresee what would be the consequences of an engagement which seemed so advantageous both for herself and for her father."

"That is just it. She thought of nothing save
what she thought advantageous," Lieschen eagerly interposed. "I cannot even pity her. She knew from
Uncle Sastrow all about that odious Egon von Ernau,
—that he was a man without heart or principle,—and
yet she was quite ready to marry him because he was
rich. It makes me indignant!"

"Ought she then to have refused to obey her father?"
asked the Lieutenant.

"Yes, she ought! No father has a right to ask his child to disgrace herself by such a marriage. I am indignant with Bertha Massenburg. I never could have believed it of her. She was so charming, so good-natured, so kind, I liked her so much when she spent nearly the whole summer with us here at Osternau, about five years ago. I cannot bear to think that she could allow herself to be so dazzled by mere wealth. She deserves her punishment."

"My child, your judgment of her is very severe," her father said, gravely. "Since her mother's death, Bertha's lot has been a sad one. She was homeless, for her father, who spent his time in all kinds of dissipation, was deep in debt, his estates were mortgaged, and he took no interest in his child. She was obliged thankfully to accept shelter with her aunt Massenburg, at Königsberg. There her life must have been absolutely wretched. I know what a hard and loveless woman Gunda Massenburg is. We must not condemn Bertha for gladly consenting at last to anything that her father proposed that could deliver her from such a home. We should rather pity her. It is your duty, Lieschen, to receive her here with all the affection which you gave her in happier times."

"You have decided to invite her here, then?" Frau von Osternau asked, anxiously.

"Yes, Emma. The poor girl ought to find a refuge with us from the gossip and slander which have attacked her good name."

"But, Fritz——"

"Indeed it is our duty, disagreeable as it may seem, so let us say no more about it except in the way of arranging how your uncle's wishes may be most speedily fulfilled. I will write to-night both to him and to

Bertha. Herr Pigglewitch is going to Breslau with Herr Storting to-morrow morning early. If he will kindly post my letters there we can have a reply by day after to-morrow night, and shall know when to expect Bertha. You will take charge of the letters, will you not, Herr Candidate?"

At this direct question Egon started as if from a dream. He had listened with intense attention to the letter, but had really heard nothing of what had since been said. It was his fault, all this wretched scandal which so painfully involved all these people, and from the annoyance of which Herr von Osternau and his family were not exempt.

When he left his father's house, as he thought forever, and succeeded in leaving Berlin without being seen or recognized by any one, he had taken genuine satisfaction in his success in vanishing without leaving a trace behind. He had derived a unique enjoyment from imagining the impression which his disappearance would produce among his acquaintances; he had never once fancied that his voluntary departure from the world could cause any real regret to a living being. He knew that his father was incapable of feeling genuine grief; there was no one to be pained by his sudden death. Egon had loved and been loved by no one. And his imagination had not played him false. Herr von Sastrow's letter described the theatric woe of the Councillor: if he had actually felt a degree of sorrow for his son's death he was more than indemnified by the opportunity for playing the part of a bereaved parent. His vanity was flattered by the sensation caused by Egon's disappearance.

The young man could see it all in his mind's eye,— his father's well-acted agony for the death of a son upon whom he had bestowed no affection, and the equally well acted sympathy of his acquaintances. All were aware of the farce at which they were assisting, but it was played because required by the customs of society, and because the actors were well pleased with their parts.

Yes, everything had happened as Egon had thought it would. What he had not thought of was that his death could cast a shade upon another human existence, —upon the reputation of his proposed bride.

He had been most disagreeably affected during the reading of the letter by the enumeration of his various characteristics, for he could not but admit the degree of truth in the written picture. A fleeting blush had passed over his cheek when he heard the terms in which Bertha von Massenburg had summed up his character, 'An unfortunate man who, bred in the lap of luxury, had lost all force of character, all capacity to shape his destiny.' She had bestowed upon him her contemptuous pity!

Lieschen had spoken of cowardice when, during their ride, she had expressed her detestation of suicide. And Bertha von Massenburg had pitied him as a coward!

He was so absorbed in these thoughts that he heard nothing of what was going on about him, and when startled by Herr von Osternau's appeal to him he was obliged to confess that he had not heard his question.

"Extraordinary absence of mind," the Lieutenant observed, but Herr von Osternau said, in his gentle, kindly way, "Herr Pigglewitch has had a most fatiguing day, and it is very natural that he should feel but a slight degree of interest in the family affairs of strangers."

Then, after repeating his request with regard to the

letters, and receiving on the instant an assurance from Egon that he would gladly undertake the charge of them, Herr von Osternau added,—

"As you must be tired, Herr Pigglewitch, and need rest, I will not detain you from seeking it. I would ask but one favour of you. We have all been moved by Sastrow's letter, which will give me at least a troubled night. Perhaps you may succeed in diverting our thoughts if you will kindly go once more to the piano and give us some of your delicious music."

An eloquent look from Lieschen seconded her father's request, and Egon willingly complied. He himself had often resorted to music for consolation, but of late this source of comfort had failed him; he had played with enjoyment to-day for the first time for months, and now so soon as his fingers touched the keys the old spell threw its charm over him. He forgot that Herr von Osternau had asked him to play, he forgot that he was among strangers, of whom one, the Lieutenant, was eying him with dislike and suspicion; he played for himself alone. Involuntarily he glided after a brief prelude into one of Schumann's wonderful reveries. He had played the studies of the immortal master so often, he had made them so thoroughly his own, that the notes came now as if from his very soul, and thus affected his hearers, who listened breathless, fairly carried away by the magic of sound.

It was over—with the last tone the spell too was broken. He knew that he was among the Von Osternaus; there upon the lounge sat the Lieutenant sullenly staring at the floor, and beside him was Frau von Osternau, her hands clasped in her lap, lost in dreamy enjoyment. And Lieschen?—there were tears in the girl's eyes! Egon saw no more, he felt his pulses quicken, any word of praise or thanks would have been intolerable to him. Rising from the piano, he would have left the room in silence, but that he suddenly remembered what was due from Gottlieb Pigglewitch to his employer. Little as he had learned of self-control, it must be exercised now. So with a courteous bow he turned to the master of the house and begged to be excused from playing anything more, he was really much fatigued and would ask permission to retire to his room. He then kissed Frau von Osternau's offered hand, bowed low to Lieschen, even bestowed a formal inclination upon the Lieutenant, and retired.

When the door closed behind him he passed his hand over his eyes as if to push away some cloud from his mind. Was he the same Egon von Ernau who had never paid the slightest regard to what others might think of him,—to anything indeed save his own whim of the moment? A strange and sudden change had come over him,—he could not comprehend it.

CHAPTER IX.

A LETTER AND ITS REPLY.

THE heavy clouds which had veiled the horizon in the afternoon had slowly covered all the skies, the night was very dark, the gloom only broken from time to time by dazzling flashes of lightning.

Egon stood at his open window. He felt easier and freer now that he was once more alone, and the spectacle of the beginning of the storm was a relief to him. The old trees waved and creaked in the blast, the rustling of the leaves, the crashing of boughs, and the moaning of the wind were as music in his ears. If only some ray of light could illumine the darkness within him, as the lightning's play lit up the world without!

He had suddenly become aware of the serious importance of existence. Hitherto he had never reflected upon the future, and but seldom upon the past. He had lived in the present, obeying the impulse of the moment, with no thought of the consequences of his actions. He had known no feeling of responsibility, he had lived for himself alone; who in all the world had any claim upon his consideration?

When the insane idea occurred to him of playing the part of Gottlieb Pigglewitch for a little while, it had indeed entered his mind that it might result in some annoyance, but he had thoughtlessly followed the impulse of the moment; he could put a stop to it all whenever he pleased, he still possessed his revolver. He had not been bored, it is true, for a moment since he had changed clothes with Gottlieb Pigglewitch and borrowed his name, but what had he gained? Was he happy? Was life any more attractive to him? No, not in the least. Formerly, when he had thought it worth while to recur to the past, he had done so without regret, without the slightest remorse, he had recalled his past with a kind of weary indifference; to-day this retrospect begot within him a sensation of shame. His whole past life seemed to him frivolous and insignificant. Bertha von Massenburg had characterized him correctly. It was only by chance that he had not fled from life like a coward. Involuntarily, as the feeling of shame grew stronger, he felt for his revolver in his breast-pocket to toss it from him, and as he drew it forth, a letter likewise was pulled from his pocket and fell upon the floor.

It was the note addressed to the Candidate Gottlieb Pigglewitch, which he had received a few hours before. Egon had forgotten it; he picked it up now and carried it to the table, where a light was burning.

His thoughts had taken another turn; the momentary disgust at the thought of his revolver vanished, he contemplated it with a half-smile, and his thoughts ran thus: "I had very nearly thrown you away forever, old friend. It was only an accident, the appearance of this wretched letter, which prevented me from yielding to the impulse of the moment. Shall I never, then, be master of myself? 'He is a man of no force of character, he has no self-control.' Those were old Sastrow's words, and, by Jove! he is right. Always the sport of the moment! Why should I toss away my revolver? There is no danger in it for me, except by my own will, by my being too great a coward to fight the battle of life. No, old friend, you shall stay by me, not as an aid in my extreme need, but as a warning to me to control myself."

He thrust the weapon again into his breast-pocket, and then turned to the letter in his left hand. It was addressed in a very fine, round hand to the "Candidate Gottlieb Pigglewitch, at Castle Osternau, near Mirbach;" but just after the name Pigglewitch two words, enclosed in brackets, were written, in a handwriting so excessively small as to escape notice at the first glance. Egon held the note near the lamp, and by its light deciphered the words "Fritz Fortune."

Fritz Fortune! It was the name that Egon had

invented and given instead of his own to the real Pigglewitch. No one else knew this name, and hence it was clear that the note was for Egon, and from the redoubtable Candidate himself. The young fellow broke the seal, and read:

"RESPECTED HERR FORTUNE,—Forgive me for once more turning to you in my extreme need; indeed I cannot help it. Wonderful indeed are the ways of the Lord! He sent me aid when with a wanton hand I attempted my own life; you, dear sir, rescued not only my body, but my immortal soul, saving it from mortal sin. And in your inexhaustible generosity you provided me with means not only to repay my uncle, but to emigrate to America and live happy there. Four thousand marks you bestowed upon me. Permit me, however, to remark that you counted out to me one hundred marks too little. I went carefully over the notes as soon as you had left, and they amounted to only three thousand nine hundred marks. I called after you, but you did not hear me; therefore you still owe me one hundred marks.

"But not for this do I now address you. A hundred marks is, to be sure, a large sum for me, but I would not mind it, I should now be in Hamburg or Bremen, ready to start for America by the next steamer, if fate had not subjected me to fresh trials.

"The spirit indeed is willing, but the flesh is weak. I have been assailed by temptation and have been unable to resist. Wretched man that I am, I have again lost everything,—everything! There is nothing left for me, Herr Fortune, but to appeal once more to your benevolence; and my heart is filled with hope that you will not let me plead in vain.

"You can probably surmise how I have been stripped of everything that you bestowed upon me. My miserable passion for play has again wrought my ruin. I could not withstand temptation. Upon arriving in Berlin, full of the brightest hopes, I encountered near the station the same men who had shortly before won all that I possessed. But why dwell upon these wretched details? In little more than an hour I was again a beggar, with hardly money enough for food for a couple of days. I sought out my former lodgings, where my landlady received me,—I had paid her up to the 15th,—and here, sitting despairing in my lonely room, it has occurred to me to write to you, honoured Herr Fortune.

"You are rich. You have with you now thousands of marks. You cannot refuse to help a miserable man who knows no help save in you. I entreat, I implore you to send me four thousand marks more, and I will say nothing about the hundred marks that you still owe me.

"What shall I do if you refuse to aid me? It is true that I promised you to reveal to no one the fact that you had under my name installed yourself in my situation at Castle Osternau, and that I had handed over to you all my credentials, but with the best will in the world it is impossible for me to keep my promise. I cannot now emigrate to America, I must stay here, and in order to live I must find a situation here; to do this I need my papers. Yes, I must lay claim to the situation promised me at Castle Osternau; only by procuring it can I ever lay by money enough to pay my uncle. This is my only hope, for if I do not pay it he will send me to jail, whereas if I make him remittances he will perhaps wait in order not to lose his money.

"You will see yourself, Herr Fortune, that I shall be forced to break my promise to you, much as it will

pain me to cause you any annoyance. I am so grateful
to you that the thought of your being arrested and
brought to punishment for assuming a false name and
presenting false credentials drives me to despair.

"'This must not happen. You will give heed to my
entreaty, and once more send me the four thousand
marks which I, miserable sinner that I am, have lost at
play. I swear to you, by all that is sacred, that by the
next mail after the receipt of the money I will transmit my uncle's money to him, and will go straight to
Hamburg without spending a day more in Berlin. I
swear to you that I will not touch a card, that I will
not yield to temptation.

"Help me this once, only this once, honoured Herr
Fortune, I implore you on my knees, lying in the dust
before you!

" Your wretched, desperate, but eternally grateful and
devoted

" GOTTLIEB PIGGLEWITCH.

"P.S.—My address is 'Candidate Gottlieb Pigglewitch, Berlin, 52 Ensel Street, care of Frau Wiebe.'"

With a face darkening as he read, Egon perused this
precious epistle, tossing it disdainfully aside when he
had finished reading it. "Miserable scoundrel!" he muttered. "What a worthless mass of hypocritical gratitude, servility, stupidity, and dishonesty the creature
must be, thus to threaten me indirectly in hopes of getting more money from me! He talks to me of arrest,
and thinks that for fear of it I shall send him another
four thousand marks that he may be plucked for the
third time by sharpers. No, my worthy Pigglewitch,
you have reckoned without your host this time; not a
mark will you get!"

He paced his room to and fro, deciding that any further thought of the miserable letter and the rogue who had penned it was foolish, and yet he could not banish it from his mind.

Was the threat so very ridiculous? If the true Pigglewitch had the courage to attempt it he might bring the false one into a deal of trouble, as Egon's sober second thought could not but admit.

The bearing of a feigned name was legally a crime, but that was of no consequence in Egon's mind. If he chose early the next morning to go to Berlin instead of to Breslau, who could succeed in finding the Pigglewitch who had vanished from Osternau? Nobody would suppose that Egon von Ernau, suddenly appearing in the capital again after a short pleasure-trip, had for a day or two taken it into his head to play the part of a Candidate Gottlieb Pigglewitch. The real Pigglewitch could not betray him, for he knew him only as Fritz Fortune. The false Pigglewitch simply vanished, leaving not a trace behind.

What would the world say if the Egon von Ernau whom it believed dead should suddenly appear safe and sound in Berlin? Egon laughed as he pictured to himself his reception in the paternal mansion, the faces of the servants, and the amazement of his father thus interrupted in his successful performance of the part of a broken-hearted parent. His poor father! But there would be some consolation for him in the sensation caused by his son's return. He could drive about town in his carriage, and, with a beaming countenance, inform all his friends, 'My son lives, I am the happiest of fathers!' Whether in joy or in woe, he could still be the model parent.

Would it not be best perhaps to cut the Gordian

knot of his foolish adventure after this fashion? Yes, it would be his wisest course to leave Castle Osternau on the morrow, never to return. And what of the future? He had never formerly thought of the future, he did so now for the first time.

He would doubtless be received with enthusiasm, would be the topic of the gossip of the capital for weeks, all the silly rumours which had been flying about with regard to him would die away of themselves, Bertha von Massenburg need not leave Berlin, for— here Egon shuddered—the betrothal could take place as agreed upon, the betrothal to which Egon had thoughtlessly consented because it was of no consequence to him what woman was the sharer of his tedious existence. All women seemed alike calculating, frivolous, insignificant. He had given his consent, it could not be withdrawn.

Why did his pulses suddenly quicken? Why did he feel a positive aversion to the girl who was described as so beautiful and amiable? "Never, never," he muttered. He could not act wisely, he could not return to fulfil his father's promise, no, he could not.

He would remain in Castle Osternau and carry out to the end the adventure in which he was embarked, if only to test his force of character, his ability to carve out a new life for himself. Was it for this alone? Did not a lovely vision hover before his mental vision, casting its spells upon him, robbing him of freedom of will and forcing him to remain, when to go would be so prudent, so sensible?

He determined to remain. But he must not expose himself to the danger of being driven forth from Castle Osternau by the real Pigglewitch. For should the latter make good his claim, as he could, to the name now borne by Egon, he would doubtless be expelled from the castle pursued by the Lieutenant's scornful laughter.

And he could not possibly explain the matter to Herr von Osternau. No, the real Pigglewitch must be disarmed. But how? There was but one course,—to grant his request. Egon bit his lip; it irritated him to be influenced by the rogue's threats, but he had no choice. He could secure himself from discovery only by sending the fellow four thousand marks. Should he then be secure? Could he trust the man in the slightest degree? No, never. But it was of little consequence, he could at all events be made harmless for a short time. It was, after all, only a matter of a petty four thousand marks.

He sat down at the writing-table and wrote: "I will help you this time, but it is the last. If you allow yourself to be led astray again by your insane love of play you have nothing further to expect from me. I ought now to leave you to your fate, for your folly in allowing yourself to be made a second time the prey of ordinary sharpers deserves punishment, the more as by your threat of breaking your promise you have forfeited all right to my clemency. You owe the money which I herewith send you to my pity for your inconceivable stupidity, not in the least to your threat as to arrest, etc., which, I would remark by the way, is absolutely futile, since your papers were given me voluntarily by yourself, and the only inconvenience to which you could subject me would be the payment of a fine which would be of no importance to me, and the abridgment of a foolish jest which I was silly ever to attempt. Your broken promise would avail you nothing here, since your letter to me would prevent Herr von Osternau from ever receiving into his house, as tutor, a low, dishonest gambler, who, according to his own confession, should be at present within the walls of a jail.

"You know now what you have to expect, and I would advise you in your own interest to keep your word and to sail by the first vessel for America. If in your new home you should ever need money to purchase a farm you may again apply to me. I may perhaps be induced to remember that I saved your life against your will. How far this remembrance will serve you in the fulfilment of a reasonable request from you your own conduct must decide.

"I wish no thanks from you for the enclosed four thousand marks. Any communication made from you to me before your arrival in America will destroy all hope of future assistance from

"FRITZ FORTUNE."

CHAPTER X.

CONTENT AND PEACE.

THE morning after the first night spent by Egon at Castle Osternau dawned so brilliantly that the light of the rising sun shining in at his window awoke him. The storm had raged itself out, and the blue sky was cloudless.

He was quickly dressed and down in the garden, where the delicious air and the dewy flowers filled him with a new delight. Although he had slept but a few hours, he felt more rested and refreshed than when rising in Berlin at noon.

He walked through the garden out into the fields, involuntarily striking into the path leading to the Oster meadows. He had time for a walk, for he was not to be ready for the trip with Herr Storting until seven o'clock, and it was now but a little after five.

He soon reached the eminence whence he had yesterday looked down with Lieschen upon the harvest-fields. The charming view seemed more lovely and peaceful than before, for the busy crowd of harvesters was absent. Labour in the fields had not yet begun. A single horseman was riding through the valley towards the castle. When he saw Egon he waved his hand, and spurred his horse on to where the young man was standing. Egon recognized Herr Storting. "Good-morning, Herr Pigglewitch," Storting called from afar. " I did not expect to meet you in the Oster meadows at five in the morning. Did you wish to be sure that the storm has done us no harm? Aha! you begin to take an interest in our harvest. You may be easy, we have come off very well. The rain was only an honest summer thunder-storm. In some places it has indeed beaten down the grain, but the injury is slight, and I can with a clear conscience fulfil my promise and go to Breslau with you this morning."

Storting was so rejoiced at the safety of his harvest that he entirely forgot his yesterday's displeasure at his companion's conduct, and he walked his horse slowly back to the castle at Egon's side, pointing with pride to the luxuriant fields on each side of them, and speaking with enthusiasm of Herr von Osternau and his agricultural foresight and skill.

His talk was most interesting to Egon, who felt an increased respect and esteem for the man of whom an intelligent inspector in his employ could speak in terms of such admiration.

Arrived in the court-yard the pair separated, Storting to superintend the arrangement of the day's labour, since, as he said, with a half-smile, "The chief superintendent will hardly appear before eight o'clock, his usual time of rising," while Egon repaired to his room. Here he found his breakfast awaiting, and beside his plate a letter addressed to Colonel D. von Sastrow, Berlin. It was the one he had been requested by Herr von Osternau to take charge of on the previous evening, and the sight of it reminded him of his own letter to Pigglewitch, which he had laid away unsealed after he had written it. He took it out and read it over once more. It did not please him, but he could not resist the longing desire that possessed him to remain for a while at Osternau. He shuddered at the thought of resuming the tedious old Berlin life. Any means were justifiable that should enable him to escape that.

With a sigh he enclosed the notes for the promised money, sealed the letter, and addressed it. Then he took from his pocket-book an additional two hundred marks. Thus much, he reflected, Gottlieb must have possessed before falling into the hands of the sharpers, and so much therefore his substitute might surely sacrifice to the exigencies of the occasion. He needed some school-books, and also some linen. That contained in the travelling-bag filled him with disgust.

Punctually at seven he started with Storting for Breslau. The travelling-bag containing Pigglewitch's old suits was carried to the station by a servant, and the travellers arrived duly at their destination, where Egon's first care was to post Herr von Osternau's letter and his own. After this he began his expedition in the town with Storting, the first visit naturally being paid to the tailor. Here it would have gone ill with him but for Storting's assistance. The tailor at first seemed disinclined to grant credit to a stranger, and Candidate Pigglewitch could not possibly pay the two hundred and fifty marks requisite for the furnishing him with two respectable suits of clothes, except by quarterly instalments. Storting, however, came to the rescue. His credit with the tradesman was excellent, and he arranged the matter, while Egon stood by, now and then biting his lip to keep himself from laughing, so ludicrous did the whole situation seem to him. In less than an hour his outfit was complete. The clothes borrowed from Storting and one of his own new suits were packed up to be sent to the railway-station. Egon paid the ready money agreed upon, and the tailor requested him to sign a paper agreeing to pay the rest in quarterly instalments as arranged. The pen was in his hand when he suddenly reflected that he had no right to sign Pigglewitch's name to a due-bill, that to do so was actually a transgression of the law. He hesitated, but when Storting said, "Sign, Herr Pigglewitch, I will write my name as surety below yours," there was nothing for it but to comply. Here was one of the consequences of coming to Castle Osternau under a false name.

His enjoyment of the occasion was disturbed, but only for a moment; when they had left the shop he felt it his duty to make a special acknowledgment to the inspector for his great kindness in so readily becoming surety for an entire stranger. Storting interrupted him with a laugh.

"You must thank Fräulein Lieschen, if you wish to thank anybody—our gracious little lady. 'Pray make

l 14*

Herr Pigglewitch look like a human being,' she said to me yesterday. Not very flattering to you, but for me a command to be obeyed under all circumstances. I tell you frankly that but for this I should have had some hesitation in going surety for you, for your conduct yesterday provoked me. To-day, however, you are a different person, and I am quite sure that I run no risk in signing your promise to pay."

"Fräulein Lieschen's word is your law, then?"

"Yes, so I told you yesterday, and so I tell you again to-day." Storting laughed as he spoke, but the seriousness in his eyes contradicted the laughter of his lips. "Fräulein Lieschen rules at Castle Osternau. Just as you controlled Soliman yesterday, Fräulein Lieschen will control you before two days are gone by. Yesterday you tried to withstand the magic of her glance, to-morrow you will obey her implicitly, as I do, as every one in the castle does."

He turned as he finished the sentence into the old-clothes shop, where Pigglewitch's cast-off habiliments were to be disposed of. If Egon had enjoyed the novelty of the transaction with the tailor, here he was infinitely more entertained. Storting defended his interests bravely. The Jew dealer declared that he should be ruined by the purchase at any price of such antiquated garments, but finally with many lamentations agreed to give twenty-four marks for the two suits. Storting was content; the porter who had carried the bag was paid and dismissed; Egon pocketed his gains with a smile, and took the empty bag under his arm.

The chief business in Breslau was completed, and Egon found that he had still half an hour before the departure of the train for Osternau. This time he em-

ployed in the purchase of linen and school-books, and
arrived with Storting at the station just in time to pack
away his various bundles in the railway-carriage and
to take his seat beside his companion before the train
started.

The events of this little expedition to Breslau were
very unimportant, and yet they exercised an important
influence upon Egon's mode of thought, his views of
life. For the first time some idea occurred to him of
the value of money. The tailor's hesitation to trust
him for the insignificant sum of two hundred and fifty
marks, the petty haggling for an infinitely less sum
in the old-clothes shop, were a lesson to him. And in
his purchase of linen and books the impossibility of his
buying, as he had been wont to do, everything that he
desired, or even everything that he thought necessary,
set him thinking in earnest.

He had smiled at the gravity with which Storting, at
the tailor's, reckoned up the cost of the clothes, at the
eagerness with which he had contested a few marks
with the Jew dealer, while his zeal was all in behalf of
another, and the same man who was so anxious to save
expense for the poor Candidate Pigglewitch did not
hesitate to pledge himself to pay a hundred and fifty
marks in case the tutor should be unable to do so. And
this when the sum in question was of great importance
to him, for, as he had frankly told Egon, he was without means except his salary as inspector, out of which
he contributed to the support of a sister who was preparing for the governess examinations in Berlin.

Under these circumstances the kindness shown to
Egon by Storting was genuine indeed, and placed the
recipient under an obligation which instead of annoying him gave him pleasure. Hitherto Egon had been

disposed to regard any favour shown him as due to his wealth and position. Storting's disinterestedness therefore made the greatest impression upon him, and weakened the morbid suspicion with which he had come to look upon all friendly advances made to him.

The elation that he felt upon returning from Breslau to Castle Osternau was not damped by the fulfilment of his duties there. His little pupil's boyish eagerness to learn, his affectionate enthusiasm for his dear Herr Pigglewitch, warmed Egon's heart, while the hours spent in giving Lieschen her music-lessons were the most delightful he had ever passed in his life.

After the daily game of billiards, in which, much to the Lieutenant's chagrin, Egon maintained his supremacy, Frau von Osternau accompanied her daughter and the tutor to the sitting-room, where the lesson on the piano was given. Egon began his instruction with an interest which the discovery of his pupil's talent for music heightened to enthusiasm, and the girl's progress was such that Frau von Osternau was charmed, and in the delight which these lessons gave her forgot that she had at first been present at them from a sense of duty. Indeed, her anxiety lest Lieschen's interest in her teacher might transcend the limits of that which a pupil should feel for a master seemed entirely groundless. The girl admired the musician, as did Frau von Osternau. She listened to every word of his, and did her best to obtain his approval. When he praised her her lovely face beamed with smiles, but it was to the teacher as such that she paid her tribute of respectful attention. The lesson once concluded, Lieschen was again the merry, artless, audacious child. She teased Herr Pigglewitch as she was wont to tease Cousin Albrecht, Herr Storting, and Herr von Wangen, the third inspector. She expressed without reserve her admiration for his skill at billiards and as a horseman, and then, when displeased by some reckless speech of his, she scolded him as unreservedly. She was as frankly familiar with him as with the others, and her conduct in this respect was at times a proof to her mother that her fears for her daughter had been unfounded. She willingly allowed the daily rides, during which the pair, of course, were never alone, Fritz always forming one of the party.

It was a delight indeed to Egon to make these expeditions through field and forest with the sister and brother. Lieschen assumed all the gravity of age as she held forth to the Herr Candidate upon the mysteries of agriculture, now and then praising the progress made by her pupil, and she was no less charming when she laughed at him for his ignorance. Herr Storting was right when he prophesied that Egon would, like all the other inmates of the castle, shortly yield Fräulein Lieschen a willing obedience. Egon smiled at his own folly, but none the less did he succumb to her charm, even putting a bridle upon his tongue when habit would have led him to utter some sneering remark. One word of admonition from Lieschen was enough to put him upon his guard.

The life he led at Castle Osternau, in utter contradiction as it was to everything that he had known hitherto, threw a strange spell around him, made him calm and content, filled him with a satisfaction which forbade for the time all idea of change.

At the noonday meal he no longer listened mutely to the agricultural discourse of the lord of the castle. His awakened interest found utterance in inquiry and discussion which afforded Herr von Osternau genuine pleasure. Frau von Osternau also would give the young man a kindly nod as she marked his growing interest in such topics. The Lieutenant alone was discontent; he never let slip an opportunity for a covert sneer at the Candidate. Egon paid no attention to his insulting words, but they called forth at times a sharp reproof from Herr von Osternau, which but served to embitter Albrecht still further against its cause.

And the evenings around the tea-table, from which Egon would rise to take his seat at the piano, were perhaps the most enjoyed of all this pleasant existence. What matter was it to the young fellow if the Lieutenant hated him? He felt that every other member of the family regarded him with kindness, that Fritz positively worshipped him, that Frau von Osternau had confidence in him, that her husband treated him as his equal in rank, as a friend of the family. And Lieschen? She was as frank and merry as upon their first meeting. She even teased him now and then about his old coat, in which she still insisted he looked like a scarecrow, but at intervals, in the midst of her girlish merriment, her eyes would meet his own with a look which, he could hardly have told why, filled him with intense, unreasoning joy.

CHAPTER XI.

GOOD ADVICE.

"BERTHA will arrive to-morrow," said Herr von Osternau, looking up from the letter which he had just received by the evening mail.

Egon alone of all the little circle had had no letter,

and he had therefore been looking over the paper, which he now dropped in dismay. Two weeks previously he had taken Herr von Osternau's letter to Breslau, and for a few days afterwards he had thought with a kind of dread of the threatened visit from Fräulein von Massenburg, but as the invitation remained unanswered, and as there was no mention made by any of the family of Bertha, he had forgotten that the peaceful life at Castle Osternau might be disturbed by the intrusion of a foreign element. His dismay was shared by Frau von Osternau and Lieschen, as was evident from their faces as they looked up from their letters.

"Indeed!" said Frau von Osternau. "I hoped that Bertha would refuse our invitation, since she has left it so long unanswered. Has she written herself?"

"No; Sastrow tells me that she is to leave Berlin early to-morrow morning, and so she will be here towards evening. You can read his letter, or I will read it to you. Albrecht and Herr Pigglewitch heard his first, and this is simply a conclusion of it." And the old Herr began :

"My dear Fritz,—Forgive me for delaying my thanks for your prompt response to my request. You must have daily expected my reply, but I could not before inform you exactly when Bertha would go to you. Almost immediately after the arrival of your letter Werner von Massenburg came to me in a state of great perturbation, to tell me that Egon von Ernau had probably not killed himself, but was knocking about in the mountains somewhere. One of his intimate acquaintances had seen him in Breslau two or three days after his disappearance. Werner had himself seen this acquaintance, a certain Baron von Freistetten, and had heard the tidings from his own lips. The Baron assured him that as he was driving to the railway-station in Breslau he had seen Ernau on the sidewalk, walking very quickly. The Baron was in a hurry to catch his train, and so had not accosted his friend, but he knew him well enough to be sure that it was he. He nodded to him from the carriage, but Ernau was looking at some books in a bookseller's window, and did not perceive him. If he had known that Ernau was reported dead, the Baron would certainly, even at the risk of losing his train, have stopped and identified the missing man; but he had been absent from the capital for some time, and knew nothing of the gossip current there. However, he is ready to take his oath that the man whom he saw was no other than Egon von Ernau.

"Werner fairly shook with agitation as he recounted this wonderful story to my wife, to Bertha, and to me; he had just come from the Councillor Ernau, whom he reported as quite as much agitated as himself by Freistetten's statement. They discussed what was best to do under the circumstances, and decided that a notice should be sent to the newspapers contradicting the report of the suicide of young Ernau, who had merely left Berlin upon a pleasure-trip. The Councillor was also to engage the police to make search for his son in Breslau. They agreed that if, as they both believed, Egon von Ernau still lived, nothing should be changed in their former arrangements. The Councillor was convinced that his son would not think of relinquishing his claim upon Bertha's hand, especially after the public scandal to which his disappearance had given rise.

"You know Werner Massenburg, and how sanguine he is; nothing that I could say as to the possibility of a mistake on Baron Freistetten's part had any effect upon him. His hopes were again high, and he thought it quite natural that young Ernau, who had always followed the impulse of the moment, should have chosen this time for a short absence from Berlin. According to the unanimous verdict of his companions, the young man was ready to commit any folly, and to carry out, regardless of the feelings of others, any project that might occur to him.

"Neither I nor my wife was convinced by what he said, but Bertha listened to him with sparkling eyes, and declared that nothing should induce her to leave Berlin until the matter of Egon's absence was fully explained; she would write to you instantly and decline your invitation with thanks. I dissuaded her with difficulty from doing so.

"Again, after her father had left us, I entreated her to pause and consider. If young Ernau still lived, his want of regard for the feelings of others had proved him entirely incapable of making a wife happy. I painted her future linked for life with so eccentric, selfish, and *blasé* a husband; but my words had no effect whatever upon her, she only smiled. Her smile is wonderfully lovely, but it did not then seem lovely to me, it made me shudder.

"She had, she declared with calm decision, no anxiety for the future if she could but attain her desire of becoming young Ernau's wife. If the young man did really, as was by no means certain, feel a certain antipathy for her, which had been the cause of his temporary flight, it should be her task to cure him of his dislike. Without vanity, she was conscious of possessing enough beauty to inflame the heart of any man susceptible to a woman's charms, if she so desired to

do. Therefore she must stay in Berlin. So brilliant a
match must not be resigned without a struggle. Herr
von Ernau's reputed eccentricities mattered nothing to
her; he was immensely rich, a gentleman, and born and
bred in the best society; these advantages outweighed
all else. She laid no claim to idyllic bliss in marriage,
she was perfectly indifferent as to whether she could
love or even esteem her future husband, if he could
but satisfy her requirements in the life she wished to
lead, and if, above all, he could deliver her father from
his pecuniary embarrassments.

"My good wife listened with positive horror to these
declarations, and I was indignant. I cannot tell you
how unlovely, with all her beauty, Bertha seemed to
us; and we have not recovered from the effects of this
impression. The girl has taken the greatest pains to
please us since then, and has been charming and bewitching, but in vain. I cannot but think, whenever I
look at her, of her sordid views of life, and I do not
trust her cordiality; it comes from calculation. She
wants to stay with us in Berlin, and therefore she
flatters and caresses my wife and myself and antici-
pates all our wishes.

"Werner supposed that the notice sent to the papers
would put a stop to all scandalous gossip, but such
has not been the case. You can have no idea of the
annoyance to which we have been subjected; my wife
actually talks of retiring from society.

"Under these circumstances Bertha must not remain
with us any longer at present. I explained this to her
to-day and told her that she really must leave for Castle
Osternau to-morrow morning. Her eyes flashed as I
spoke, and she was evidently tempted to make an angry
retort, but she possesses immense self-control: she

thanked me most amiably for allowing her to stay with us until now in spite of the annoyance she had caused us. She declared herself quite ready to start for Castle Osternau to-morrow, but at the same time begged that she might return to us if Egon von Ernau ever made his reappearance in the capital. This request was preferred so bewitchingly that I could not but accede to it.

"So Bertha will arrive at Castle Osternau towards evening to-morrow. I know, my dear Fritz, how much I ask of your wife and yourself when I beg you to keep her with you for some time, but I cannot help hoping that this visit may turn out well. Bertha can be extremely delightful if she chooses to be so, and I am sure she will so choose in this case. Farewell. I send a thousand affectionate messages to your wife from her grateful old uncle,

"SASTROW."

"A charming prospect!" said Frau von Osternau when her husband had finished. "If our good-natured uncle Sastrow is so indignant with Bertha von Massenburg, she must have behaved badly. Can you ask me—can you ask Lieschen, Fritz, to make her welcome here for months?"

"You look only on the dark side, Emma. Sastrow says expressly that she can be enchantingly amiable if she chooses."

"Any one who is amiable only when she chooses is not amiable at all," his wife replied. "Indeed, Bertha von Massenburg does not seem to me a fit companion for Lieschen. I am afraid we have been somewhat hasty about this invitation."

"It has been given and accepted, Emma. Bertha is

coming to-morrow, and hospitality demands that she be kindly received. Neither you nor Lieschen, I hope, Emma, will forget that."

"Must I play the hypocrite, papa? How can I receive Bertha kindly when I am indignant at her conduct? I think it detestable in her to insist upon marrying that miserable Egon von Ernau when she knows that he does not like her and that he is a worthless man. I cannot tell you, papa, how odious Bertha's greed for wealth seems to me, and you tell me to receive her kindly. I cannot pretend to what I do not feel."

"I do not ask you, dear, to lavish affection upon her or to adopt her as your confidential friend, but to treat her as a relative of the family who has come to live with us for a while. You are no longer a child, Lieschen, and you must learn to fulfil the conventional requirements of society. I never desire you to play the hypocrite, and a courteous silence as to what we are thinking at the moment is not hypocrisy. You must accustom yourself, my dear, not to wear your heart upon your sleeve, and to bridle your tongue."

Lieschen was unaccustomed to so serious an admonition from her father, and she replied, meekly, "I will try, papa," while her mother did not look up from her work, but knitted faster than ever.

All were a little put out of tune by the news of Bertha's arrival, with the exception of the Lieutenant; he expressed the hope that the beautiful Fräulein von Massenburg would put fresh life into the old castle. He took Bertha's part; he could not see how she was to be blamed for wishing to be wealthy for her father's sake. Certainly Lieschen least of all ought to find fault with her frank expression of her sentiments as to wealth. As in royal families, so also in the higher aristo-

cratic circles, marriages were contracted without the
sentimental affection talked of in novels; Bertha was
only conforming to the laws of good society if she over-
looked Egon von Ernau's trifling defects and showed
herself ready for a union which would relieve her father
from pecuniary embarrassment. Even judging from
Herr von Sastrow's prejudiced description, young Ernau
was a talented man of unstained honour, and it would
be inexcusable folly in Bertha not to overlook any little
faults in one so richly endowed.

Although the Lieutenant delivered himself thus with
a degree of enthusiasm, no voice was raised in sympathy with him; Frau von Osternau maintained an obsti-
nate silence, seeming to be absorbed in her knitting,
Lieschen frankly declared that she could not understand a nature so coldly calculating, and thought it
detestable, and all that Herr von Osternau said was
that he could not judge Bertha until he had seen her,
and that, whatever she might be, no member of his
family was justified in showing her anything save kindness; it would be best for the present to drop all discussion of her, and he therefore begged Herr Pigglewitch to go to the piano and soothe their troubled
minds.

Egon complied, but he himself was so filled with all
kinds of conflicting thoughts and emotions that his
heart was not in his music, and he soon arose from the
instrument. It was impossible to resume the customary
happy evening talk, all were absent and uncomfortable
in mind, and the circle broke up at an unusually early
hour.

On the following day both Lieschen and her mother
were depressed in spirits. They scarcely spoke during
dinner, and but for the talk between the master of the

house and his inspectors there would have been absolute silence.

When the time came for the afternoon ride Fritzchen was about to rush off to order the horses, but
Lieschen detained him.

"Let us take a little walk to-day, Herr Pigglewitch,"
she said. "My father wishes me to arrange some flowers
in Bertha von Massenburg's room, so I cannot be away
from home long, and yet I have a great deal to say to
you. I do not want to ride to-day, we can talk so much
more easily on foot."

"Oh, Lieschen, it is delightful to gallop across the
fields, and you always talk all the time to Herr Pigglewitch," Fritz cried out, with a discontented air, but
Egon pacified him by promising to ride with him after
their walk, and the little fellow ran on before the pair
who sauntered slowly out into the fields.

In the narrow path along which they strolled Lieschen walked close by Egon's side. She had said that
she had much to say to him, but she seemed unable
to begin, and even when Egon asked the name of a
distant hamlet she gave a brief, hasty reply, and then
walked on with downcast eyes, until her companion,
eager to put an end to the uncomfortable silence, asked,
directly, "What have you to say to me, Fräulein
Lieschen?"

She looked up at him.

"You are right to remind me; it is folly to delay
asking your advice, since I have made up my mind to
do so. I do not often need advice, my own feeling tells
me what I ought to do, and I follow its promptings,
but to-day it leaves me in the lurch, I am doubtful
whether I feel and judge rightly, wherefore I want to
ask your advice, only you must promise me, Herr Pig-

glewitch, to tell me your opinion frankly, even at the risk of offending me."

" I promise you."

" It really is strange for me to turn to you for advice. When you came to us two weeks ago, I had no confidence in you, you talked so oddly, and ridiculed what I held sacred,—I was almost afraid of you. I thought you could not be a good man. Do you remember I told you so the first day you came?"

" I have forgotten none of your words."

" I was wrong. You have been very different since. When I see you now and hear you talk I can hardly believe you are the same man who talked so frivolously about self-destruction. You looked strangely and your laugh was so bitter that it hurt me, but now you laugh from your heart, and you look so kind and sincere that I cannot help having faith in you. I beg your pardon for what I said. You certainly are a good man, or Fritzchen would not be so fond of you. None but good men win the affection of children."

Egon's heart beat as he listened to her simple words. She was right; fourteen days had made another man of him. Formerly such praise from girlish lips would have excited his ridicule, now it delighted him. " I hope your opinion of to-day may prove as correct as was your former one," he said. " I am trying, at all events, to improve."

Lieschen looked up at him gratefully. " Yes, you shall advise me. To whom should I turn when I am at odds with myself? To my parents? Oh, I know how ready they are to help me, but upon this point they do not agree. To Albrecht? Never. He is not good. I never could trust him. But you wish me well,—I know you do,—and you will be frank with me."

Egon did not speak, but his eyes were more eloquent than words.

"You shall hear how I am at odds with myself," Lieschen went on. "It is about Bertha von Massenburg. My father wishes me to receive her affectionately, to let no word or look betray how indignant I am with her, with her sordid views, her odious conduct. My dear father is so gentle and kind, he cannot bear to think ill of any one. He does not believe in Bertha's low motives. It is easy for him to receive her kindly, but in me it would be hypocrisy. Must I be a hypocrite? Should not truth be our first consideration? Ought I to be false to myself out of conformity with conventional ideas of courtesy? Nothing makes me so indignant as falsehood, and now I am asked to act a falsehood myself. My mother thinks as I do, but she submits. In whatever my father seriously desires she always obeys him. He yields to her in all small matters, but when he has formed an opinion upon any important question my mother always conforms to it. I know that she is as indignant as I am about Bertha von Massenburg, but she never will allow it to be seen; my father's wish is her law, and it has always been mine, but now I am sure he is mistaken. Advise me what to do. What would you do if you were in my place?"

Egon's gaze was bent upon the ground. He did not dare to look into the clear eyes that were questioning his face. 'Nothing makes me so indignant as falsehood,' the girl had just said, and her words yet sounded in his ears. Was not his whole life at Castle Osternau a falsehood? She did not dream of the sentence she had passed upon him. She hated falsehood, and asked advice of him! He commanded his voice with difficulty, and, without lifting his eyes, said, "You wish to

know what I should do? I cannot tell you. I do not
know. It has always been my misfortune to yield to
the impulse of the moment. How can I tell what that
impulse might be?"

"Is that all you have to say? You have no advice
to give me?"

"What ought I to say? Can I advise you to dis-
obey your father? Should I be tempted to do so I
might perhaps sin grievously, not only against Herr
von Osternau, good and kind as he is, but against
Fräulein von Massenburg. It is easy to pronounce
a harsh judgment upon those who have not acted
rightly according to our convictions, but what do we
really know of their springs of action? How do you
know that it has not cost Fräulein von Massenburg a
bitter struggle to insist upon her union with Herr von
Ernau, whom you call a miserable fellow, judging him
no less harshly than you judge her? Do you know
him at all except from the description of a man who
is not acquainted with him? And if he is, as Herr
von Sastrow says, at odds with life, do you know what
has made him so? I can imagine a wretched man
satiated from earliest childhood with every pleasure
that money can procure, with no wish ungratified
save that for affection, never having known the love
of either father or mother, miserably lonely, surrounded by flatterers and parasites who feign friend-
ship for the sake of his riches, but who care nothing
for him in reality. Is it his fault if he has become
disgusted with his fellow-men, if he is vain, *blasé*, dic-
tatorial, destitute of self-control? How do you know
that deep in the soul of the man whom you have condemned there do not slumber the sparks of nobler and
truer sentiments, beneath the ashes of the ruin wrought

m

by his ill-spent life? It needs but a breath, perhaps, to make this spark a flame, a breath of self-inspection or a breath of affection, and yet you condemn him. If he should judge himself as you judge him, the spark would surely die beneath the ashes, and he would be lost without hope of rescue."

Lieschen stared at the speaker in wonder. "How strangely you speak," she said, "exactly as if you knew Herr von Ernau! And how agitated you have become! you have grown quite pale. Oh, you must know Herr von Ernau, or you would not thus defend him."

"I did not mean to defend him," Egon replied, in some confusion. "He may not deserve any defence. I only wished to point out to you the harshness of your judgment both of him and of Fräulein von Massenburg, and to show you that your knowledge of them is insufficient to allow of your forming such a judgment."

"That means that you advise me not to receive Bertha Massenburg coldly, but to suppress my dislike for her and comply with my father's wishes?"

"I am not worthy to advise you to do anything save to act according to the dictates of your own heart."

Lieschen shook her head. "You are a very strange person, Herr Pigglewitch," she said, with a smile. "You do not wish to advise me, and yet you have given me advice which I shall follow. You have shown me clearly that I was wrong in condemning Herr von Ernau and Bertha, and that my dear father was right in asking me to receive Bertha kindly. I am glad I came to you for counsel. I shall think of what you said about Herr von Ernau, and I should like to hear more of him from you, for I am sure you know him; but I cannot now, for it is time to return to the castle."

CHAPTER XII.

BERTHA VON MASSENBURG.

AFTER a long ride with Fritzchen, Egon returned to the castle later than usual. As they rode into the court-yard a dusty carriage was standing before the carriage-house, and old Wenzel informed them that the Fräulein from Berlin had arrived a little while before.

During the ride the talk of his lively young pupil had left Egon small time for reflection, and he really felt a desire to be alone for a time. Much as he usually enjoyed the evenings spent with the family, he preferred to pass this one in his own room, and he suspected also that his kind employers would be quite willing to dispense with his society upon this particular occasion. He therefore commissioned Fritzchen to tell his father that he would not intrude upon the family this evening, but would remain in his own apartments. Scarcely had he reached them, however, before Fritz made his appearance to say that his father had sent him to tell Herr Pigglewitch that he could not possibly intrude, and that he should expect him at the tea-table. After giving his message the boy hurried away, declaring that he must go instantly to his 'lovely new cousin.' She seemed to have quite supplanted his adored tutor, for the while, in the child's affections.

Of course Egon could not but comply with Herr von Osternau's expressed desire. Reluctant as he was to confront Bertha von Massenburg, he knew that he must meet her sooner or later, and he resigned himself with the best grace possible to the inevitable. He dressed quickly and repaired to the tea-room.

Before he reached it he heard the notes of a popular *Conzertstück* played with great execution. He paused in the corridor and listened. He knew the thing well enough, he had played it several times himself, but always with distaste, for he did not like this style of music, but he listened attentively, for he knew how much practice it must have required before it could be rendered thus clearly and brilliantly.

He did not listen long, for there could be, he thought, no better moment in which to enter the room unnoticed than just when every one was occupied in listening to the music; he softly opened the door and entered.

His first glance fell upon the performer, whose back was towards him, his second upon a tall mirror opposite that reflected her face and figure. Involuntarily he stood still.

He had heard that Bertha von Massenburg was beautiful, and Herr von Sastrow's letter had confirmed the report, but the image reflected in the mirror amazed him by its wondrous, transporting beauty,—beauty consisting not only in faultless regularity of feature, but much more in the strange loveliness of expression, in the gentle smile of the delicately-chiselled mouth, in the dark, fiery eyes that sparkled beneath long lashes, in the grace which informed every motion of the full yet slender figure. A piano-player is seldom graceful in the exercise of her art, but with Bertha von Massenburg even the rapid movement of hands and fingers as they flew over the keys seemed natural and beautiful; therein lay one charm of her playing, and yet, masterly as it was, it lacked something,—it lacked depth of feeling. Was it really lacking? or was there no opportunity for its revelation in a brilliant drawing-room piece of music, which was calculated to display merely the execution and skill of the performer?

Egon remained standing near the door, after bowing to Herr and Frau von Osternau, and exchanging glances in the mirror with Lieschen, who stood with her back to him, turning over the leaves for her cousin. At last the piece was concluded; the performer arose, and was greeted with enthusiastic applause from the Lieutenant, who advanced from the recess of a window. Herr von Osternau also expressed his admiration of the performance. "Brilliant indeed," he said. "You are an artist, not a *dilettante*. You will have all the more pleasure in making the acquaintance of another artist in our Fritz's tutor, Herr Pigglewitch, whom I beg leave to present to you."

The smile which Egon's assumed name when first heard was sure to provoke hovered upon Bertha's lips as she turned to the tutor, looking at him with evident interest and curiosity. Her glance took in his entire figure, his movements, his bow upon being presented, in short, she observed him so closely as almost to embarrass him, as she said, easily, "My kind uncle pays a very high compliment to my indifferent performance in ranking me with you, Herr Pigglewitch,"—the smile deepened on the charming mouth. "I have heard that you are a true artist, and had I known that you were standing behind me I might have hesitated to continue my performance and subject myself to your criticism."

She had seen Egon in the mirror upon his first entrance, and he knew that this was so, for their glances had met. "I hate falsehood!" Lieschen had said. Why

16

was Bertha untrue? Where was her inducement to be
so? Had untruth become to her a second nature, as
to so many women of the world of society? Egon
suddenly felt himself transported to the old life which
he knew so well,—Herr von Osternau's pleasant room
changed to a brilliant ball-room, and before him stood
one of the ball-room puppets whom he so hated and
despised, particularly when they tried to make themselves attractive by flattering him.

Involuntarily he stood more erect. The disdainful
smile which Lieschen had so disliked, and which she
had not seen of late, appeared on his lips as he replied,
"Is it possible that you fear criticism, Fräulein? A
mastery of technique is the ideal of our modern art.
You are certainly aware that the sternest critic would
not withhold his recognition of the brilliancy of your
execution, but must pronounce you a virtuoso indeed."

"A virtuoso? My kind uncle called me an artist,
and I was proud that he did so."

"Who makes such subtile distinctions nowadays?
The virtuoso is the only true artist. He alone rep-
resents the true modern ideal; he is never led astray
by the genius, now so out of fashion, of wearisome
classical music."

Her eyes flashed. "You think you can interpret
this genius, or you would not pass such a criticism
upon modern art," Bertha replied, sharply. "Pray
take my place at the piano. He who pronounces such
sentences must justify them by his own performance."

Her cheek flushed slightly as she spoke, her dark
eyes glowed, she seemed to Egon at the moment enchantingly beautiful. Her tone and her words were
not those of a ball-room puppet. Bertha was not of
them, then; she could be vexed and angry and could

transgress conventional forms, as was proved by her request to him and by its manner.

He obeyed, dominated by her glance. He took her place at the piano, but for a few moments his hands rested idly upon the keys and his eyes were downcast. The glow in those large black eyes recalled to him the memory of old days which he had thought half forgotten, when suddenly the eyes into which he gazed turned, in his vision, from black to dark, melting blue, and were filled with sympathy for the mental struggles through which he was constantly passing. The spell of the moment that had summoned up the past was dissolved; he belonged again to the peaceful present. Involuntarily the hands upon the keys began to give expression to the gladness that arose within him. He played he knew not what, the various melodies awoke and resolved themselves to harmony beneath his touch, he played as if in a dream, uttering in tones all that he would have said to the lovely child to whom he owed a new and delicious content of soul,—exulting words of joy, gentle words of gratitude, tender words of love.

"Bravo! bravo!" The Lieutenant, desirous of showing his impartial love of art by applauding the detested tutor, clapped his hands loudly. His 'bravo!' roused Egon from his dream as the last notes died away.

He arose. His first glance sought Lieschen, who had been standing behind him, and who involuntarily held out her hand to him, while tears stood in her frank eyes.

Bertha seemed no less affected. "Thank you," she said, and her voice faltered. "I promise you that you never shall hear a drawing-room performance from me again."

"Splendid! wonderful!" exclaimed the Lieutenant.

"Herr Pigglewitch, you have surpassed yourself, you never played so delightfully before. It is your work, Fräulein von Massenburg. Of course, Herr Pigglewitch did his best not to disgrace himself before such an artist. You must play us something else, Herr Pigglewitch."

But this Egon was not to be induced to do, and to cut short the Lieutenant's persistence he closed the piano, and just in time, for Frau von Osternau at that moment called them to the tea-table.

Herr von Sastrow had declared that Bertha von Massenburg could be charming if she chose to be, and she certainly chose to be this evening; she captivated every member of the Osternau family, even, at last, Lieschen and Frau von Osternau, in spite of their prejudices. She did not appear to notice that at first Frau von Osternau's manner was but coolly courteous, and that Lieschen scarcely spoke at all, and never addressed her. She talked on innocently and gaily, and was so cordial and amiable that Frau von Osternau could not but abandon her reserve, and Lieschen became herself once more. As for the head of the house, Bertha had charmed him from the very first, while the Lieutenant was quite enraptured by her, although she paid him less attention than she bestowed upon any other of the little circle. She was more gracious even to the tutor than to Cousin Albrecht.

Indeed, the manner in which she included Egon in the conversation was especially pleasing to Herr von Osternau. In every word which she addressed to the young man she showed the estimation in which she held so accomplished a musician. She said not one flattering word to him with regard to the pleasure he

had given her, but there was a respectful acknowledgment of his superiority in the way in which she
listened to everything that he said when the conversation turned upon modern music.

With infinite tact she avoided dwelling upon her
late stay in Berlin when the Lieutenant clumsily
alluded to it. She spoke of her uncle von Sastrow with
the greatest affection, but speedily contrived to change
the subject.

The evening passed delightfully. The head of the
house was late in giving the sign for retiring, and did
so at last only in view of his wife's admonition that
it was time to bid good-night, since he generally paid
for so pleasant an evening by some hours of sleepless-
ness.

"Well, Emma," he said when he and his wife were
again alone together, "do you now think that Bertha
will be a disturbing element in our little circle? I
fancy you are cured of your prejudice against her."

Frau von Osternau did not immediately reply, perhaps she would gladly have been relieved from the
necessity of doing so, but when her husband repeated
his question she said, "I have not yet made up my
mind about Bertha. I confess that so long as I was
with her, and listened to her gay, innocent talk, and
looked into her dark, sparkling eyes, I was charmed
with her; she captivated me as she did you and
Albrecht and Herr Pigglewitch, and even Lieschen,
who finally treated her as affectionately as she used
to do when Bertha visited us years ago. But now
that she is no longer present, and that I am not subject to the magic of her eye, I am doubtful about her.
Was her amiability from the heart? She seems unaffected, but is she so in reality? I must defer giving

16*

you my opinion of Bertha until we have known her longer."

The same doubt that troubled the gentle mistress of the castle tormented Egon, as he paced his room to and fro, pondering upon the evening he had just passed. Frau von Osternau was right in saying that Bertha had captivated him; she seemed to him so wondrously beautiful that even Lieschen's lovely image paled beside her.

"If you had seen her a while ago you would not have fled from Berlin, and she would have been your wife," he said to himself, and his imagination ran riot in picturing what might then have been his future. To call that exquisite creature his own, to love her and be loved in return, to spend his life beside her,—the thought quickened his pulses and his temples throbbed.

He opened the window. The cool night air refreshed him. As he looked out into the black night of the garden, two strips of light were marked distinctly upon the dark lawn. The one was thrown there by the light in his room. Whence came the other? Involuntarily he wondered, whence? Ah, from Lieschen's window. Was she too gazing out into the dark night? Her image suddenly arose in his soul as clear and distinct as Bertha's, it looked at him reproachfully, the lips parted to say, "I detest nothing so much as falsehood!" He almost heard the words.

Clearer and more brilliant grew Lieschen's fair and lovely image, while Bertha's faded into night and darkness. He turned from the window calmed and cheered.

CHAPTER XIII.

A WISE YOUNG JUDGE.

THE spell which Bertha von Massenburg had cast around the inmates of Castle Osternau upon her first appearance within its walls did not fade, but grew stronger, and embraced in its charm every individual of the household, with the exception of Lieschen. Both the inspectors, Herr von Wangen and Herr Storting, and even all the servants succumbed to it. Her sweetness and gaiety were unvarying; she had a word of kindness for all, and knew exactly when to utter it.

She talked with Herr von Osternau of his farming, and displayed a degree of knowledge and judgment in such matters rare indeed in a young girl. Her entire childhood before the sequestration of her father's estates had been spent in the country. She had kept alive all her interest in country pursuits and occupations, and was never weary of introducing a discussion of her uncle's favourite topic. It was a genuine delight to the old man to be able to explain his theories and practice to her, while her large black eyes gazed intelligently into his own; and not less did he enjoy her gay talk of Königsberg and Berlin, and her affectionate, caressing way of leaning her head on his shoulder and stroking the gray hair from his forehead as she called him her dear, dear uncle Fritz.

Nor could Frau von Osternau resist the influence which Bertha exercised upon her also. There was no withstanding the girl's innocent, amiable readiness to assist in any occupation in which her aunt was engaged. She was sure to place the footstool just in the right place for Frau von Osternau's feet, and was always ready to take up dropped stitches in her knitting, or to ring the bell just when the servant was wanted, or to make herself useful and indispensable in the household in a thousand ways. Cultivated and well bred as she was, she disdained no feminine occupation. Indeed, she was a pattern for Lieschen, who had been allowed, her mother thought as she watched Bertha's ways, to run wild altogether too long. And then how perfect was her behaviour towards the gentlemen of the family! She received their homage with genuine pleasure, but never exacted it, and armed herself with a dignified reserve whenever there was the slightest risk of their attentions becoming importunate. This was especially the case with her treatment of the Lieutenant, who paid her decided court, and this often in a way which annoyed Frau von Osternau, although Bertha was never thrown off her guard, but preserved her maidenly dignity intact. On the other hand, she encouraged the shy young inspector, Herr von Wangen, by a charming degree of kindly interest in his labours.

Herr von Wangen was the only son of a wealthy landed proprietor in West Prussia. His father had sent him to Castle Osternau to learn agriculture upon a model estate, and in the hope of conquering his great natural shyness by a stay among strangers. The bashful young fellow, who at table scarcely spoke unless he was spoken to, and who rarely accepted an invitation to join the family at tea, for fear of transgressing some rule of social life, was suddenly metamorphosed by Bertha's arrival. He began to converse at dinner with Bertha, who sat next him, and as she kindly encouraged him he soon took part in the general conversation, and gladly joined the family in the evenings.

Frau von Osternau was grateful to the girl for thus drawing out the young man. She had frequently regretted that the son of one of her husband's oldest friends should spend almost all his leisure time in his own apartment. She observed with great satisfaction the signs in Herr von Wangen of a budding attachment for her charming guest. Bertha grew in favour with her as the good lady began to indulge in such plans for the future as are dearest to the feminine mind. Herr von Wangen was, to be sure, rather young,—only a couple of years older than Bertha,—but he was an excellent match for her, since she had given up all thoughts of Herr von Ernau. It seemed doubtful to Frau von Osternau, however, whether Bertha would smile upon the young fellow's suit; there were signs that her fancy had been suddenly caught by one who, of all the men in the house, paid her the least attention,—Herr Gottlieb Pigglewitch. She must be sure about this, and so she carefully watched them both.

She soon made up her mind that Bertha was greatly interested in the tutor; her tone of voice changed when she addressed him; she never jested with him as she did with Herr Storting and Herr von Wangen, or even with the Lieutenant; she was more reserved with him, although she listened eagerly to everything that he said. When engaged in lively conversation with others she nevertheless heard every word uttered by the Candidate, and she watched him when she thought herself unobserved. She was always present during Lieschen's music-lessons; she had asked permission to be in the room, saying, with a smile, that she could not ask Herr Pigglewitch to give her actual lessons, but that he

could do so indirectly if he would allow her to observe
his method with Lieschen. And she also joined the
afternoon walks and rides which Herr Pigglewitch took
with Lieschen and Fritz. She was a bold, fearless
horsewoman, and especially enjoyed the rides. She
certainly knew how well she looked in her riding-habit,
and how the hat upon her black curls became her.

And it was a significant fact, Frau von Osternau
thought, that Bertha was never to be induced either to
play on the piano or to sing when the Candidate was
present, while in his absence she was always amiably
ready to do so. She evidently feared his criticism.
When he played she listened in rapt attention.

All these observations confirmed Frau von Osternau
in her suspicion that Bertha was in danger of falling
in love with the tutor, but she was led to doubt this
again by certain observations and remarks of the
young girl's, which gave her much food for reflection,
—remarks similar to those which had so shocked her
uncle Sastrow, and which were exceedingly singular
in the mouth of a lovely young girl, since they be-
tokened a perfectly materialistic conception of life and
its duties.

Bertha was wont in conversation to play the part of
a listener; she was usually reserved in the expression
of her own views, and it was only when very much
interested that she took a lively part in any discussion, but then she was apt to become eager and to
express herself with reckless frankness. Thus at times
she advanced opinions which shocked Frau von Osternau no less than they had Herr von Sastrow.

One evening, when the conversation turned upon a
distant relative of Herr von Osternau, a beautiful young
girl of an ancient noble family, who had just become

the wife of a poor young *bourgeois* councillor, with
whom she had long been carrying on a compromising
love-affair, a sharp war of words had arisen between
Herr von Osternau and the Lieutenant, the former expressing his great satisfaction in the marriage as the
only atonement for the past, while Albrecht severely
denounced the *mésalliance* with a poor man from the
people. Bertha agreed eagerly with the Lieutenant,
declaring that a daughter of an ancient and noble race
might be pardoned for yielding, in a moment of weakness, to an impulse of the heart, in bestowing her love
upon a man her inferior in rank, but that she acted un-
pardonably in degrading herself and her family by a
marriage with this inferior, especially if he were poor.
There was only one thing which could justify such a
mésalliance, and that was immense wealth on the part
of the inferior in rank,—wealth that could reinstate in
splendour an impoverished family of noble descent.
The present Frau Councillor had been both unprincipled
and foolish : unprincipled in forgetting what was due to
her noble descent, and foolish in forgetting what was
due to herself. The highest aim of existence was enjoyment, and it was unpardonable folly to resign all the
delights which wealth could procure for the sake of
indulging in a brief dream of love from which one must
soon awake to bitter repentance and misery.

Frau von Osternau listened in dismay; her favour-
able opinion of Bertha was shaken by her avowal of
such sentiments, but the unpleasant impression faded
when Bertha immediately afterwards showed herself
so sweet-tempered and charming that it was impossible
to resist her. Frau von Osternau could not but think
that in her interest the young girl had been led to say
more than she meant; it was a pity, but excusable;

she was sure that Bertha herself would never conform her actions to the opinion which she had asserted, and the girl's evident interest in Herr Pigglewitch seemed to her suspicious.

The good lady could not decide as to the sentiments entertained by the tutor for her guest, indeed the young man was more of a puzzle to her than ever. Immediately after his arrival at the castle he had become quite a different creature, had been transformed from an awkward, uncouth Candidate into a courteous, well-bred gentleman, a restlessness of manner peculiar to him had entirely vanished, and now since Bertha's arrival he had undergone another metamorphosis.

His eyes again showed the same restless gleam that animated them when he was agitated, the scornful smile, so long absent from his lips, again often hovered there, accompanying some sneering remark, and there was a want of repose about him which made itself especially apparent when he improvised upon the piano. Frau von Osternau often seemed to hear the cry of a wounded heart in the strange, wild melodies that echoed beneath his fingers, and anon she would be carried away by the din and strife of a chaos of tones which harassed and troubled her, and from which there was no escape save by a crashing dissonance. His playing was always admirable, but it no longer brought refreshment to the mind, it was bewildering, confusing. Lieschen was profoundly aware of this; her eyes did not fill with tears as she listened, but her cheek paled and her downcast glance would avoid that of the player when he had finished. When he noticed this he would turn away with a shiver, and pass his hand across his eyes as if to brush away some cloud, then, seating himself again at the instrument, he would evoke from it such touching sounds as quickly reconciled Frau von Osternau to the artist.

His conduct towards Bertha grew to be as contradictory as his music. When he gazed at her his eyes would glow darkly, but when they were turned upon Lieschen their fire faded, a happy expression took its place, too often to be banished again by the mere sound of Bertha's voice. He seldom appealed directly to her in conversation; he even avoided all *tête-à-têtes* with her, but what he said to others was constantly addressed indirectly to her. And this was frequently the case, as Lieschen told her mother, during their rides. The Herr Candidate addressed Fritzchen or herself, but what he said was meant for Bertha.

In short, Pigglewitch had become entirely changed since Bertha's arrival; he was the same only in one respect,—his duties were most scrupulously fulfilled. Over Fritzchen he exercised the same affectionate superintendence, beneath which his little pupil made extraordinary progress, and he acted with the same conscientiousness in his instruction of Lieschen. During the music-lessons he had neither eyes nor words for the lovely Fräulein von Massenburg, he seemed to live only for his pupil, and Lieschen showed her gratitude by giving him her undivided attention.

These lesson-hours had come to be the happiest time of the day for the young girl, who had so lately been little more than a careless, happy child. Since Bertha's coming to the castle there had been a change in the daughter of the house, which filled her mother with anxiety. The girl no longer ran races with Fritzchen when lessons were over, her merry laughter no longer came floating up every day from the lawn, the charming romp, who had deserved and received many a loving

reproof from her father, had vanished, and in her stead
there was a serious, gentle, sensible maiden, almost too
serious, her mother thought, remembering her former
playfulness. It did not please Frau von Osternau that
Lieschen had suddenly lost all pleasure in her childish
games, that she would sit for a long while at times over
her embroidery, not always working, sometimes in a
profound revery, with hands clasped in her lap. Of
what could she be thinking? Her mother would have
given much to know; such knowledge might have relieved her of a great dread,—a dread never quite laid
to rest in her mind,—lest Lieschen should cherish a
warmer affection for her music-teacher than her parents
could approve,—an affection now shown, perhaps, by an
awakening jealousy of Bertha von Massenburg.

This really seemed the only explanation of the change
wrought in the young girl. This might be the reason
why Lieschen withstood the charm which Bertha exercised upon all the other members of the household.
She alone treated Bertha with a scrupulously courteous
reserve, which was not to be overcome by any effort on
the part of the guest to win her affection.

"What is your objection to Bertha Massenburg?"
Frau von Osternau asked her daughter one morning
when they were alone together, Bertha having accompanied her uncle in his walk in the fields. "You treat
her with a coldness and reserve that she really does not
deserve at your hands. She will surely be offended by
your manner some day."

"I think I show her all the courtesy that is her
due," Lieschen replied, gravely, looking up from her
work. "She has never heard an unkind word from
me."

"That is not what I mean. It only seems to me that

you might be more cordial and frank to so amiable a girl."

"I cannot feign what I do not feel."

"I do not understand you, Lieschen. Bertha treats you with special sweetness. She is fond of you, and shows that she is so by not being hurt by your coldness."

"I do not believe in the sincerity of her sweetness and cordiality. Now and then when she forgets herself in the heat of conversation she betrays her real thoughts and feelings, and a curtain suddenly seems lifted from before her inner self. Do you not remember how she spoke a while ago of Valerie Laupe?"

Frau von Osternau looked at her daughter in surprise, and, more for something to say than from a desire to defend Bertha, replied, "We ought not to weigh every hasty word with such nicety. One often says more in the heat of argument than reason would justify; you do so sometimes, as every one does. What, for example, should we think of Herr Pigglewitch, if all his words were so harshly criticised?"

Lieschen's cheek flushed slightly, but she looked up at her mother and replied, without embarrassment, "They are both puzzles to me. In a certain way they are alike,—the true self of each seems hidden behind a veil; but when this veil is slightly lifted in his case I seem to see a poor, harassed heart, a spirit longing for the noble and the true. In Bertha's case the veil covers an abyss of selfishness, avarice, and love of pleasure."

"Good heavens, child! what puts such thoughts, such words into your head?" Frau von Osternau exclaimed in dismay.

"I cannot tell, mother. I have been thinking a great

deal about these two people, and I have come to this conclusion."

Her mother did not continue the conversation, but at night, when she was alone with her husband, she repeated to him word for word what Lieschen had said. "If that extraordinary man had only never come inside our doors,"—it was thus she concluded her tale. "He, and not Bertha, is to blame for the sad transformation which our child has undergone. For my sake, Fritz, dismiss him. Pay him his salary for an entire year; only let him leave the house."

Herr von Osternau shook his head. "Do you think Lieschen conceals anything from you?" he asked.

"No, assuredly not."

"Did she ever complain that he had spoken to her otherwise than as a teacher should speak to a pupil, or have you ever observed that he has in his lessons or in social intercourse with us transgressed any law of good breeding?"

"I cannot say that he has, but——"

"Has he ever neglected the duties which he undertook to perform when he entered our house? Is he not a conscientious and affectionate tutor for Fritzchen? Has he ever done anything for which he could justly be reproved?"

"No. I do not ask you to dismiss him abruptly. If you would pay him his salary for an entire year——"

"Do you suppose that a man of honour could be compensated by a year's salary for being turned from our door? I think there was a great deal of truth in what Lieschen said of him, and I should never forgive myself for wounding him by injustice. He certainly is not a happy man. So long as he does his duty we must do ours. Good-night, Emma."

CHAPTER XIV.

PASTOR WIDMAN AS A CORRESPONDENT.

THE Lieutenant had returned from Berlin, whither he had gone upon business for Herr von Osternau. He had driven over from the station without waiting for the sorting of the mail, because he was in haste to tell his cousin of the results of his mission, so he said at least to excuse himself for not bringing with him the post-bag, but the excuse was a very lame one, since he had but little to tell and his news could easily have waited for an hour.

Apparently the Herr Lieutenant had found waiting at the lonely station too tedious; he was in a mood on this particular evening to find such waiting very irksome, for he was possessed by a spirit of unrest that did not leave him even after he had reached the castle. Scarcely had he taken his place at the tea-table, and communicated to Herr von Osternau certain insignificant details relating to his visit to Berlin, when he arose quickly and hurried to the window, declaring that it was so warm that his head ached. After cooling his forehead against the panes he returned again to his place, only to arise in a few moments and pace the room hastily to and fro as he detailed some vapid anecdotes which he had heard in Berlin.

His restlessness was so evident that Herr von Osternau looked at him with some anxiety. "Are you not

17*

well, Albrecht?" he asked, kindly. "You look pale
and your eyes are feverishly bright. Would you not
rather go to your room?"

"No, no; nothing is the matter with me," the Lieutenant replied, hastily. "I am only a little upset
by my Berlin visit; it always is so when I leave the
quiet and repose of the country for the whirlpool
of city life and sit far into the night with my old
friends."

After this he forced himself to suppress all sign of
the unrest which possessed him, but he could scarcely
bear his part well in the conversation around the tea-
table. After staring for a while absently before him,
he would suddenly make some remark which showed
that he had paid no attention to what was going on,
and even Bertha, to whose slightest observation he was
wont to pay great heed, could not to-night succeed in
fixing his attention.

He was usually vexed when Pigglewitch was entreated to play, but to-night he hailed with joy Frau
von Osternau's request for some music from the Candidate. He seemed to be glad to be relieved from the
necessity of taking part in the general conversation.
As soon as Egon had struck the first chord he left his
place at the tea-table, and, exchanging a rapid glance
with Bertha, retired to the recess of a window. Contrary to her habit, Bertha rose immediately afterwards
and joined the Lieutenant in his retreat, where they
were soon deeply engaged in a whispered conversation.
They might easily have continued this unnoticed, for
Herr and Frau von Osternau were absorbed in the
music, if Herr von Wangen had not followed with his
eyes Bertha's every movement. It did not escape him
that the girl's cheeks were suddenly suffused by a burn-

ing blush at the Lieutenant's first whispered words, and
that she instantly listened with the greatest eagerness
to all that he said.

Herr von Wangen heard not one note of Egon's
music, his entire attention was bestowed upon the pair
whispering together in the recess; what would he not
have given to overhear what they were saying? Several
times during the month which Bertha had already
passed at Castle Osternau Herr von Wangen had been
tormented by the suspicion that there was a greater
degree of intimacy existing between the Lieutenant
and the beautiful guest than either cared to have
observed; he had surprised one or two meaning glances
exchanged by them, but Bertha had always succeeded
in allaying these suspicions by the easy indifference
with which she received the Lieutenant's homage. He
had hovered between fear and hope, the hope inspired
by every gentle word addressed to him by Bertha, the
fear aroused by every look exchanged between Bertha
and the Lieutenant; to-night fear was in the ascendant,
his jealousy was aroused, he felt desperately wretched,
but in another moment he was lifted to heights of
supreme delight, for Bertha looked across the room at
him, and there was such enchantment in her glance as
he had never seen there before. She spoke a few hasty
words to Albrecht and then returned to her place at
table, excusing herself in a low whisper to her neighbour for leaving him to learn from the Lieutenant how
her father was. Herr von Wangen was enraptured, his
jealousy of a moment before vanished, he was ashamed
to have felt it. Never had Bertha been to him so gentle,
so kind, so engaging as on this evening after her conversation with the Lieutenant. Herr von Wangen was
so intoxicated with delight that he did not notice the

depression of spirits of all the other members of the circle, Bertha alone excepted.

This melancholy mood had been induced by the contents of the post-bag, which had brought a letter for Herr von Osternau and one for Pigglewitch. The latter had indeed thrust his unread into his breast-pocket, but the mere fact that it was addressed in a hand unknown to him worried and annoyed him. Herr von Osternau, on the other hand, read his letter not only once, but several times; it must have contained some very depressing intelligence, for Herr von Osternau grew graver at each perusal, now and then casting a peculiarly searching glance at the tutor, and then continuing his reading with a shake of the head. The contents of the letter must have occupied his mind during the entire evening; he took scarcely any part in the conversation, and when Egon bade him good-night he did not respond with his usual cordiality.

Just as Egon was leaving the room Herr von Osternau recalled him: "Excuse me for a moment, Herr Pigglewitch, I have a few words to say to you."

Egon turned round and awaited his employer's pleasure, divided between anxiety and curiosity with regard to what had induced Herr von Osternau to adopt so unusual a tone in addressing him.

The old man paced the room silently to and fro for a while until the rest of the family had retired and left him alone with the tutor. Then, turning to Egon, he said, gravely,—

"I have received a very surprising letter that concerns you nearly, Herr Pigglewitch, and I do not deny that its contents have affected my good opinion of you. I do not wish to discuss them with you at present, such a conversation would probably agitate me, and rob me of my night's rest, which is very important for me, and then, too, I might under the immediate influence of the letter treat you with injustice. I must give you time to defend yourself; therefore I beg you to come to me to-morrow morning at nine o'clock, and we will quietly talk the matter over. Here is the letter, take it to your room and read it. You can return it to me to-morrow. No more for the present. Good-night, Herr Pigglewitch."

Egon was dismissed. He took the ominous epistle and repaired to his room, where, his curiosity on the stretch, he lit his lamp and read as follows:

"Most Respected Herr,—Pardon a stranger for venturing to intrude upon you with a complaint and a request. In the unfortunate situation in which I am placed no other choice is left me. I must appeal to you, most honoured Herr, if I would not run the risk of losing forever a sum of money hardly earned and accumulated only by constant self-denial. Permit me to lay the case before you.

"Some years ago I loaned the Schulze Brandes, in Wilhelmshagen, the sum of four hundred thalers at a reasonable rate of interest, knowing him to be an honest man. He has justified my estimate of him as such, for although impoverished and forced to emigrate to America, he sent me before his departure all that he owed me, both capital and interest, but in such a manner that I am in danger of losing my hard-won savings entirely. Before leaving for America he gave it to my nephew, Gottlieb Pigglewitch, commissioning him to hand it to me. Whilst on the ocean he conceived a suspicion that Gottlieb had not fulfilled his trust, and therefore he wrote me immediately upon his arrival in

New York to ask me if I had received the sum in question. Unfortunately his fears were but too well grounded; my nephew has never paid me the money, it is probably squandered, or lost at cards.

"My nephew, the son of my sister and the deceased Pastor Pigglewitch, of Wilhelmshagen, has repaid by the basest ingratitude the benefits conferred upon him by me when he was left a friendless orphan. He has never concerned himself about me since he left my house to enter upon an independent existence. He has forgotten my teachings, he has squandered his substance, leading a dissolute life, and given over to a passion for cards. His conduct lost him a good situation in Wilhelmshagen, since which I have heard nothing of him until the arrival of Schulze Brandes's letter, which has filled me with anxiety concerning my money.

"More than four weeks had passed since this money was intrusted to Gottlieb Pigglewitch. I did not know his address, and therefore wrote to his patron, Herr Director Kramser, from whom I learn that my nephew is receiving a high salary in your worshipful household as tutor to your son. I have now written to him to beg him to restore my property to me, but I fear that my request will be vain if it is not seconded by yourself, respected Herr. It is not probable that the money is at present in my nephew's possession, therefore he could not pay it even if he wished to do so. I might easily bring him to justice, but a feeling of kinship restrains me; I could bring myself to adopt such extreme measures only in case my nephew should refuse to pay me the money with interest. He can do this if he chooses.

"I learn from Herr Director Kramser that my nephew

receives from your highly-respected self a salary of three hundred thalers cash. A young man can get along extremely well upon one hundred thalers yearly; 1 myself as a Candidate did with much less than that sum; he can then pay me at least two hundred thalers every year, if he only will.

"My humble request to you is, respected Herr, that you will compel my nephew thus to fulfil his duty by giving him only one hundred thalers yearly of his salary, and transmitting the two hundred to me, until the debt is liquidated. My nephew will, I am sure, be content with this means of returning to me my money; he will not force me to appeal for justice to the law of the land, and you, respected Herr, will establish a claim upon my everlasting gratitude by yielding to my entreaty.

"With devoted respect, your obedient servant,

"WIDMAN, *Pastor of Wennersdorf.*"

"A most edifying document!" Egon said to himself, when he had read the letter. "I suppose the communication which I received this evening and put unread into my pocket also comes from Uncle Widman." He took out the letter and read it. Yes, it was from Widman, and contained threats of arrest and exposure if his nephew refused to devote two hundred thalers of his salary each year to the payment of his debt.

Egon indignantly crushed the letter together in his hand. "Gottlieb Pigglewitch has lost his money for the third time," he muttered. "There is no helping him, he must be left to his fate. He probably knows this, and therefore has made no further attempt to extort money from me by threats and promises."

Once more the young man read the letter to Herr

von Osternau; it filled him with a vague apprehension. What should he say to the kind old man on the morrow? In his eyes, his tutor was Gottlieb Pigglewitch, the confirmed gambler, who had actually appropriated money intrusted to him for his uncle. 'I do not deny that this letter has affected my good opinion of you,' Herr von Osternau had said, and certainly he was justified in saying so.

"It is high time that this farce were ended," Egon murmured. "I must leave this house, and break the spell that has been cast about me!"

He had often of late made this resolve; almost nightly, after he had retired to his solitary apartment, and thought over the events of the day, he had determined to tear asunder the bonds that were being woven about him, but the next morning found him powerless to carry his determination into execution. Yes, a spell had been cast upon him which paralyzed his will, and whose this spell was, he could not rightly tell.

When Bertha's wondrous beauty filled his mind, a wild feeling of delight thrilled through him, his pulses throbbed, his thoughts made chaos within him, he longed to clasp in his arms as his own her whom he had so foolishly insulted and scorned.

But in the midst of this rapturous intoxication he was recalled to a sober certainty of waking disgust when he remembered various expressions of Bertha's which had revealed to him her true self; he turned away from the thought of her, chilled and repelled, and in her place there was a very different image,—Lieschen gazed at him with a look of reproach, and yet of love! In thought of her he was calmed and cheered, she incited him to continued exertion, she called forth all his better nature,—she, the good angel who had led him out from the slough of an existence into which the beautiful fiend with the glowing eyes would fain drag him back!

Did he love Bertha? Did he love Lieschen? He did not know. Bertha exercised a demoniac influence upon him, Lieschen's spell was fairy-like, but mighty. His soul hovered between the two, in a conflict which robbed him of repose, subjugated his will, and made any firm resolve impossible for him.

Perhaps chance would befriend him.

CHAPTER XV.

RENEWED CONFIDENCE.

HERR VON OSTERNAU passed a miserable night. Pastor Widman's letter had excited him more than he cared to confess to himself. If he could have told his faithful partner of the wretched epistle, he would soon have been soothed to rest, but he could not do this for fear lest his Emma should find in the Pastor's letter fresh reasons for urging her oft-repeated desire for the tutor's dismissal. Herr von Osternau's sense of justice revolted against condemning the accused without allowing him a hearing.

As he had frankly confessed, his faith in the Candidate was shaken, and the more he thought, during his sleepless night, of the Pastor's letter, the more he suspected that he had bestowed his confidence upon one quite unworthy of it. The Pastor's accusation of his

18

nephew did not seem like an invention, and if it were well grounded, Pigglewitch could no longer be retained as Fritzchen's tutor. The man who could lose at play money not his own was unfit for such an office, whatever might be his intellectual acquirements. But perhaps he was not so guilty as he seemed. He should not be judged before he had been allowed to speak in his own defence.

The next morning Herr von Osternau awaited the tutor's visit with the greatest impatience, continually consulting the clock as he walked to and fro in his sitting-room. It was only half-past eight; there was still half an hour to wait, since he had appointed the interview at nine o'clock.

He was pleased and surprised when thus early, nevertheless, a knock was heard at the door. Upon his "Come in," however, he was equally disappointed by the entrance not of Pigglewitch, but of the Lieutenant.

"Is it you, Albrecht? I thought you had gone to the meadows," he said, rather testily, but the next instant, perceiving that the Lieutenant looked downcast and unhappy, he continued, kindly, "What is it, Albrecht? You look out of sorts. I hope nothing is the matter."

The Lieutenant did not reply immediately. He had meant to look desperate, and not merely out of sorts, and it cost him some effort to make his features convey the desired impression. Perceiving in an opposite mirror that his efforts were crowned with a degree of success, he said at last, in a trembling voice, "I come to you, Cousin Fritz, a prey to remorse and despair. On the day before yesterday evening I actually had my revolver in my hand to put an end to my wretched existence, but I thought of you, and of the contempt which you feel for a man who lays violent hands upon himself; the pistol dropped from my grasp, I had a glimmer of hope. I remembered your inexhaustible kindness. You have helped me so often that I cannot but look to you in my extremity."

Herr von Osternau's face had grown dark as the Lieutenant spoke. He had heard words like these too often not to know that they were the preface to a demand for money to pay some extravagant or gambling debt. He replied, indignantly, "Spare your words, cousin; they are useless. I must remind you of what I told you last year when I paid two thousand thalers for you. I assured you then that it was for the last time, and the money was paid upon your solemn promise never again to contract a debt which you could not pay yourself. It is of no use to continue this conversation. I shall be true to my word."

"I implore you, Cousin Fritz——"

"I will hear nothing further. I should wrong my daughter by sacrificing fresh sums of money to you. I felt free to do for you what I have done, but now it is time that I should lay by Lieschen's portion, since I have been spending my whole income all these years upon the improvement of the estate."

"All that is needed is three thousand marks, an insignificant sum for you. Would you for such a trifle drive me to suicide, Cousin Fritz?"

"It is sacrilegious to talk thus."

"Do you not force me to it? Can I live disgraced? I have signed a note of hand. I must pay the money in fourteen days, or I shall be dishonoured."

"You told me a year ago that you owed nothing."

"It was true, but—I am ashamed to confess my

folly—I was insane enough to be tempted to play. I fell in with some of my comrades the day before yesterday inBerlin, and cards were proposed. I refused for a long time to join the game, but I was overpersuaded. At first the stakes were very low, and I won, but the luck changed, I lost my head, and I came away with a debt of honour for three thousand marks. If it is not paid in fourteen days I shall be dishonoured."

"You are dishonoured already, even though your debt were paid; you promised me never again to touch a card."

"I was mad! I was mad!"

"Your word of honour should have kept you sane. But I shall not depart from what I told you a year ago. You have no help to expect from me."

"At least lend me the three thousand marks. You can easily do so; you have ten thousand there in your desk; the trifling sum can readily be paid from my salary in two years at the latest."

"That cannot be done, either; you must learn to help yourself."

"You drive me to suicide."

"That threat is useless. It will not move me to break my word to you."

An evil look was the Lieutenant's only reply; he saw that further entreaty would be of no avail. There was no need, then, to subject himself to further humiliation. The expression of despair in his face gave place to one of sullen defiance. Without another word he left the room.

Herr von Osternau had been calm and decided so long as Albrecht was present; but now that he was alone he grew restless and anxious. Had he perhaps been too hard? No, he could neither speak nor act otherwise. For years he had been far too much influenced by the reflection that Albrecht had been deprived of an inheritance which he had long considered as his own. The sums which had been sacrificed for this dissipated, reckless relative were enormous; the sacrifice had been made in vain, Albrecht was utterly ungrateful. He seized every opportunity for a visit either to Breslau or to Berlin to resume his dissolute career, to contract fresh debts. There was no helping him, least of all by compliance with his demands. Only by being thrown upon his own resources, with no hope of assistance from his cousin, might he perhaps be induced to resist the temptation to play.

Herr von Osternau was sure that he had acted for the best, but nevertheless he felt very anxious. The thought that his cousin might fulfil his threat of self-destruction, filled him with dread. His kindly nature gave him no repose. He sat down at his writing-table and scratched off a note to Herr von Sastrow begging him to write to Albrecht and offer to lend him the money he needed upon his promise to repay him from his salary. The money, Herr von Osternau assured his uncle, should be repaid him,—for that he would go surety,—but of this the Lieutenant must be kept in ignorance. He must believe that the offer of help came unsuggested from Herr von Sastrow alone.

When the note had been handed to Wenzel, with orders to take it directly to the post at Station Mirbach, Herr von Osternau felt relieved, but so occupied had he been with the Lieutenant's case for the last half-hour that it was only when the Candidate presented himself punctually at the appointed time that he was reminded of Pastor Widman's miserable letter, according to which the Candidate, like the Lieutenant, had squan-

dered his patrimony; like Albrecht, he was an inveter-
ate gambler, who had lost at play money not his own.
Involuntarily Herr von Osternau compared the two
men in his mind. There was no trace in the Candidate's face of the theatric despair which Albrecht had
laboured to display. Herr Pigglewitch was so calm
and collected that Herr von Osternau was half convinced of his innocence before he had spoken a word,
and not until the young man avoided his searching
glance did he again doubt him.

Did Egon suspect this? He looked up again frankly,
and in a clear, calm voice, without embarrassment,
without waiting to be questioned, he opened the interview which was to decide his future relations with the
lord of the castle.

"You made use of harsh language to me last evening, Herr von Osternau. You told me that you had
lost confidence in me——"

"No, I only said that my confidence in you was
shaken. It was best to be frank, and you could not but
see that I was justified by the Pastor's letter. The
importance to be attached to that letter depends entirely upon the explanation which I expect from you."

"I am ready to give you an explanation. I assure
you that every word which I am about to utter shall
be perfectly true, but I do not deny that the circumstances in which I find myself forbid my telling
the whole truth. I am forced to be silent with regard
to these circumstances, whilst I could by a single word
prove the falsehood of the ridiculous charges—ridiculous so far as I am concerned—contained in the letter.
This word, however, I shall not speak. If the explanations which I am able to give you do not satisfy you,
then, Herr von Osternau, I must remind you of our

agreement when I first came to your house. We reserved for each of us perfect liberty to dissolve at any
given moment a connection which cannot continue to
exist if you withdraw your confidence from your son's
tutor or believe him capable of appropriating to himself money confided to him by others."

"This is a strange preface to your explanation, Herr
Pigglewitch; it can be answered only when I have
heard you further."

"I do not ask a reply until then. I understand perfectly that this letter, which I beg now to return to you,
has shaken your confidence in me. Your knowledge
of me is of too recent a date to convince you that in
spite of grievous defects of character I am incapable
of a dishonourable act, and Pastor Widman's letter,
containing as it does a mixture of truth and falsehood,
may well give you cause for reflection. Let me refer
to the letter in detail. It is untrue that Pastor Widman befriended his sister's orphan boy. He treated
him with great severity, only sending him to school
when he was forced to do so, the expenses of his education being defrayed from the orphan boy's patrimony.
On the other hand, it is true that the weak, thoughtless
young man squandered the rest of his inheritance, and
sacrificed his first situation to his passion for gaming.
Later, in another situation, he so won the esteem of his
employer that Doctor Kramser felt himself justified in
recommending him to you for your son's tutor. I candidly confess to you, Herr von Osternau, that I have
led a life far from blameless, that I have foolishly
squandered both time and money, but I swear to you
that I have never been involved in any dishonourable
transaction. It is true that the Schulze Brandes gave
the sum in question to the nephew of Pastor Widman

for transmission to his uncle, and that this money has not yet been paid him, but I have neither appropriated this money nor have I lost it at play. The reason why this money has not been paid I cannot now disclose to you, all I can say is that I have a perfect right to refuse to give this sum to the Herr Pastor. Nevertheless, he shall have his money without abatement of a penny; here it is, and I beg of you, Herr von Osternau, to transmit it to him."

As he spoke, Egon took out his pocket-book and counted out the notes upon the table.

Herr von Osternau was amazed. "You have the money? Why then did you not send it to your uncle long ago?"

"I regret that I cannot answer this question, for in doing so I should be obliged to refer to matters which were best passed over in silence, at least for the present. I can only assure you that I never even dreamed of depriving Herr Pastor Widman of his property. If this does not suffice you, Herr von Osternau, I can no longer remain in the castle; I must resign my situation here, much as I regret to do so. I can no longer be your son's tutor if you have lost faith in me."

"No, I have not lost it. I believe you to be incapable of anything dishonourable, but I tell you candidly that I do not like your wrapping yourself up in mystery."

"I regret being forced to do so. At present I cannot tell you the whole truth, and I will not tell you a falsehood."

"I have no right to force your confidence or to lay down the law to you, but, as a man much your elder, I have a right to tell you honestly what I think. The manner in which you speak of your uncle displeases me as much as does your foolish mystery. You speak of him as Herr Pastor Widman, in the most formal way; however harshly he may have treated you years ago, you are wrong thus to bear malice. When there has been a coolness or a quarrel between relatives, it is the duty of the younger to take the first steps towards a reconciliation. If my good opinion is worth anything to you, you will accept my advice to put back into your pocket-book the money you have counted out upon the table. I will not undertake to mediate between uncle and nephew. You ought to return his property to him; if you comply with my wishes, you will take it to him yourself. Wennersdorf is only a few hours' journey from Breslau. The journey thither is neither difficult nor expensive. Take your uncle his money, pay him a visit of a few days, and be reconciled with him. I will gladly give you leave of absence for a week. Will you not start early to-morrow morning?"

Egon hesitated to reply. He had not expected such a proposal. Could he accept it, since he could not possibly deliver in person Pastor Widman's money? He could not positively reject it without wounding Herr von Osternau, and, besides, it had a certain attraction. If he could be delivered for a few days from the spell that bound him, if he could make a short excursion in the Riesengebirge, he might perhaps come to some clear conclusion in his own mind. After a short pause for reflection, he said, "I can give you no decided promise, Herr von Osternau. If you will allow me leave of absence for a few days, I shall be grateful for it. I shall then go to Breslau to-morrow, but whether I shall go thence to Wennersdorf, or employ the time granted me in making a pedestrian excursion among the mountains, I cannot at present tell you."

"I do not ask you to tell me. I hope that calm reflection will show you the right path to pursue. At all events I am glad that our interview has had the effect of entirely restoring my confidence in you, in proof of which I beg you to transact a little business for me in Breslau to-morrow. A manufacturer in Breslau, whom I have known for many years as an honest, industrious man, became some time ago so involved in his pecuniary affairs as to solicit of me a loan of some ten thousand marks, for which he gave me his note. It falls due to-morrow. I do not wish this note presented at the bank, it might injure the man were it known that he had borrowed money of a private individual; nor do I wish the note to be protested if he should not be quite ready to pay the money. I have entire confidence in his honesty, and I do not wish to embarrass him. I thought of sending my cousin Albrecht to-morrow to Breslau to attend to this affair for me, but since you are going I should be much obliged by your undertaking it. Will you do so ?"

"With pleasure."

"Use your own discretion. I do not want to have my debtor harassed. If he pays the money, please send it to me immediately by post, I shall receive it to-morrow afternoon; if he does not, send me back the note."

Herr von Osternau went to his secretary and opened it. In one of its centre partitions stood an iron-bound box with a patent lock. From it he took first a pile of bank-notes representing a considerable sum; these he laid on the desk of the secretary until he had found the note, then returning them to the box, he locked it and the secretary, and turned to Egon. "I hope," he said, kindly, "that our conversation to-day, painful as it was at first, has left no unpleasant impression on either of us. I shall be glad if it is the means of reconciling relatives at present at odds. And now, Herr Pigglewitch, I will detain you no longer. Fritzchen is, I am sure, awaiting you."

He dismissed Egon with a friendly grasp of the hand, and when the young man had left the room, gave himself over to reflection as to whether he had not been somewhat hasty in putting so much trust in him. "I am sure he will justify it," he concluded. "If he had not held sacred the money intrusted to him for his uncle he would have used it in Breslau to purchase what he so greatly needed; he would not have paid for his clothes by instalments. I would far sooner trust him than Albrecht with ten thousand marks. Still he is a strange, incomprehensible fellow, and I detest mysteries. He said himself that he could not tell me the whole truth. I wonder what he suppressed." Upon this he pondered for some time without coming to any conclusion.

CHAPTER XVI.

ROBBED.

IT was an uncomfortable, wearisome evening. A conversation like that of the morning between Herr von Osternau and the tutor always leaves traces, even although it has ended satisfactorily for both parties; for some short time at least it leaves behind it an uncomfortable sense of restraint, and this was evident now. Herr von Osternau could not recover from the effect upon his mood of the interviews with the Lieutenant and the tutor. He tried to be as cordial and kindly as usual, but he did not succeed very well, and his efforts were by no means seconded either by Albrecht or by Pigglewitch.

The Lieutenant was so absent-minded and self-occupied that he took no part whatever in the conversation, and the Candidate was noticeably taciturn. He did not add to the evening's entertainment either by playing or by singing; he declined, indeed, to sing when asked, pleading fatigue, even when Lieschen added her voice to the general petition for a song.

"He is jealous," Frau von Osternau whispered to her husband, and it really seemed as if she might be right. Herr von Osternau noticed that the Candidate was watching Bertha narrowly, and if he really were in love with her she certainly gave him abundant cause for jealousy.

Bertha alone of the little assemblage was in the rosiest mood, she was so gay, so absolutely charming, that Herr von Wangen was to be pardoned for having eyes and ears for nothing save her radiant self. The young fellow, who was wont to be so shy, now conversed with readiness and ease, nay, he and Bertha monopolized the talk. He did not find the evening wearisome, he could have wished that it might last much longer when Herr von Osternau declared that it was time to separate for the night, since Herr Pigglewitch would be obliged to rise early for his journey the next morning.

"You are leaving us?" the Lieutenant asked, suddenly becoming interested. "Where are you going, and for how long?"

Lieschen looked at Egon in surprise, awaiting his reply.

"I do not yet know how long I shall be gone," Egon

replied. "My leave of absence is for three or four days."

"Oh, no, Herr Pigglewitch," Herr von Osternau interposed, "I leave that entirely to you; if you wish to remain longer with your uncle you need not return for a couple of weeks. Herr Pigglewitch, Emma, is going to visit a relative of his, Pastor Widman, in Wennersdorf," he added, in reply to his wife's look of surprised inquiry.

An odd smile hovered about the Lieutenant's features for an instant. His sullen mood was suddenly dissipated, and with a good grace he wished the tutor a successful journey and a speedy return. In this he was joined by Bertha and Herr von Wangen, but Lieschen said not a word; there was only a dreamy, faraway look in her eyes as she bade him good-night, and her hand rested in his a moment longer than was usual.

Herr von Osternau had another interview on his hands this evening. He had his confession to make to his wife. She had a right to know the meaning of this sudden visit of the Candidate to his uncle. Her husband could not but acquaint her with Herr Pastor Widman's letter, and with his conversation of the morning with Herr Pigglewitch. As he did so he expressed his conviction that Pigglewitch was a thoroughly honest man, and he added an account of the commission with which he had intrusted him.

Frau von Osternau did not share her husband's faith. "I am afraid, Fritz," she said, shaking her head, "that you have allowed yourself to be carried away again by your kind, unsuspicious nature. Had you not better recall the commission? Ten thousand marks is a large sum, quite sufficient to tempt a poor Candidate who, as we now learn, has a passion for play. Let Albrecht go to Breslau to-morrow, or Herr Storting, or Herr von Wangen."

"To change my messenger now would be a positive insult to Herr Pigglewitch. I was perhaps imprudent, but it is done now and cannot be altered."

The old Herr, however, was not quite easy in his mind. He slept but poorly, and awoke the next morning so weary that in spite of the glorious weather he did not go out, but sat at his favourite window in his arm-chair. Lieschen and her mother kept him company, but they could not enliven his gloomy mood, which was partly caused by his confinement to the house and partly by a vague feeling of anxiety. His thoughts dwelt upon the Candidate. Would the money arrive punctually from Breslau?

Towards eleven o'clock the Lieutenant entered the room, and seemed confused and not quite agreeably surprised to find Lieschen and Frau von Osternau with his cousin, but quickly collecting himself he said, "I come to you at a rather unusual time, Cousin Fritz, to ask you for leave of absence for a few days. I must attend to that money matter of which I told you. I must spend a short time in Berlin."

"You know I never wish to put any restraint upon you," his cousin said, kindly; "still less would I do so in this matter, in which I wish you all success. When would you like to go?"

"With your permission, immediately after dinner. I wish to leave Breslau by the night-train, and so have the entire day in Berlin to-morrow."

"I am quite willing. I beg you, however, to go to see Sastrow to-morrow as early as possible. I know that you are not on very good terms with him. I ask you as a favour to me to see him yourself, and learn from him about Bertha's affairs: whether anything has been heard of young Herr von Ernau, and whether there is any abatement of the disagreeable gossip of society. Write me to-morrow what you hear."

"It will hardly be necessary. I can tell you the latest news of the affair without having seen Sastrow. You must pardon me for not letting you know before what I heard from a friend in Berlin, who accompanied me to the railway-station when I was last there. I was so preoccupied with my own affairs that I quite forgot Fräulein von Massenburg's. However, I told Fräulein Bertha herself soon after my arrival that there was no longer any doubt of the death of Herr von Ernau, his body has been recovered from the Spree."

Herr and Frau von Osternau uttered an exclamation of surprised dismay. Lieschen was not at all surprised. "Now I understand," she said, "Bertha's excited manner on the evening of her conversation with Cousin Albrecht in the window-recess, and her great amiability towards Herr von Wangen after it. As Herr von Ernau is certainly dead, Herr von Wangen is to take his place."

"How can you speak so unkindly, child?" said her father.

"I only speak the truth. I know that she would have preferred the millionaire, but since she must give up all hopes of him, Herr von Wangen will do."

"Not another word, Lieschen!" Herr von Osternau exclaimed. "Hush! If you cannot conquer your childish, unfounded dislike for Bertha, at least do not give it utterance. Go on, Albrecht, tell me what else you heard."

"Nothing else, except that the body of the unfortunate man had been found in the Spree. Whether

Herr von Ernau was murdered or had drowned him-self my friend did not know. The chief of police, from whom he had his information, did not know either, but suspected he had been murdered, since none of the money which he had drawn from his father's bank on the morning of his disappearance was found upon the body. Doubtless all this has tended to in-crease the talk about Fräulein von Massenburg, so it is scarcely necessary for me to go to inquire of Herr von Sastrow."

"You will, however, oblige me greatly by doing so, and by letting me know what he says."

"Your wish shall be my law, Cousin Fritz. My first visit to-morrow morning shall be to Herr von Sastrow. I shall leave, then, immediately after dinner, and I must ask you to advance me five hundred or a thousand marks. I dislike to ask this favour, but if I am to make any settlement of the matter I spoke of to you I must have some cash in hand."

Herr von Osternau frowned. He would fain have refused the young man's request. He suspected that the money would be used to attempt to recover his losses at play, but he did not wish to expose the Lieu-tenant before Lieschen and her mother, and he could not explain to them his reason for wishing to refuse a demand apparently so reasonable.

He rose slowly and went to his secretary. It was usually opened with great ease, but now something seemed the matter with the lock, he was several moments in unlocking it, and he had the same difficulty with the money-box. "Strange!" he said, trying to turn the key in the last; "either I am very awkward to-day or these keys are growing rusty." As he spoke the lock yielded and the lid of the box opened. One glance showed him to his dismay the reason why he had found so much difficulty in turning his keys. His secretary had been forced in the night by means of false keys, and the money had been stolen from the iron-bound box. The bundle of bank-notes which Herr von Osternau had returned to it on the previous day, after giving the note of hand to the Candidate, was gone.

One look sufficed to tell Herr von Osternau that he had been robbed, and by some inmate of the castle; no one else could have known of the considerable sum in the money-box, no one else could have used false keys in the night without a forcible entrance into the castle, of which there were no traces.

It was not the loss of his money, but the thought that there was a thief beneath his roof which so disturbed Herr von Osternau that he tottered, and might have fallen had not his wife and the Lieutenant hastened to his assistance and helped him to his arm-chair.

It was but a momentary weakness, however, to which the old Herr succumbed; in an instant he was on his feet again, examining the secretary and the papers left in his box. They were all there, even a package of certificates of stock in a sugar-refinery, worth some ten thousand thalers; everything was there save the bundle of bank-notes. The thief had been too cunning to take anything which might lead to his detection.

But who was the thief?

This question Herr von Osternau put to himself and to his wife, after informing her of his loss, and of his belief that he must have been robbed by some one of his household.

Frau von Osternau was no less shocked than her husband, she did not reply. The Lieutenant made answer in her stead. "It can be no other than that fellow, the Candidate, who left the castle this morning with the booty obtained thus in the night."

He had scarcely finished speaking when Lieschen, flushed with indignation, confronted him. Her little hand was clinched and her eyes flashed as she said, in a voice which she vainly tried to steady, "It is a vile, cowardly calumny! You would not dare to say it to his face if he were here! I should sooner believe that you were the thief than that he could be guilty of a dishonourable act!"

The Lieutenant started and turned pale at this sudden denunciation; unable to meet Lieschen's indignant eyes, he cast down his own and answered not a word.

"My child, my child, of what are you thinking?" Frau von Osternau exclaimed.

But Lieschen was not to be stopped. With flashing eyes still riveted upon the Lieutenant, she went on, " I will not have an innocent man slandered when he is not here to defend himself, and by one, too, who has always shown himself his enemy, and who may have his own ends to serve by this accusation."

"Cousin Fritz, can you allow your cousin to be thus treated by your daughter?"

Herr von Osternau had entirely recovered from the shock of his discovery, and he replied calmly and gravely to the Lieutenant's complaint: "No, neither can I allow an unfounded charge to be brought against one who, as Lieschen says, is not here to defend himself. My child is right in espousing the Candidate's cause, but her manner of doing so I cannot approve. Go to your room, Lieschen, and stay there until Cousin Albrecht consents to pardon you."

Lieschen silently obeyed the father whom she loved,

but her glance at Albrecht, as she left the room, spoke of anything save a desire for pardon at his hands.

"It is infamous!" the Lieutenant exclaimed, when Lieschen had left the room; "just to whitewash a vagabond, an adventurer, dropped down among us from nobody knows where, I am exposed to such vile insinuations! This Pigglewitch——"

"Has done nothing to lay himself open to the charge of a midnight robbery," Herr von Osternau interposed.

"But, cousin, you yourself said that the thief must have been one of the household. Whom else can you suspect save this fellow? The servants are honest and tried, and have been here for years, while the tutor has been here but for a short time. We know nothing of his past, he never mentions it. Such reserve betokens an evil conscience. I never trusted him. I will not repeat my suspicions, but surely they are justified by his absent-minded manner yesterday, his strange behaviour, and the fact that the robbery occurred the very night before his departure. I shall avail myself of my short time in Breslau to-day to notify the police of what has happened, and beg them to try to arrest the thief. He probably has the money still in his possession; to-morrow he will have hidden it in some safe place or will run off the day after from Hamburg or Bremen for America. Whatever is done must be done quickly."

"I strictly forbid all notice to the police. I will not have an innocent man insulted by their interference in his affairs."

"But, Fritz, will you let the thief escape with his booty? How are you to discover him if you do not call in the police, whose business it is to catch thieves?"

"I do not wish to discover him," Herr von Osternau quietly replied to his wife.

"You will let the money go?"

"That is the least of my loss, although the sum was a considerable one. What I find hardest to bear is that among those whom I have trusted there is a scoundrel, a thief. I do not wish to know him, to bring him to punishment. I can do without the money. I would rather lose it than have Castle Osternau made the subject all over the country of the talk which I hate. Therefore, I beg you to say not one word to any one about the robbery. You hear, Albrecht? You understand?"

"As you really desire it, I will promise to be silent."

"Enough. Now I will detain you no longer. Before you start I will find means to give you the advance you have asked for, and to do this I must drive to Mirbach myself. Pray have the horses put to the light, open wagon, and brought round to the door as soon as possible."

"Do you mean to drive yourself, cousin? No, you must not; you look pale and ill. The discovery has agitated you, the drive might do you harm. Permit me——"

"You have preparations for your journey to make."

"But, Fritz, I pray you let Albrecht go with you," Frau von Osternau said, anxiously, but her husband shook his head impatiently. "Do not oppose me," he said. "I have reasons for wishing to go alone. The wagon must be at the door in five minutes; pray see to it, Albrecht."

There was no gainsaying the old Herr when he was thus decided, and the Lieutenant left the room to do as he was requested. No sooner had the door closed behind him than Herr von Osternau said to his wife, "I must go to Mirbach myself. If Pigglewitch has received the money on the note and sends it immediately by post, it will arrive with the mid-day train. I must see for myself whether he has sent it."

"I am afraid you will have your drive in vain. All excitement is, as you know, injurious to you; why will you not let Albrecht go?"

"Let him go? Do you forget what Lieschen said, Emma?"

"For heaven's sake do not tell me that you share the suspicion at which Lieschen's words pointed so unjustifiably?"

"Lieschen's look probed her cousin's soul, he could not endure it, an evil conscience spoke in his eyes. Do you guess now why I would rather lose the money than ask the police to interfere? Their investigation might result in what the Lieutenant would hardly like. I have made many a sacrifice to preserve the name of Osternau from dishonour, I shall make this one also. There must be no whisper of even a suspicion that an Osternau could be guilty of theft."

"But you cherish such a suspicion, while your confidence in Pigglewitch, whom there are quite as many reasons for suspecting, is unshaken."

"I hope in a short time to bring you proof that the Candidate deserves my confidence; this is why I am going to Mirbach."

Frau von Osternau said no more, but accompanied her husband to the hall door, before which the light wagon was waiting.

As he drove off she followed him with anxious eyes, and then applied herself to waiting patiently for his return. Fortunately, she had not long to do so; hardly

P

three-quarters of an hour had passed when the vehicle again drove up to the hall door, and her husband sprang from it with an elasticity and vigour which showed that he felt stronger than before his drive.

"I was not deceived," he whispered to his wife, who had come from the sitting-room to receive him. "I do not deny, Emma," he went on, when they were alone together, "that I could not help being somewhat doubtful as I drove to Mirbach. I thought of Lieschen, of her implicit trust in Pigglewitch, of her fearful disappointment if he should be discovered to be a scoundrel who might well be suspected of theft. My heart beat faster when I asked for my letters at the post-office, and when they handed me the envelope with five seals, I was delighted. Here it is. Pigglewitch is all right, he has executed his commission promptly and well. If he had committed the robbery, he would surely have added to his gains the ten thousand marks which he sends me here, that he might carry away in his flight everything he could get. This letter is the best proof of his innocence. Do you suspect him now?"

"No; but I cannot tell whether to rejoice that I do not, and I cannot see how you can be so glad. How can you look so happy when, as you cease to suspect a stranger, your next of kin takes his place in your suspicions?"

"I gave *him* up long ago," Herr von Osternau replied. "I keep him beneath my roof because my duty and the honour of our name link me to him, and because I owe him some indemnification for the annihilation of his hopes. The unhappy event which has just occurred does not relieve me of this duty, it must remain a secret between us two."

CHAPTER XVII.

TWO LETTERS AGAIN.

THE day was an eventful one for Herr von Osternau. Scarcely had he recovered from the effects of the robbery and of the hurried drive to Station Mirbach, when he was surprised by an unexpected visit.

Herr von Wangen was formally announced by old Hildebrandt, and when he made his appearance in full dress, with a white neck-tie, and a silk hat held in his left hand, when he bowed with ceremonious observance to the mistress of the mansion and her husband, and, accepting the seat offered him on the lounge, stared into space for some minutes with an air of confusion, evidently searching in vain for words in which to explain the purpose of his coming, Frau von Osternau began to suspect what those words when found would be.

At last the young man cleared his throat and raised his eyes to Frau von Osternau's face as he began : " Pardon me, madame, pardon me, Herr von Osternau, if I express myself ill, but I come—yes, I come to you as the relatives and protectors of my betrothed—no, pardon me, I have begun at the wrong end, I ought first to tell you that I am the happiest man in the world. An hour ago I had the good fortune to meet my beloved Bertha, pardon me for not saying Fräulein von Massenburg, but she is now my betrothed. She was going for a walk to the Oster-ford, where I am superintending the work, and she allowed me to walk with her. Her heavenly kindness emboldened me to confess to her my love; she, to my intense delight, did not reject it, and we are betrothed."

Herr von Osternau was unpleasantly surprised, he could not help remembering what Lieschen had said, and whilst his wife warmly congratulated the happy lover he was silent. He could not altogether approve this hasty betrothal, and after a short pause he said, " I cannot yet congratulate you, Herr von Wangen, or consider you betrothed to Fräulein von Massenburg. Your father is my old friend, I should not be doing my duty by him if I did not beg you to reflect before taking so irrevocable a step. Do you know that Bertha von Massenburg came to Castle Osternau to escape the——"

Herr von Wangen interrupted him, saying, in a tone of entreaty, "Do not, I beg of you, allude to that slander, I know everything. Bertha has told me how magnanimously she sacrificed herself for her father, how she consented to be betrothed to a man whom she knew only by reputation, and how evil tongues attacked her upon the disappearance of Herr von Ernau. She has acknowledged to me that she struggled against her love for me so long as there was any possibility of Herr von Ernau's being alive; she was determined to sacrifice her affection to her duty. But she is free; she learned yesterday from the Lieutenant that Herr von Ernau is really dead, and she can obey the dictates of her heart, can be happy herself and can make me so. She is mine, my own fondly-loved betrothed."

"No, Herr von Wangen, I can allow of no such betrothal beneath my roof until your father and Bertha's have given their consent."

"My father has already given his," the young man rejoined, eagerly. " I should not have ventured without it to declare my love. I wrote him more than a week ago that I should try to win my Bertha, and he answered me instantly, and told me he was rejoiced that I had chosen a lovely girl of an old family. He cares nothing for worldly possessions, but he wishes his only son to marry his equal in rank. I should love my dear Bertha all the same if she were a peasant's daughter, but I am glad that she is a Von Massenburg. I am glad of this for my dear father's sake."

"But Bertha's father has not yet given his consent."

"That is why I am come to you with an urgent request. I know it is asking a great deal, for there is so much to do at harvest-time, but I come to beg you to give me leave of absence for two days, that I may ask Herr von Massenburg's consent in person. I can leave after dinner to-day, and take the night-train for Berlin. I can be back at Castle Osternau by noon of the day after to-morrow."

There was no refusing such a request. Herr von Osternau granted it, but upon the condition that he should be allowed to speak with Bertha before the young man's departure. The lover was quite agreed to this, he was too sure of his good fortune to dread any interference. And the event showed that he was right. Herr von Osternau had a long interview with Bertha; he asked her if she were sure of her own sentiments, if it were possible for her to be happy with a husband who was in all respects the opposite of Herr von Ernau, possessing none of the latter's brilliant qualities to fit him for playing a conspicuous part in the world. He reminded her that she was undertaking to pass her life in the depths of the country, remote from all social excitement, with a husband who was content to lead the life of a simple country gentleman upon his

20

own estate. To all which Bertha replied, with her own charming smile,—

"I really did not expect such an admonition from you, Uncle Fritz, who are always extolling the joys of home and the home circle. I should be happy with 'the man of my choice' in any solitude, and, besides, I shall not be so very lonely. One can always assemble one's friends about one in the country in summer, and the long, tiresome winters we can spend in town. Country life may be made very delightful with plenty of money. Let me choose my own lot, Uncle Fritz; it will be a happy one."

What could Herr von Osternau reply to such arguments? he did not try to reply, seeing that Bertha's mind was fully made up.

That afternoon Herr von Wangen and the Lieutenant both took their departure, and at noon of the following day a lengthy dispatch was received at Castle Osternau. It announced the full and free consent of Herr Werner von Massenburg that the betrothal should be made public, and also stated that Herr von Wangen would certainly return by noon of the next day to his fair betrothed.

He did so punctually, beaming with delight, overjoyed at the reception he had met with from his future father-in-law. In truth, Werner von Massenburg had bestowed his paternal blessing upon the union so soon as he was informed that no dowry was looked for. Of course, Herr von Wangen's delicacy led him to suppress this last fact, as also the slight circumstance of Werner's explanation as to his present pecuniary embarrassments, in view of which Herr von Wangen had signed a checque for two thousand marks to relieve the worthy gentleman from his temporary trouble.

On the other hand, he told with great delight how Werner had hastened to present him to several of his friends, among whom were Herr von Sastrow and his wife, whom he had called upon, and from whom he had received cordial congratulations. Herr von Sastrow had declared that this betrothal would put an instant stop to all malicious gossip.

Herr von Wangen was in such a state of rapture that there were positively no shadows in the picture which he painted of his journey. The Lieutenant had been the most delightful travelling companion, only unfortunately they had not seen each other after parting at the Berlin railway-station. Werner von Massenburg was a fine, open-hearted man, just such a father-in-law as he had always wanted, and Herr von Sastrow and all the father-in-law's friends were most delightful people. But what filled the young man with the wildest joy was that Werner had expressly desired that the marriage should take place as soon as possible, since he disliked long engagements.

When Bertha declared with a blush that she should be guided entirely by the wishes of her betrothed, and when Herr von Osternau expressed himself willing to dispense with the services of his third inspector so soon as harvest should be over, that the young man might immediately betake himself to West Prussia and undertake the charge of the family estates, Herr von Wangen was transported to the highest heaven of felicity.

He adored his charming betrothed, and never noticed that Lieschen's manner towards her was more coolly reserved than ever, nor dreamed that he was the object of the sad, compassionate expression that sometimes appeared in the young girl's eyes. He was fairly intoxicated with bliss. He was perpetually with his betrothed. She paid him visits in the fields, she went to meet him when he returned to the castle. And then the evenings, the delicious evenings! Herr von Wangen did not observe that the little circle was in general silent and monosyllabic, that Lieschen bent silently over her embroidery, and that Herr von Osternau frequently resigned himself to revery. So long as he could exchange glances with Bertha and hang upon every word she uttered, his cup of happiness was full to the brim.

Herr von Osternau was far from easy in his mind. He could not forget the sad event that had so lately occurred, and he shared his wife's anxiety upon another point. Since Lieschen had so boldly entered the lists for Pigglewitch against the Lieutenant, Herr von Osternau had agreed with his wife in believing that the young girl's feelings for the tutor were warmer than those of a pupil for a teacher. He took a lively interest in the young man, indeed he was surprised to find how much he missed his conversation and his charming music, but he could not but see that his wife was right in regarding the tutor as a most undesirable son-in-law. Lieschen's attachment to him caused him all the greater anxiety since he could not reconcile it with his sense of justice to dismiss the young man as his wife advised.

The old Herr really dreaded, therefore, the Candidate's return, and he had a sense of relief when day after day passed and the tutor did not come back to the castle.

Five days had thus gone by without bringing tidings of either the Lieutenant or the Candidate, when the post-bag brought two letters for Herr von Osternau, one from Berlin addressed in the Lieutenant's hand-

writing, and the other postmarked Hirschberg and
addressed by Pigglewitch. This last Herr von Osternau opened first, read it, and then turned to his wife.
"A strange letter!" he exclaimed, "as strange and enig-
matical as its writer. Only listen." And according to
his custom of reading aloud to his family all his letters
which contained nothing private and confidential, he
read aloud: "Farewell! I cannot tell you how hard it
is for me to part from you, from the generous, high-
hearted man whom I so respect, from my dear pupil
Fritzchen, who has grown into my heart, and from the
kindly family-circle where I have passed such happy
hours. But it must be done in spite of the pain it gives
me, pain increased by a sense of guilt. You trusted
me and I deceived you. My entire life in your home
was a lie. Even now, when I am going from you, I cannot tell you the truth, I can only pray you to forgive a
most unhappy man, who never can forget the gratitude
he owes you. Farewell!"

"There is no signature," said Herr von Osternau,
handing the letter to his wife. "The man is in all respects a riddle, only one thing seems clear, and that is
that we shall not see Herr Pigglewitch again."

"I knew he would not return," Lieschen said, with a
strange quiver in her voice. "He could not."

"He could not?" her father asked, in surprise.

"No, he owed it to himself to flee. He was on the
brink of an abyss. It was well for him that he had the
strength to save himself."

"Lieschen, what nonsense are you talking?" her
mother exclaimed, in dismay. "You do not know
what you are saying!"

"I wish I did not," Lieschen replied, glancing for an
instant with scorn in her eyes at Bertha, who paying

no apparent attention to what was going on, was engaged in a whispered conversation with her betrothed.

"There is no use," Herr von Osternau said at last, after reading the letter again over his wife's shoulder, "in our beating our brains over this mystery. The Candidate's going, like his coming, will always be a riddle for us."

After this he opened the Lieutenant's letter and began to read it, but he had not read far before he turned to his wife again, with: "This is absolutely incredible, Emma! Only hear what Albrecht writes: 'My dear Cousin,—First of all forgive me for not returning, and for delaying to write until now. After many tedious transactions, of which I will inform you more minutely by word of mouth if you desire it, I have concluded the affair you know of, and should have returned to you to-morrow, but that I think it best to remain here a day or two longer in the interest of our family. You will allow this, I am sure, when I tell you of the astounding news which I have learned to-day. Herr Egon von Ernau, whose body it was affirmed was found in the Spree, has returned from quite a long journey, and is now here in Berlin!'"

An exclamation of surprise from Bertha interrupted Herr von Osternau. He turned towards her. She had grown very pale, and her large eyes were riveted upon his face. "He is alive!" she almost whispered.

"He is alive, and you are betrothed to Herr von Wangen," Lieschen said, quietly.

A look of positive hatred was Bertha's only reply. The next instant her colour came again, and she turned with her own lovely smile to her lover: "Yes, Hugo, and I thank God that I am so, and that I am saved the struggle between duty and affection which I must have undergone if Herr von Ernau had reappeared before I was betrothed to you."

Herr von Osternau looked rather dubiously at her as she spoke, but he said nothing, only continued the reading of his letter: "I could scarcely credit this when I heard it this afternoon from an acquaintance. Yesterday there was no doubt but that his body had been found in the Spree. It had, to be sure, been too long in the water to allow of the features being recognized, but Ernau's body-servant identified the summer suit of the dead man as positively his master's, and there was in one of the pockets a small silver card-case, which both the servant and the Councillor recognized as young Ernau's. The Councillor was so convinced that the body was that of his son that he arranged an imposing funeral, at which half the aristocratic society of Berlin was present; and yet here was the dead man alive and well. I went directly to Sastrow for further information.

"From him I received confirmation of the incredible report. Herr von Ernau did really return yesterday from a tour among the mountains. He employed his time this morning in visiting his acquaintances, apparently to convince them that he is alive. He has nothing to say of where he has been or why he left Berlin so abruptly, but he ridicules his own splendid funeral and thanks the mourners profusely for their sympathy. He is as reckless and extravagant as ever. Werner Massenburg, who has just seen Sastrow, gave him all these particulars. I shall go to him again to-morrow, when I may have more to tell you, but for the present the subject must give place to certain revelations I have for you concerning the redoubtable Herr Pigglewitch, who I was quite certain was what he proves to be,— an adventurer and deceiver."

"What a shameful calumny!" Lieschen exclaimed, indignantly.

"Hush, my child!" her father rejoined, gravely. "I neither can nor will believe that your cousin's harsh expressions are justifiable, but I hardly know what to think. Listen to what Albrecht says:

"You forbade me to put the police upon the fellow's traces, and I obeyed you, but you did not forbid my instituting inquiries as to his previous life and circumstances. This I have done, and as I have an acquaintance who is one of the superior officers of the police force, I easily learned from him the following particulars: The man calling himself Pigglewitch, who brought you a letter from Herr Director Kramser, and who lived so long at Castle Osternau, has no right to the name he bore there, and must be a mere adventurer.

"I remember perfectly well that the so-called Candidate Pigglewitch arrived at Castle Osternau on the 6th of July, and on that very day the real Pigglewitch is proved to have been in Berlin. He had informed his lodging-house keeper—a woman by the name of Wiebe—that he had obtained a situation as tutor, and that he was to be at Osternau, in Silesia, on the 6th, but after leaving Berlin on the 5th he returned on the evening of the 6th and took possession of his old quarters. Here he stayed for several days, expecting, as he told his hostess, a letter containing money, which would enable him to sail for America, and in fact on the 9th of July a letter did arrive, addressed to Herr Gottlieb Pigglewitch, and containing a large sum of money, some four thousand marks, Frau Wiebe says. She further states that Pigglewitch was overjoyed at the arrival of the letter, and told her that he should spend a few days longer in Berlin to take some recre-

ation before sailing; that he left home early in the
morning and returned late at night until the 12th of
July, when he went from the house at eleven in the
forenoon, and has not since been heard of. As there
were no charges against him, and as it was more than
probable that he had sailed for America, no search
was made for him. Thus much at least is certain,
that the real Pigglewitch was in Berlin from the 6th
to the 12th of July, and that therefore the man who
was at Castle Osternau must have been an adventurer
and impostor, wearing an assumed name.

"The conclusions to be drawn from this fact I leave
to you. If the sham Pigglewitch has returned from
his journey, give him this letter to read. I am curious
to know whether he will defend himself against the
charges it contains, and whether you, Cousin Fritz, will
still refuse to call in the aid of the police. I have no
doubt that they would find in his possession skeleton
keys and a considerable sum of money, unless he has
been prudent enough to conceal them during his absence
from the castle.

"Day after to-morrow I shall return to Osternau,
and in the mean time I may perhaps learn something
further of Herr von Ernau and of the sham Pigglewitch.

"With great regard, faithfully yours,
                    "ALBRECHT VON OSTERNAU."

"These are terrible revelations!" Frau von Osternau
said, when her husband had finished reading the letter.
"Who would have thought it? But yes, I always suspected that something was wrong. I never trusted
Herr Pigglewitch. While he sat at the piano and played
or sang I forgot, it is true, all my doubts, but they re-

turned as I looked into his restless, dark eyes. You know, Fritz, how often I have warned you against him and begged you to dismiss him. Now he is proved to be an adventurer and an impostor. In his own letter he confesses that he has deceived us, that his life was a lie. He knew that discovery was imminent, and so he has not returned. Now you will change your opinion of him, and no longer delay sending an account of the robbery to the Breslau police inspector."

"No, Emma, I am as thoroughly convinced of his innocence now as I always have been," her husband replied. "Whoever the thief may have been, it was not the Candidate. I wish for no clearing up of that mystery."

Lieschen arose, went to her father, and, putting her arm around his neck, kissed him tenderly, and said, "Thank you, my own kind, darling papa!" Then she ran out of the room to hide the tears which Bertha must not see.

CHAPTER XVIII.

A FORCED RESOLVE.

On the morning of his departure from Castle Osternau Egon had packed up enough clothing to last him for a few days, and carried it himself to Station Mirbach, whence he took the next train to Breslau.

He did not know himself what course he should take. He trusted, as he had formerly been wont to do, to the impulse of the moment. Only one thing was clear to him, he needed rest and solitude, and a forcible severing of the ties which bound him to Castle Osternau, before he could come to any clear decision as to his conduct.

Arrived in Breslau, he first attended to Herr von Osternau's commission, and dispatched the money to him. At the same time he enclosed to Herr Pastor Widman, in Wennersdorf, the sum owing him. "No need of a letter of explanation," he said to himself, as he sealed the envelope. "I am a fool to send this money, but I promised Herr von Osternau, and I wish the Herr Pastor joy of his good luck."

As he sauntered through the streets of Breslau after posting his letters, whiling away the time before the departure of the noonday train, which was to carry him to the mountains, he tried in vain to collect his thoughts, to arrange his ideas. It was in vain, his mind was a chaos; he seemed walking in a confused dream; old impressions recalled by the busy life of the streets, from which he had so long been absent, struggled with those of the last few weeks, and he attained some degree of calm only when, after a couple of hours in the railway-carriage, he arrived at the little mountain village whence he was to set out upon his pedestrian excursion. He strapped upon his back the knapsack which he had purchased at Breslau to contain his few effects, and set out; it was not long before the physical effort necessary for mountain-climbing had its usual beneficial effect.

His rebellious thoughts would still revert to Castle Osternau, and refuse to be held captive by the changing landscape on either hand, but they were no longer so confused and unsteady as they had been early in the day, and when, after a long walk, he retired for the night, tolerably late in the evening, at a little mountain inn, he soon fell into a dreamless sleep.

He waked in the early morning refreshed and invigorated mentally and physically. The weather was glorious, and most propitious for mountain travel on foot; Egon felt awaken within him an old longing for some days alone with nature in her grand, careless mood. It was long since he had felt so fresh and strong, and as he walked upwards among the odorous pines he calmly reflected upon his life at Castle Osternau. Could he return thither? He was able now to ponder the question quietly. His position there was uncertain; Pastor Widman's letter had raised doubts in Herr von Osternau's mind which an accident might reawaken, he might naturally make investigations as to his tutor's past, and then? The inevitable consequence would be the ruin of the false structure erected, as Egon was forced with shame to confess, upon falsehood. The unmasked impostor would be thrust in disgrace from the castle, despised by those whom he held so dear.

No, he could not expose himself to such a peril; if he returned he must confess the whole truth to Herr von Osternau. But could he do this? There rang in his ears all the words of disapproval and condemnation uttered by almost every member of the Osternau circle with regard to Herr von Ernau. Lieschen had called him a wretched, detestable man, and her father and mother had openly expressed their contempt for him. Should he say to them, "I am that Egon von Ernau whom you so despise!" Could he defend himself against the accusations brought against him? He had tried once to do so to Lieschen, and how incredulously she had shaken her lovely head! with what surprise, nay, dismay, she had looked at him! Had not his former life justified all that was said of him? Had he not given additional reason for it by carrying on a deception for weeks, living under an assumed name among those who had trusted him?

In imagination he saw Lieschen turning from him indignantly, as she exclaimed, "There is nothing I detest as I do falsehood!" He heard the Lieutenant's scornful laughter. And Bertha! Should she too witness his humiliation?

No; he could not return and run the risk of being discovered, nor could he confess his deceit. Both were alike impossible.

But if he did not return to the castle, what was he to do? Go back to Berlin! And why not? Formerly the thought of falling in with his father's plans had filled him with disgust; now his heart beat quicker at the thought of calling Bertha von Massenburg his wife.

And yet he hesitated and could come to no decision. Always in the midst of the intoxication of the senses that accompanied the remembrance of Bertha, a lovely girlish image would rise before his mental vision to calm and soothe him, and no sacrifice seemed to him too great to purchase a gentle word of pardon from Lieschen, one look of love from her eyes.

He could not decide. For three days he wandered about the mountains, pursuing those paths least frequented by tourists, and lodging at night in some lonely, retired little inn, determined to avoid any chance encounter with acquaintances. But on the fourth day of his wanderings he was slowly descending the agate rocks towards Hermsdorf, lost in thought, his eyes bent upon the ground, when he was roused from his revery by a clear, merry voice: "All *good spirits praise the Lord!* Positively this is a capital joke! Day before yesterday we buried you, Herr von Ernau, and to-day I meet you, sound in body and limb, upon this far from delightful ascent!"

Egon looked up startled. Before him stood an old acquaintance from Berlin,—Baron von Freistetten, a wealthy young nobleman, whom he had often met in society, and whom he had liked rather better than most of his associates, since in the preference shown him by the young fellow there could be no suspicion of interested motives.

Freistetten was in the act of making the ascent of the agate rocks, in company with a guide, and had paused for a moment to take breath, when he perceived Egon coming down towards him and instantly hailed him. All fatigue was forgotten; he hurried to meet him, and shook him cordially by the hand. "Upon my word, Ernau," he said, "this is the greatest pleasure I have had for years! I never believed you were dead, for did I not see you a month ago in Breslau? But when everybody insisted that your body had been found, and when I followed it to the grave, the day before yesterday, I thought I had been mistaken, and sincerely mourned you. Thank God! I was right at first. I am indeed delighted."

The young fellow's joy was so sincere that Egon could not but reciprocate his cordiality. Disagreeably surprised as he was at first at the encounter, several of the Baron's expressions had aroused his curiosity, and he agreed readily to the young man's proposal that they should find some shady spot for a half-hour's talk.

Beneath an overhanging rock they threw themselves down upon the soft green moss.

"I cannot get used to it," said Freistetten, shaking Egon again by the hand. "This is what I call a surprise indeed. But now tell me all about yourself.

Where in the world have you been hiding? What reasons could you have for vanishing so suddenly and giving no sign of life?"

"I was tired of the stupid society life of the capital, and I have been spending a few weeks quietly in the country. I really have nothing to tell. But you must satisfy my curiosity. What was it you said about finding my body and going to my funeral? What did you mean?"

"That you were buried, and have risen from the dead. But no, the matter is too serious for trifling. You shall hear the consequences of your flight from Berlin."

And he went over the whole story; how he had not been believed when he said that he had seen Egon in Breslau, how every one said that young Ernau had taken his life because of an unhappy love-affair. "You have deeply grieved your friends, Ernau," he added.

"Have I any friends?" Egon rejoined. "The few who felt some slight regret at my death were more than indemnified by the interesting gossip to which it gave occasion."

"I don't envy you such sentiments as those," Freistetten said, gravely. "They can only be entertained by one who is no man's friend, and who thinks only of himself. I am no moralist, but I cannot understand how you could make up your mind to play so reckless a game with your friends, among whom I count myself, and, above all, with your father."

Egon had no reply to make to this reproach, and Freistetten continued his narrative, telling how the dress of the corpse found in the Spree had been identified by the servant and by Councillor von Ernau, and how magnificent had been the funeral.

Egon listened eagerly, and when he heard how the

body had been identified, he had a sudden conviction as to who had been so ceremoniously consigned to earth in his stead. He remembered that he had forgotten to take his empty silver card-case from the breast-pocket of the coat which he had exchanged for Pigglewitch's. The Candidate had not been heard from for weeks. Doubtless he had gambled again, had again lost all, and his second attempt at suicide had been more successful than his first. His body was now at rest in the church-yard.

"You are really dead in every one's estimation," Freistetten concluded. "It is fortunate that I chanced to meet you, and could tell you of the result of your flight from Berlin,—else you might not have thought of returning thither to put a stop to the wild rumours about you. Or were you going down to Hirschberg, to start thence for Berlin?"

"No," Egon replied, "I did not think of that. I have not yet decided what to do, and I must pray you to keep my secret, and inform no one that you have seen me."

"I shall do no such thing!" Freistetten exclaimed, indignantly. "That would be to make myself an accomplice in what offends my sense of right. Indeed, Ernau, you must return to Berlin; it would be unpardonable to allow your father to believe any longer that he has lost his only son. I know that your relations with him were never very cordial, but he is your father, and you owe him a son's duty. If you refuse to return to Berlin, I shall cut short my mountain excursion and go there myself to tell your father that his son is alive."

Freistetten had arisen, and now signed to his guide that he was ready to go on.

"Decide, Ernau," he said, gravely; "your decision will govern mine."

Egon had hoped for some chance that should force him to a resolution; his wish was fulfilled; his hesitation between Castle Osternau and Berlin was at an end. He was not angry with Freistetten for his severe, almost insulting, words : he was justified in using them.

"I thank you, Freistetten," he said, likewise rising. "Your admonition is harsh, but I will lay it to heart. Continue your tour; I promise you to go directly to Berlin from Hirschberg. Since I am, half unwillingly I admit, forced to take upon me the old yoke, I will do so without delay. Farewell!"

The young men separated with a warm grasp of the hand, and Egon walked on down into the Hirschberg valley. With a heavy heart he went his way back to the old life. Now that he was resolved not to return to Castle Osternau, existence there appeared to him in the rosiest light; he longed for each one of those of its inmates who had grown dear to him; he could not bear the thought of parting from them without one word of farewell, one prayer for pardon for having deceived them.

Lieschen's image accompanied him on his way; it seemed to beckon him on. He felt an intense desire to hasten to Castle Osternau, if only for a day, an hour, that she might decide whether he should remain there, or return to Berlin.

He lodged for the night in a little inn seldom visited by strangers. He could not sleep when he first retired to his room; the effort to abide by his resolve chased sleep from his eyelids. At last he sat down and wrote two farewell letters, one to Herr von Osternau, the other to Herr Storting. In the latter he enclosed the

payment of the little debt for which Storting had so
readily gone surety in Breslau.   Both letters he posted
the next morning before starting for Berlin, thus destroying all possibility of a return to Castle Osternau.
He then grew calmer; the struggle was over, he hesitated no longer.

CHAPTER XIX.

THE PRODIGAL'S RETURN.

PRIVY COUNCILLOR VON ERNAU was sitting in his
dining-room, at the little round table, which was to-day
set for but one person.   He was not fond of dining
alone; guests were always invited to join him at this
meal, which was on table punctually at four o'clock.
Certainly gay conversation is the best seasoning for
delicate viands.   Neither well-prepared food nor excellent wine delighted the Councillor's palate if partaken
of in solitude.   He therefore reflected sadly, as he
sipped his soup, upon the number of days upon which
he should now be obliged to dine alone,—fourteen, at
the very least.   He sighed profoundly.   Fourteen days
appeared an endless time to him.   Since the finding of
Egon's body had established the fact that the unfortunate Councillor von Ernau had lost his only son, eight
days had passed; for eight days he had worn deep
mourning.   Until eight days ago there had been some
doubt as to his calamity, and he had not felt it necessary
to deny himself all social pleasures; but now there was
no help for it.   As a father overwhelmed with grief, such

joys were not for him. He glanced sadly enough at the broad band of crape that encircled his left arm.

During the first few days after the finding of the body there had been some satisfaction in the sensation produced in Berlin by the actual death of Egon von Ernau. It had been very interesting to read the accounts in the papers, to receive visits of condolence, to show to each new-comer how profound was the grief that wrung the paternal bosom; then came all the arrangements for the funeral, which was magnificent. Thus occupied the time passed quickly, and the sacrifice of a solitary dinner was a matter of course, but now? The visits of condolence had ceased, the funeral was over, the newspapers said nothing more with regard to the death of Herr Egon von Ernau, the Councillor felt very lonely, and the thought that he must yet pass at least fourteen days secluded from all the delights of the capital made him very sad. It really was a hard fate to lose an only son in the bloom of youth, and to have to go into mourning for him besides!

The soup was delicate, but he did not relish it. He looked up with a sigh——The spoon dropped from his fingers and fell clinking into his soup-plate, as he gazed with staring eyes at the ghost which suddenly confronted him in broad daylight,—a ghost the very presentment of his dead son. There it stood in the open door-way. No, it did not stand; it moved as if made of flesh and blood; it walked with the elastic step that had been Egon's, through the room and directly towards its solitary occupant.

"Good-day, sir," Egon remarked, as quietly as if he had just returned from a short walk; and then, turning to the servant, who stood staring in no less terror than his master, he said, "Bring me a plate, Johann, and be quick, for I am desperately hungry."

No ghost speaks thus; no ghost coolly draws a chair up to a table and sits down.

"Good God!" exclaimed the Councillor, who could not yet collect himself, "is it really you, Egon? and alive?"

"As you see, sir, alive, and very hungry. Will you have the kindness to order Johann to bring me a plate and not to stand there staring at me? I think my appetite will soon convince both you and him that I am alive."

Johann hastened to obey the order, and the Councillor no longer doubted that his son was before him. He took up his spoon again, wiped a spot of soup off the handle with his napkin, and as he did so eyed his resuscitated son with an air of anything but delight. "You are alive, then," he said, peevishly; "and that you are so destroys the only satisfactory excuse that there could be for recklessly plunging me into the greatest embarrassment by your sudden disappearance, just when your betrothal was announced."

"Did I embarrass you, sir?" asked Egon, upon whom the paternal reproof appeared to produce but a slight impression. "I am sorry, but I should not have believed it. You are not wont to be easily embarrassed. So far as I can learn, you have had a very agreeable time. The variety which the sensation caused by my disappearance, by the discovery of my body, and at last by my funeral must have introduced into your monotonous existence has certainly been entertaining. The crape upon your arm becomes you admirably; it is a pity to have to take it off, but then you will be indemnified for its loss by the fresh sensation which the prodigal's return will excite. We shall both form the topic of Berlin gossip for at least a week. Dead men do not rise from their graves every day. The funeral, I hear from Freistetten, was really brilliant, quite worthy of your distinguished taste. I regret not to have witnessed it. However, I can go to the church-yard tomorrow to look at my grave and admire the flowers with which you have adorned it. I must beg you to accept my thanks for them."

"Always the same," the Councillor murmured, "a venomous sneer in every word; you return as you departed."

"Does that vex you, sir? We have always got along very well together. You never troubled yourself about me, and I never annoyed you. I think we can do as well for the future. You never shall be disturbed in your enjoyment of life by me, not even now. Pray do not let your soup get cold; here comes mine. We will dine together, and consult comfortably how we can introduce to the living world in the manner most agreeable to you the son risen from the dead. But before I say another word I must take my soup; I am as hungry as a wolf."

He applied himself to his task with an excellent appetite, and the Councillor followed his example.

The Councillor did not speak until the soup was removed and Johann was busy changing the plates for the next course. Then he availed himself of the interruption of the dinner to say, "It seems high time that you should inform me of your reasons for leaving me so suddenly, of where you have been, of what you have been doing, and why we have heard nothing from you for all these long weeks? Certainly, as your father, I have a right to an explanation from you."

"There we differ, sir," Egon replied, in the same tone of cool contempt which he had thus far used in addressing his father. "Our relations have hitherto not corresponded to those usually existing between father and son. You never desired any confidence from me. You have pursued your pleasures without troubling yourself to think whether your son might not perhaps need a father's affection, and you have never required of me any explanation of my actions or sentiments. You gave the boy perfect liberty to commit any folly he chose; how can the man possibly be called to account by you? We had better continue our relations as you have arranged them. It can be of little moment to you where I have been and why I went away. It is enough that I am here again, and that you are relieved of the duty of mourning for my death. It is true that you are also deprived of the inheritance of my estate, but this is a matter of indifference to you. You never attached any great value to money, and you have probably never even remembered that my maternal inheritance fell to you at my death."

"You do me but justice. I certainly never thought of that when I saw you alive before me. I did think of what I could reply to the countless inquiries that will be made of me as to where you have been and what you have been doing all these weeks."

"Tell the truth, sir. Say that you do not know, that your son is an incorrigible fellow, with no regard for the opinion of the world or for his father's feelings, and that he is resolved to act as he himself sees fit. Say this to all eager inquirers, and if they are not satisfied send them to me, and I will so answer them that they will not repeat their questions."

"You will make yourself impossible in society!"

"Precisely. I shall remain only a few days in Berlin, and may not return here for years."

The Councillor stared at his son with a comical expression of dismay. To him it was inconceivable that a young and wealthy man should propose voluntarily to leave Berlin. A visit to London, Paris, or Vienna was all very well in its way; he himself had never cared to see those cities, but he could understand how they might interest some men for a while; but to leave Berlin for years without being forced to do so! the thought was preposterous. "You are going away again?" he asked, incredulously.

"Yes; I shall be here but a few days. I returned only to show you and all my acquaintances that I am alive. I am tired of this insignificant existence, and am resolved to devote my future life to some serious pursuit. I shall, I think, pursue the study of agriculture for a year or longer, and so soon as I am capable of the management of a large estate I shall retire to Plagnitz, where I hope to play the part of an able agriculturist."

"I believe you are insane!" the Councillor exclaimed. The idea that Egon von Ernau, the spoiled darling of society, could desire to establish himself upon a West-Prussian estate as a simple agriculturist was monstrous, incredible!

Egon smiled involuntarily at his father's dismay. "You see, sir, I have very sensible and rather commonplace plans for the future. I hope you will approve them, although they surprise you at present. Of course I shall also want a wife. Here I shall meet your wishes. During the few days which I shall spend in Berlin, my betrothal with your choice for me, with Fräulein Bertha von Massenburg, can be announced publicly and cele-

brated by a brilliant *féte* after your own heart. As
soon as it is over I shall leave Berlin, and my marriage
will take place when my castle in Plagnitz is put in
a condition to be a worthy abode for my young wife,
and when I am fitted to undertake the management of
the estate."

Were the surprises which Egon had prepared for his
father never to come to an end? The shock of this last
announcement was too much for the Councillor's self-
control. He tossed aside his napkin, rose from his chair,
and hastily left the room, to return in a moment with
a note, which he handed to Egon. "Read that!" he said.

"I have the honour to announce to you the betrothal of my only daughter Bertha to Herr Hugo von
Wangen.

"Werner von Massenburg.

"Bertha von Massenburg.
"Hugo von Wangen.
"Betrothed."

The blood rushed to Egon's cheeks and there was a
mist before his eyes as he read these words. Bertha
betrothed to that insignificant, unintellectual, good-
natured young fellow! And this was the end of the
struggle through which he had passed in his sleepless
night at Hirschberg, where he had at last resolved
upon his future career! His plans were all annihilated
by a paltry bit of paper, on which was printed "Bertha
von Massenburg, Hugo von Wangen, betrothed."

If the Councillor's amazement at all that he had
seen and heard on this day could have been increased,
it would have been so by the alteration visible in his
son's features as he read this note. "What now?"

he exclaimed. "You are absolutely incomprehensible! When you could have had Bertha von Massenburg for a wife by simply saying 'yes,' you ran away to be rid of her, and now you look as if the lady's betrothal to another man were an immense disappointment to you. You have never seen her; it can make no possible difference to you whether you have her or somebody else for a wife, since you are resolved to marry and settle down as a country squire."

"True, sir, it can make no possible difference to me," Egon said, slowly, his eyes still fixed upon the note in his hand.

"Besides," the Councillor continued, "betrothed is not married. If your heart is so set upon this girl, which I never should have suspected, I will speak to Werner Massenburg about it. He consented to the present betrothal only to put a stop to disagreeable gossip. It will be easy to retract his consent, especially since your appearance gives him a reason for declaring the engagement to Wangen null and void. He will be glad, and so shall I, to have matters take the course we decided upon two months ago. Since you wish it, Egon, I will speak to him."

Lost in thought, Egon had not understood a word his father had uttered. The syllables had struck upon his ear without conveying any impression to his mental sense. When he heard his name spoken he started from his revery and rose. "I must now leave you, sir," he said.

"But you cannot possibly have eaten enough. Sit down and let us consult what is to be done."

"I really am unfit for discussion at present. I will go to my room. You can employ the afternoon in acquainting your friends with my return. To-morrow I

22

will pay the requisite visits, and then try to evoke some order out of the chaos that now reigns in my mind."

He left the room, and slowly walked through the familiar rooms and corridors until he reached his own apartments. Here nothing had been changed during his absence, and it seemed to him that he had been away but for a few hours. His lot appeared as empty and forlorn as when he had decided to put an end to his tedious existence: life was as comfortless and devoid of interest now as then. He threw himself upon a lounge, and buried his face among the cushions. He wished neither to see, to hear, nor to think. He sank into a half-unconscious state between waking and dreaming. Pictures from the past arose, mistily indistinct, before his mental vision. He saw himself as a little lonely child in his luxurious nursery, longing for affection, filled with childish envy of other children who might kiss and caress their father or mother; then he saw himself a youth among the throng of his fellow-students, all ready to flatter and fawn upon him so long as he lavished money upon them; then in society among women whom he despised and men who wearied him; then came the scene on the shore of the lake,—Pigglewitch's confession, and his own sudden impulse that led him into so wild an adventure. All these pictures were cloudy and vague, when suddenly there emerged from among them, in startling distinctness, Lieschen's image. He saw her as she looked upon the afternoon when she had asked counsel of him as she turned to him trustfully. How could he ever have forgotten for a moment that pure, confiding look?

And as once the reality, so now the remembrance affected him profoundly. He felt suddenly invigorated, strengthened for the further conflict of life; the dull despair that had assailed him when he saw all his plans crumble to ruins vanished; he was ashamed that the thought of Bertha should so have moved him, and that he should have again blindly followed the impulse of the moment. "Lieschen's pure memory shall be my guiding star," he said to himself, "in all the conflicts to come!"

He arose from the lounge, and just in time, for steps were heard in the corridor, his door was flung open, and there appeared on the threshold a man, tall and still handsome in spite of his years, followed by the Councillor. Egon recognized his visitor instantly, although he had never seen him before, so decided was his resemblance to his daughter.

"My son Egon, Herr von Massenburg," the Councillor said, introducing the young man to the stranger. But Werner von Massenburg put aside all formality, and, offering Egon his hand, said, with the greatest cordiality, "Pardon the informality of my visit, Herr von Ernau; its excuse is my great pleasure when I heard from my friend, your father, that our mourning for you is at an end, that you are restored to life. I could not but come to you immediately to express my joy."

Why should Egon be repelled by this frank display of cordiality? He could not tell. As Herr von Massenburg spoke, the resemblance between his daughter and himself increased; but this did not lessen Egon's distaste for the man. Every friendly word that he spoke seemed to the young fellow a conscious falsehood, and he reciprocated but coldly the other's kindness.

Nothing deterred by Egon's reserve of manner, Werner continued to pour forth his joy upon the occasion of this 'resurrection,' as he called it, and his self-congratulations that it was not too late to prevent the mischief which might have ensued upon any longer continuance in the belief of Egon's death. "Your father knows," he said, "how pained I was to be forced to resign all our delightful schemes for the union of our families, and that I am all the more rejoiced now that the hope of their fulfilment blooms afresh."

"If I am not mistaken, Fräulein von Massenburg is betrothed to a certain Herr von Wangen?" Egon said, quietly.

"True," Massenburg replied, no whit embarrassed. "In the distressing situation in which my daughter was placed, I was forced to have recourse to some means to vindicate her imperilled reputation. A very well-to-do landed proprietor, an honest but rather insignificant young fellow, proposed for her. I gave my consent, hard as it was for me, and harder still as it was for my daughter to submit to the lot thus decided upon for her. She considered herself, so she wrote me, as the widow of one so suddenly snatched from her and from the world. The supposition under which both Bertha and myself, as Herr von Wangen well knows, were induced to give our consent to the betrothal proves to be erroneous, and the betrothal is consequently void. I gladly consent to declare it so, since your father informs me of your readiness to accede to our old plans."

"But Fräulein von Massenburg and Herr von Wangen?" Egon asked.

"Bertha will be happy to be liberated from a tie that is odious to her, and Herr von Wangen must resign himself to the inevitable. I will write to him to-day, and shall rejoice to welcome you, my dear Ernau, as my future son-in-law."

"I regret, Herr von Massenburg," Egon said, quietly, but firmly, "that I can make no claim to the title with which you would honour me. I could never consent to be the cause of the rupture of an engagement which has been publicly announced."

"What new whim is this?" the Councillor exclaimed, angrily. "Why did you send me to Herr von Massenburg?"

"I did not send you, sir."

"But you made no reply when I told you that I would arrange that the betrothal should be declared void."

"I do not remember hearing you say a word upon the subject."

"Incredible!" the Councillor exclaimed, indignantly. "I expressly told you that I would dissolve the engage ment which seemed so obnoxious to you. For your sake, to fulfil your wishes, I went directly from the dinner-table to Herr von Massenburg, and now you leave me in the lurch, for the sake of heaven only knows what insane idea. It is too much, too much!"

"Indeed, Herr von Ernau," Werner von Massenburg went on to say, "your father's anger would be justifiable if you were in earnest in what you say, but that I am sure you are not. I respect the delicacy which makes you hesitate to be the cause of the rupture of a betrothal which has been publicly announced. But my daughter's engagement to Herr von Wangen was only a sad means of putting an end to much scandalous gossip. It was but an empty form, and owes its existence to the force put upon my daughter's will by myself."

That it was an empty form Egon knew only too well. He knew how gladly Bertha would escape from it did she but know who Herr von Ernau really was. Gottlieb Pigglewitch, the tutor at Castle Osternau, had learned thus much from many a glance of the large, dark eyes that had often robbed him of his rest. One word of his, a simple 'yes,' and she might yet be his wife.

'Lieschen's pure memory shall be my guiding star in all the future conflicts of life.' These words, which he had murmured to himself a few moments before, echoed in his soul. In imagination he saw her eyes bent on him in pity,—pity for the weakness of a nature prone to yield so readily to the impulse of the moment.

He hesitated no longer. "I deeply regret," he said, gravely, "if I have been the cause of Fräulein von Massenburg's contracting an engagement to which her heart is not a party, but in my opinion, and I trust in that of the young lady, a betrothal is no empty form. I should consider it an insult to Fräulein von Massenburg to suppose her capable of being false to her betrothal vow. I certainly never can give her occasion for being so, and I beg you, Herr von Massenburg, to consider this as my irrevocable resolve."

Werner von Massenburg had much ado to preserve his self-possession. He arose, and, with rage in his heart, said, coldly, "After so decided an expression of opinion there is no reason for another word upon this subject. I can only regret having been induced to comply with your request, Herr Councillor."

He then took a formal leave of Egon, and left the room, followed by the Councillor, who did not deign to bestow one farewell glance upon his son.

When Egon was once more alone he drew a deep breath of relief. For the first time in his life he had absolutely controlled an impulse to yield to the whim of the moment. He had resisted temptation in a most alluring form, and he might hope to date from this moment the dawn of a truer and nobler existence.

CHAPTER XX.

LINAU.

THE mansion-house of Linau, the German corruption of the Polish Linorov, is by no means an imposing residence. Many a wealthy peasant in Saxony can boast of a home grander in appearance than the seat of the ancient noble family which Hugo von Wangen inherited from his father, and in which he was living at present with his young wife and his orphan sister, four years after his marriage. Before his father's death the young couple had occupied a small but comfortable farm-house on the estate, to which Hugo had brought his bride, and where, in accordance with his father's ideas as to the frugality and economy proper to be observed by young people just beginning life, they would still have been residing, had not his father died two years after his son's marriage and bequeathed to him the large manor-house itself.

The old Herr left only two children behind him, a son and a daughter, the latter a child twelve years of age. His will declared his son Hugo the heir of his landed estate, and arranged that the daughter, whose inheritance consisted of a mortgage upon the estate, should find a home in her brother's house.

Hugo von Wangen gladly fulfilled the duty thus imposed upon him. He loved his sister dearly, and needed no injunction from his father to induce him to act the part of an affectionate protector to the girl, whose mother died shortly after her birth, having received

her son's solemn promise that he would be a faithful
brother to little Clara.

Thus, since the death of his father, Hugo von Wangen,
with his wife and sister, had inhabited the manor-house
of Linau.   It was a low, rambling assemblage of build-
ings, quite large enough for Hugo's wishes, as it had
been for those of his father, who had for many years
lived happily in it with his family and kept open house.
The guest-chambers were seldom empty, the hospitality
of the host had always been generous, and although
the style of living had been devoid of pretension to
modern elegance, there had never been any lack of
comfort in the old Von Wangen manor-house.

For Hugo, every piece of the quaint, old-fashioned
furniture, every nook and corner of the house, suggested some incident of his childhood, some tender recollection of the mother and father whose memory he
revered; but to his young, pleasure-loving wife the
place was odious. She begged that at least the old
furniture might be banished, to give place to what was
more worthy of a Herr von Wangen. To this Hugo
would in no wise consent, and it was with great reluctance that he yielded so far to his wife's wishes as to
have the finest of the rooms—one which opened by folding doors upon a large balcony built out over the garden
—given over entirely to her and newly furnished and
decorated according to her taste. In all the other
rooms the old articles of furniture in which he delighted
remained untouched, contrasting oddly enough with the
gorgeous arrangements of the garden-room, as it was
called. Here Bertha spent most of her time, sitting
in the balcony when the weather was fine, and receiving there the frequent visitors, who now as formerly were seldom wanting at Linau.

The tin roof of this addition to the garden-room protected it from sun and rain, and that it might be thoroughly warmed in winter Bertha had it enclosed with sashes of glass, which could be opened and closed at will.

Here, on a sultry day in August, we find Bertha, something more than four years after we last saw her in Osternau. The glass doors and sashes of the balcony were all wide open to admit every breath of air, and the fair mistress of the house was leaning back in an arm-chair, fanning herself lazily with a large lace fan, and evidently wearied and discontent.

There was not the faintest breeze stirring, and, low in the west, dark masses of clouds were slowly gathering; the afternoon sun was already hidden behind them, and they were mounting high above the tall shrubbery that bounded the lawn of the garden below the balcony.

"It is insufferably hot and sultry," Bertha sighed, laying aside the novel she had been reading. "In this wretched climate one either freezes with cold or melts with heat. Such a thing as a fair, mild summer afternoon is positively unknown in this odious Western Prussia."

Did she speak in soliloquy, or were her words addressed to the young lady who, seated at some distance at a table in the centre of the spacious balcony, was busy correcting a sketch by Clara, Hugo's young sister, who stood by intensely interested in the operation? It was impossible to say, for, as she spoke, Bertha's glance was directed to the distant horizon, and she fanned herself uninterruptedly. Nevertheless she expected an answer, and, receiving none, the movement of her fan grew more energetic, and there was a degree of ill

humour in the voice with which she said, sharply,
" Elise!"

There was such a tone of command in the word that
she who was thus addressed, and who was bending over
the drawing on the table, looked up from it startled.
Her charming face flushed slightly as she left her place
and approached Bertha in obedience to her call.

" I really think you might reply to me when I speak
to you," the latter said, as if aggrieved.

" I beg pardon! I really did not know that your remark was addressed to me."

" To whom else could I be speaking? You cannot
think me so silly as to sit here talking to myself. Do
try to pay a little attention to me."

Every word was uttered with an evident intention to
be disagreeable, but no retort was provoked from the
person addressed. In fact, she had no time to reply
before her young pupil eagerly took up her defence.
Clara threw down her pencil and turned sharply to her
sister-in-law: "What is it, Bertha? What has Elise
done to provoke you? How should she know that
your criticism of West Prussia was addressed to her?
It might as well have been uttered for my benefit, and
you may be sure I should have taken up the cudgels if
I had not been so busy over this miserable drawing."

The child was most attractive in her eager defence
of her teacher, but Bertha's ill humour made her blind
to any charm in her little sister, to whom she administered a sharp rebuke for want of respect to her brother's
wife, adding, " I cannot see, Elise, that your teaching is
likely to produce any very fine results here. Clara
grows too pert and insubordinate. I really must ask
Hugo to have her sent to some one of our many admirable boarding-schools, where she may have the

advantage of stricter discipline than any that can be exerted over her at home."

"No need to try that," Clara retorted; "Hugo never will consent. Papa has taken care of that, I know."

"Clara, Clara!" her governess interposed.

"Let me speak, Elise," Clara went on, putting aside the warning hand extended to her; "I must for this once. I cannot see why Bertha should treat you as she has so often done since you came to us, a month ago. I cannot help speaking of it. I love you dearly, and I will not have any one unkind to you if I can help it."

"Surely, Elise," Bertha said, angrily, "you must see that I am not called upon to endure this patiently. Fortunately, there comes Hugo: he will know how to put a stop to Clara's impertinence."

Hugo von Wangen was returning from an expedition to the neighboring town of G——. He had driven thither in the early morning, and had hastened his return to Linau that he might escape the storm threatening in the west. His vehicle was just entering the court-yard, whence he came immediately through the garden-room out on the balcony.

Hugo von Wangen had changed greatly in the past four years; the shy, retiring youth had developed into a strong, capable man. The good-natured expression of his kindly face was, however, unaltered, it was even more pronounced than it had formerly been. He could hardly be called a handsome man, but he certainly was pleasant to look upon.

As he appeared upon the balcony he was so pleased with his speedy return and the happy termination of his business in town, that he did not observe the frown upon his wife's brow.

"Fortunately back again before the storm," he called

out, gaily. "How are you, darling?" As he spoke he
bent above his wife and gave her a resounding kiss upon
her forehead, took Clara's head between his hands and
kissed her likewise, and then bowed to the governess
with a cordial, "Good-day, Fräulein Lieschen."

"Indeed, Hugo, I must beg you to dispense with the
babyish 'Lieschen' in addressing a young lady of
twenty-one," his wife said, sharply.

"You're right, my dear," he replied, good-humouredly.
"I forget myself, Fräulein Lieschen comes so naturally
to my lips; but I shall learn not to use it; so good-day,
Fräulein von Osternau. I am so glad to be at home
again, and I have had such a pleasure to-day. I met
an old acquaintance, or rather an old friend, most un-
expectedly in G——. Guess who it was, my dear,—you
know him, and so do you, Fräulein Lieschen,—I mean
Fräulein von Osternau."

Bertha had no desire to guess. She was contemplating
preferring a complaint of Clara's disrespect, but her interest was aroused when Wangen went on eagerly,—

"No, you could not possibly guess. Just as I had
got into the carriage to drive off from G——, whom
should I see coming striding down the street but my
dear old friend Storting? I jumped out of the carriage, and he was as much delighted as I was at our
meeting. I should have liked to talk for an hour with
him, but the skies looked so threatening I had to leave,
and he too was in a great hurry to get back to Plagnitz
before the storm came up."

"Plagnitz?" Bertha asked. "Is not that Herr von
Ernau's estate?"

"Yes, and that is the strangest part of the whole
story: Storting is now Herr von Ernau's head inspector."

At the sound of the name Ernau, Elise's attention was evidently attracted.

"Herr von Ernau?" she said. "Is that the same man——" Her glance fell upon Bertha, and she hesitated slightly. "I mean the Herr Egon von Ernau who——"

"You need not hesitate, Fräulein von Osternau," Wangen interposed with a laugh. "You can with an easy mind ask whether it is the same Herr von Ernau who ran away from the most charming of women, who was declared dead, and who afterwards came to life again, and has since been travelling or something of the kind. I am far too grateful to him for his folly, and I think Bertha is likewise, to find anything disagreeable in the recollection of him; indeed, I am quite curious to make his acquaintance."

"Does he live in this neighborhood?" Elise asked, evidently greatly interested.

"His principal estate, Plagnitz, is scarcely two miles from Linau, but he is not living there at present. No one knows exactly where he is. All his letters and papers are sent to his father's banking establishment in Berlin. Herr von Ernau has hitherto seemed to take very little interest in the management of his estates, except that a few years ago his requirements as to the accounts and remittances from Plagnitz became much more strict than they were formerly. His old superintendent, Sieveking, told me that he had never been there but twice, the last time about four years ago. On that occasion he made a very exact inspection of the entire estate, informed himself of every particular of its management, and took copious notes in his note-book, since which time he has never revisited the place, nor have any orders been received from him. He

informed the superintendent when he left, at the end of
two weeks, that he was about to undertake an extensive
agricultural tour, and that he intended at some future
time to assume the superintendence of his estates himself, but that in order to do so he must acquire a thorough knowledge of agriculture. Since then nothing has
been heard of him at Plagnitz. He must be a queer
fellow. I really am curious to know him. I suppose
he will be back here some day. What do you say,
Bertha, should not you like to see this eccentricity face
to face?"

" I really care nothing about it," Bertha said, shrug-
ging her shoulders indifferently.

" But I do. I should like to know how Storting will
get along with him," her husband went on; " he has
never seen him, he has not even corresponded with
him. Five weeks ago he saw in one of the country
papers that a head inspector was wanted on the
baronial estate of Plagnitz, further particulars to be
obtained at the office of the banking firm of A. C. Ernau
& Co., Berlin. He addressed a letter to that office, in-
quiring as to the terms upon which the place could
be obtained, declaring himself an applicant for the
situation, and offering to furnish testimonials as to his
capacity to fulfil its duties. Two weeks after sending
this letter he received a most amazing reply; any stipu-
lations which he might make were acceded to before-
hand, including the amount of his salary; it was en
tirely unnecessary to send in any testimonials; it was
desirable that he should enter upon the duties of his
office as soon as possible, to which end he was directed
to report at his earliest convenience to Herr Sieveking,
the administrator, who was instructed to comply with
all his requirements and to conclude the engagement

with him. The letter enclosed three hundred marks
for travelling expenses. Of course Storting instantly
betook himself to Plagnitz; old Sieveking, who has been
ailing for some time, and greatly in need of assistance
in his duties, received him with delight, and thus Storting has been installed at Plagnitz as head inspector
for more than two weeks, without ever handing in a
single testimonial as to his ability."

"He deserves such confidence," Elise said. "He is
an honest, excellent man, prudent, conscientious, diligent, and an admirable superintendent. My father
trusted him entirely."

"And he merited it, as I know well," said Wangen.
"Had I known that he was unemployed I should have
engaged him at any price; but how in the world did
they know of his admirable qualifications in the Ernau
counting-room? It is unprecedented, the engaging of
a head inspector without any examination of his testimonials."

Elise made no reply, but the shadowy smile that
hovered about her mouth seemed to indicate that she
had her own opinion with regard to what was so incomprehensible to Wangen, who dwelt at length upon
the unaccountable bestowal of Herr von Ernau's confidence. He was very sorry that he had been able to
have only five minutes of conversation with Storting,
but he was resolved to drive over to Plagnitz shortly
and have a talk with his friend about the dear old
times.

At mention of the dear old times Elise sighed, whereupon Bertha bestowed upon her a glance of displeasure:
she too remembered them, but they were anything but
dear to her. Suddenly recalling in her displeasure her
cause of offence with Clara, she said, ill-humouredly,

" We have had enough of your Herr Storting for the present: the account of your meeting him drove out of my head for a while the urgent request I was about to make you that Clara should be sent to boarding-school. You have no idea how pert and headstrong the child is becoming. Elise seems quite unable to govern her, and I really must appeal to you, both for the girl's sake and my own. Elise's incapacity is a great disadvantage to her pupil."

" That is not true !" Clara declared.

" Hush, Clara! I am talking with your brother and guardian."

" But, Bertha, I cannot hush when you say what is not true. You began our quarrel, and Elise did all she could to prevent it. It was your fault that I was pert; you made me angry by threatening to ask Hugo to send me away from here——"

" That is precisely what I ask of him," Bertha angrily declared. " You hear, Hugo, how impertinent the child is. You cannot hesitate as to what should be done."

She was angrier than her husband had ever before seen her, but her anger became her. To Hugo she looked adorably beautiful, with her large black eyes flashing, her cheeks flushed, and her lovely lip curled. He did not like angry people, he was too easy and good-natured himself, but even anger charmed him in his wife. He said, smiling, " My darling, my darling, you exaggerate. Fräulein von Osternau, will you have the goodness to take Clara to her room for a while, that I may quietly discuss this matter with my wife ?"

Elise inclined her head in assent and withdrew, taking Clara with her. The girl went willingly, but cast a glance of defiance at her sister-in-law as she left the room, thus further exasperating Bertha's angry mood. "Surely, Hugo," she said, when the husband and wife were alone together, "you cannot wish to expose me to such insult at the hands of a child? I cannot have Clara in the house any longer."

"You will listen to reason, darling," Wangen replied, in his easy, good-humoured way, "when your present irritation has subsided. You know how gladly I comply with every wish of yours if I can do so, but you must not require of me the impossible. Clara is my only sister. I promised my mother on her death-bed to be a father to her, and I promised my father never to allow her to leave me, except to become the wife of some worthy man. I cannot break such promises; and really the child is good at heart and affectionate; she is a little pert and forward, perhaps, but she responds instantly to kindness. You see how devotedly attached she has become to Elise."

"That is just it. Although you will not see it, they are leagued against me. Elise hates me. Years ago, at Castle Osternau, she showed only too plainly her invincible dislike of me. I never can forget how I was forced then to feign affection for her, and how she never neglected an opportunity to repulse me. Then I was dependent, now it is her turn,—her turn to feign and dissemble, although I can see how it galls her pride to do so."

"My dear Bertha, what do you mean? If I did not know how really kind and good you are, such words as these would make me doubt you; but I know you better. It was your proposal to engage Lieschen for Clara's governess, and to give her a salary so large as to enable her to support her poor mother. Your unwillingness to suffer the unfortunate girl to go among strangers bore testimony to your goodness of heart."

Bertha's expression of face, as her husband spoke thus, was not pleasant to see. "We'll say nothing more of Elise," she said. "She can remain here as my companion, but Clara must be sent to boarding-school."

"I told you that I could not break my promise. I must tell you now that by the conditions of my father's will I could not if I would. I did not wish to annoy you, and so I have hitherto refrained from explaining these conditions to you, but there is no help for it. You must know that it is impossible to send Clara away if we would retain possession of the estates."

"But how can this be? Explain to me exactly how your father's will is expressed."

"I should greatly prefer not doing so, but, since there is no help for it, you must know that in the last years of his life my father regarded you with a certain suspicion which I could not allay. He conceived an idea that when he was no longer here you would use your influence with me to induce me to remove to Berlin, and that you would find in Clara an obstacle to your schemes. I did all I could to disabuse him of his mistrust of you, dear, but in vain, and he gave it expression in his will, by which I am not the proprietor of the estates; their income is mine only so long as Clara is brought up beneath my roof. Upon the day of her marriage, if she lives until then with me, the estates become my own. My father had a horror of boarding-schools for girls, and expressly forbade my sending Clara to any such. Should I transgress the injunctions laid upon me by his will, Clara becomes his residuary legatee. The value of his property is legally appraised, and my share will be only that which the law allows me. The same result will ensue should Clara, through my own or my wife's unkindness, be forced to leave my house before she is of age; as to the sufficiency of her provocation the courts would decide. My father provided for all possible contingencies. The will is drawn up by an admirable lawyer, Councillor Herder, and I could not possibly evade its provisions, even should I be so lacking in filial respect as to endeavour to do so."

"Does Clara know of all this?"

"I believe Councillor Herder has informed her upon the subject. She is a great pet of his, as you know, and he is her godfather. You know, too, that he has always been somewhat prejudiced against you; indeed, dear, you have not treated him with quite the respect due to an old friend of the family. And now you see that I could not send Clara away from home if I would, and I frankly confess to you that even if I could I would not. Only try to win the child's affection and it will be given to you without reserve, and you will be glad to have her with us."

"I am, then, to kiss the hand that smites me?" Bertha rejoined, with bitterness. "It does not make me love the child any better to have her thus forced upon me. But you may rest easy, Hugo, I understand it all now, and you may be sure that I never shall give your sister an opportunity to use her power against us. She is quite aware of the extent of it, and would doubtless hail an occasion for exercising it. Be sure that I will so conduct myself that no court in Prussia would justify her in leaving your house and defrauding you of your inheritance."

Wangen was deeply grieved by his wife's words and her manner of speaking; for the first time he entertained suspicions as to the genuineness of her kindness of heart. All such he had hitherto banished, reproaching himself at her first kind word for even allowing their shadow to cross his mind. To-day he could not lay them to rest, he was so hurt by his wife's open expression of her dislike of his pet Clara.

CHAPTER XXI.

AN ACCIDENT.

THE rain rattled against the glass enclosure of the balcony, flash after flash of lightning illumined the darkness, and the crashing thunder shook the walls of the old manor-house of Linau to their foundations.

Hugo von Wangen was pacing the spacious room restlessly to and fro. The storm had been raging for more than two hours. The rain was falling in torrents, and through it could be heard the rushing noise of the brook at the end of the garden,—it was plainly overflowing its banks.

"The storm is increasing," said Wangen, and his words instantly received confirmation from an intensely vivid flash of lightning, followed by a reverberating clap of thunder. The panes in the windows shook almost to breaking, and the howling of the blast all but drowned the sound of his voice.

"You make me very nervous," Bertha said, "by pacing backwards and forwards in that manner, like some wild animal in a cage. Come and sit down with us, your restlessness can do no good."

Wangen did not heed her; he quickened his steps, his anxiety evidently increasing every minute. "I hope there has been no accident," he said. "The Dombrowker bridge is unsafe at the best of times, and very dangerous in a storm like this."

"Don't worry yourself, Hugo," Clara rejoined, leaving the table where she had been seated at her embroidery and affectionately putting her arm through her brother's as he pursued his restless walk. "Herr Kämpf is with the men, and he is so prudent he will see that nothing happens. Perhaps he has not started from the station, but is waiting there for the storm to abate."

"Clara is right," Bertha said, kindly. Since Elise and her charge had made their appearance again at supper the mistress of the house had been once more all sweetness and amiability, and had seemed desirous of effacing any unfavorable impression produced by her previous ill humour. "Herr Kämpf is certainly waiting at the station. He must have seen the storm coming up all the afternoon."

"That is just why he will surely have driven over,—it came up so very slowly, and then burst forth with such sudden fury. Something must surely have hap——"

He interrupted himself to listen. The noise of the rain beating against the glass panes was fainter for the moment, and Wangen distinctly heard the rolling of wheels in the court-yard.

It ceased, and the next moment the door of the garden-room was hurriedly opened, and Inspector Kämpf appeared on the balcony. The water was dripping from his wet and muddy overcoat, and his hair hung in damp, straight strings over his sunburned forehead.

"Thank God you are back again!" Wangen exclaimed, hastening to meet him, but pausing as he looked into the troubled face of the man, who turned in some hesitation from him to the ladies.

"We are back again," the inspector said, after an instant's pause. "The first carriage is here, the other is directly behind us, nothing has happened to us, but —I should be sorry to startle madame and the ladies, but—there has been an accident. A stranger left the station a short time before us in a one-horse light wagon, and wagon and horse fell over the cliffs in the Dombrowker Pass. The driver is dead, and the stranger is senseless. He fell but a short distance, but there is a wound upon his forehead,—he must have struck his head against a stone. We put him into our foremost wagon and brought him here; there was nothing to be done for the unfortunate driver. The storm was furious, and we have been obliged to drive very slowly. The stranger may revive, but I fear——the men are now bringing him into the hall."

As he spoke, the sound of many footsteps and a murmur of low voices were heard in the hall, whither Wangen instantly went, followed by the inspector, Elise, Clara, and last by Bertha.

The spacious hall was filled with men-servants and maids, who had hurried hither from all parts of the house and stables upon hearing of the accident. The unconscious stranger had been carefully brought in from the wagon and laid upon various wraps on the floor of the hall, where men and maids were crowding about him, whispering their pity and dismay, and wondering who the unfortunate man could be lying there as pale and lifeless as the poor driver, whose body had just arrived in the second wagon.

No one knew him, not even Herr Berndal, the second inspector, who had lived at Linau for years, and who knew every one in all the country round. One of the men affirmed that he had seen the gentleman get out of a first-class carriage when the train arrived at the railway-station. He must be a rich man, he thought, for he had a very grand air, and the station-master had bowed low to him and had sent one of the porters to get him a conveyance immediately.

There was nothing of the grand air to be seen now in the senseless figure lying there, his clothes muddy and disordered, his face ghastly pale and stained with the blood that trickled from a wound in the forehead, now half concealed by the thick dark hair. The features were scarcely distinguishable in the fitful light of the candles in the hall and of a stable lantern held by one of the men, but the maid at the man's elbow whispered that the poor gentleman would be very fine-looking if he were not so horribly pale, and he could not be over thirty at most.

The whispering suddenly ceased when Herr von Wangen appeared, and the servants respectfully made way for the new arrivals.

Wangen looked down compassionately upon the unconscious man; Bertha, after one timid glance at the motionless form, hid her face in her hands and turned away in horror; while Elise stooped, and, gently brushing aside the hair from the wound, listened eagerly, in hopes of catching some faint sound of breathing from the parted lips.

"There is hope," she said, gently: "he is still living." Then, as the light of the lantern held by the man beside her fell full upon the stranger's face, she started, grew very pale, and with difficulty suppressed a cry of horror. "Good God!" she whispered, "it is he! Oh, horrible!"

Her start, her change of colour, and her whispered words attracted Bertha's attention again, and Wangen, no less amazed, bent over the prostrate figure and eagerly examined the lifeless features. "You know him?" he asked, hurriedly. "Yes, yes; I too have seen that face before, but where? Now I remember —at Castle Osternau. Surely it is the Candidate who disappeared so suddenly, the tutor with the odd name, —yes, I remember it now,—Pigglewitch."

The name, even at this moment, called forth a smile from some of the servants, but Wangen exclaimed, eagerly, "There! his lips moved, he will recover! Help me, Hans, instantly to take him up gently and carry him to the blue room, it is ready for guests. Be careful! he is coming to himself."

And, all alert in the hope of the stranger's recovery, Wangen himself supported the head and shoulders of the wounded man, and, with the help of the groom, carried him slowly up the steep staircase to the designated guest-chamber and laid him upon the huge old-fashioned bed. Elise walked beside the bearers, lending what aid she could, and never heeding that the blood, which was beginning to flow freely from the wound in the unfortunate man's forehead, was staining her hands and her dress.

"We must have medical aid immediately," Wangen said, when his burden had been safely deposited in the blue room; "every minute is precious."

He was interrupted by a vivid flash of lightning and a terrific clap of thunder, the echo of which was drowned in the dashing of the rain against the rattling window-panes.

"No servant will venture to drive to Ostrowko in such a night as this," Inspector Berndal declared; "we shall have to wait until the storm abates. It would be impossible to brave its fury."

Elise had occupied herself in arranging the pillows about the wounded man's head, after sending a maid for water to wash the wound, but as the words of the inspector fell upon her ear she turned to him, and said, quietly, "I know the road to Ostrowko perfectly well. I will drive over there and bring the doctor if you will have a vehicle made ready for me."

"What! you drive to Ostrowko in this storm, Fräulein Lieschen? Impossible!"

"You forget that I am a country girl, and accustomed from my earliest childhood to drive alone over the roughest possible roads. My sight is keen, my hand is sure. I know the road, and am not afraid either of the darkness or of the storm. Delay may imperil a human life; you have just said that every minute is precious, Herr von Wangen. You must not prevent my going to Ostrowko."

The inspector looked admiringly at the girl, who announced her daring resolve as quietly as if it were the easiest and most natural of undertakings.

"I really believe you would do as you say, Fräulein von Osternau," he said, "but it is out of the question. I never could look any one in the face again if I allowed you to go. I will go for the doctor, and bring him back with me as soon as may be."

"You have just got home," Elise remonstrated.

"All the more reason why I should be the one to go out again,—I could not possibly be wetter than I am. I shall bring the doctor back with me."

He was so evidently resolved to go that Elise did not gainsay him, but quietly declared her intention to stay beside the wounded man until the doctor arrived.

Wangen suggested that, since the poor fellow was unconscious, the housekeeper or one of the maids might just as well relieve her of this duty; but Elise was firm, and Bertha supported her in her decision, although in a mocking way that was very irritating. "Let her do as she wishes," she said to her husband, quite loud enough to be heard by the self-constituted nurse. "It will be a comfort to her. Do you remember her enthusiasm for her music-teacher when she was but seventeen? She preserved his image faithfully in her heart and recognized him immediately. We ought not to interfere with her."

Elise blushed painfully, but she suppressed the bitter retort that rose to her lips. Clara threw her arms round her and whispered to her, "Don't let her distress you, darling Elise. She grows worse and worse; you must not mind her."

Wangen, too, was grieved by Bertha's tone and manner, reminding him as it did of his late interview with her, and his voice was not so cordial as usual as he rejoined, "This is no time for jesting, Bertha. Come, let us leave Fräulein Lieschen to her work of mercy. The poor man could not be in better hands."

CHAPTER XXII.

AN OLD ACQUAINTANCE.

EGON awakened as from a long, deep slumber. He opened his eyes, and was conscious of a dull pain in his head, and of a burning, pricking sensation in his forehead; he raised his hand to it, and his fingers encountered a wet linen bandage, while he observed that the place in which he was was entirely strange to him. He had never before seen the blue and white draperies of this room, nor had he any recollection of its rather quaint but comfortable furniture.

How had he come here? and why was his head bandaged? He closed his eyes again and tried to collect himself, finding that, in spite of the pain in his head, he was able to think connectedly. He had certainly arrived shortly before at Station R——. He had asked a porter to get him a conveyance to take him to Plagnitz. The man had been eager to serve him; but had not some one warned him against driving along so rough a road in such a storm? Yes; he remembered this quite well, and that he had laughed at the speaker's warning, and had driven off in the pouring rain, and in a pitchy darkness which was illuminated every moment or two by vivid flashes of lightning. The driver had grumbled and sworn in a mixture of Polish and German, and the vehicle had dragged on at a snail's pace, because its one horse scarcely sufficed to pull it through the mud that came up to the hubs of the wheels.

Egon had shivered in his wraps, which did not avail to protect him from the drenching rain, and then—what happened then? He remembered a jolt, a cry, and nothing more. But yet—yes, there were flitting, vague visions still haunting his memory. Had not he been faintly conscious of a light flashing in his eyes? And he had seen a crowd of dark, dim forms about him, not all quite strange to him. Surely, while he had been powerless to move a limb, he had felt rather than seen the compassionate gaze of two dark blue eyes in an angelic countenance. Was it a dream? Ah! during the last four years that face had often haunted his dreams, —the face of the fairy of Castle Osternau. It was her face, and yet not the same,—even more lovely than ever. Yes, this too was a dream, this touch of her soft, cool hand upon his forehead, and it so absorbed him that he could not rouse himself to a sense of reality; he went on dreaming, and a voice which he had surely heard at Castle Osternau said, at last, "We have been longing for you, doctor."

And another voice, which Egon did not know, replied, "I am very sorry, Herr von Wangen, but I could not possibly be here before. I trust I am not too late."

"I hope not, indeed." Egon recognized this voice perfectly: it was Herr von Wangen's. "The poor man's condition is unaltered. His kind nurse has just informed me that during her watch all night beside him he has never awaked to consciousness, although his breathing has been quite regular. The door on your left, doctor; he is in the blue room."

Egon opened his eyes again as the door of the room was opened and the speakers entered. One of them was Herr von Wangen. Egon recognized him immediately, in spite of the increase of manliness which the past four years had imparted to him. The other was an elderly man, an entire stranger.

This was no dream; here was Herr von Wangen in the flesh. Egon roused himself. He was on a bed, with a wound in his forehead, in a perfectly strange room; but how he came there, or what had happened, he could not divine.

"Aha! our patient is entirely conscious, a very cheering sign," said the doctor, approaching the bed. "No fever! Why, he'll soon be all right. You have distressed yourself very unnecessarily, Herr von Wangen."

He proceeded to examine the wound in the young man's forehead, which he pronounced of no consequence. "The shock of the fall had stunned him,—had produced unconsciousness. You have had a very lucky escape."

"What happened to me?"

"Herr von Wangen will tell you all about it. You really do not need my aid; you're a little weak from loss of blood, and I dare say you still have some headache. Be careful for a few days to take no amount of exercise, and you'll be all right. I must bid you good-by immediately and return to Ostrowko, where they really need me."

"May Herr Pigglewitch get up?" asked Herr von Wangen.

"If he feels like it; he can do as he pleases. Goodby, Herr—— Pigglewitch, I believe?" and a faint smile hovered about the doctor's lips.

"No, my name is Von Ernau," Egon rejoined, simply.

"What the deuce! Herr von Ernau, the long-expected proprietor of Plagnitz?" the doctor exclaimed, evidently much pleased. "Ah, this will delight my old friend Sieveking; and Herr Storting, too, has been very

24*

Involuntarily Egon's slow steps were stayed. There was something about the child that reminded him of Lieschen as he had first seen her. For an instant the present vanished, and he was standing, in the form of 'the new tutor,' at his window at Castle Osternau. Merry laughter floated upward from the lawn, and two children came flying out of the shrubbery. Lieschen's image as he had then seen it arose vividly before his mind's eye in all its innocent charm; but another moment brought him back to reality, and he knew that he was in a strange house, and that courtesy required that he should show himself aware of the presence of the new-comer. He bowed as ceremoniously as he would have done to a woman grown, and surveyed the pretty girl with great interest. Indeed, there was something of Lieschen in the arch sparkle of her eyes and in the girlish grace of her movements.

Clara paused also as she became aware of the stranger's presence, and returned his bow with a charming little courtesy. Then, suddenly approaching him, she said, "Are you Herr von Ernau, of whom I have heard so much? Oh, I thought you would look so different!"

"Indeed? And in what does the reality differ from the picture you condescended to frame of my insignificance?"

"I can't exactly say, but you are very—— Of course that bandage disfigures you, and you will look better when you have recovered from losing so much blood. Do you feel better? Are you strong enough to go alone, or shall I support you? Oh, you think I am too little to be of any use; but indeed you are mistaken, I am very strong. Lean on me. Indeed you do need help, you look so terribly pale and tired."

"I thank you for your kind offer of help, but——"

large a share of her attention upon the Candidate, or had listened in rapt admiration to his singing.

All these thoughts passed like lightning through Wangen's mind while recovering from his astonishment. "Are you then Herr Egon von Ernau?" he said, at last.

"Yes, Herr von Wangen, you find an old acquaintance under this name. I will explain the metamorphosis to you; but first gratify my burning curiosity, and be kind enough to tell me how I came here and what has happened to me. The past night is a blank in my memory."

Egon's questions restored Wangen's equanimity; he seated himself by the bed, and told his guest the whole story of his inspector's arrival with the wounded stranger, and of the accident that had occurred, finally depicting his wife's and his own anxiety, now happily dispelled by Egon's return to life.

He found an eager listener; when he alluded to his wife Egon remembered the vision of the past night. Now he knew whose was the gentle hand that had lain so cool and soft upon his forehead. How strange that he should, in his vague semi-consciousness, have taken Bertha for Lieschen! But it had sometimes happened during the past years that the two had been confounded in his dreams, although Bertha's image had gradually faded from his memory, while Lieschen's lovely face still frequently haunted him. He felt something akin to disappointment on learning that Bertha had been his kind attendant, but he banished the feeling as rank ingratitude; he thanked Wangen warmly for his kindness and hospitality, adding a short explanation of the manner in which he had come to play the part of Cand'date Pigglewitch at Castle Osternau.

beautiful even than the picture of her which he had preserved in his memory. Her figure had not lost one whit in grace, while it had gained in fulness and finish. Her dark eyes sparkled and she smiled bewitchingly as she held out both hands to him, with "Welcome! a thousand times welcome, Herr von Ernau! Ah, what an anxious night you have given us!"

'You'd better be careful with Bertha.' The words occurred to Egon as he kissed the fair hand extended to him and felt its lingering pressure. The ordeal through which he was passing could hardly have been imagined by the child who had just left him, and yet her words helped him to suppress all evidence of emotion, although his heart did undeniably beat faster and louder.

"Your kind welcome, madame, gives me courage to hope that you forgive me for once deceiving you with a name and personality not my own, and——"

"I will not hear one more word that bears reference to the past, Herr von Ernau. It lies far behind us, and I have made a vow to forget it and to think only of the present and the future. Promise me to follow my example."

"It shall be as you please, madame."

"And I please to forget everything that is not delightful. We are near neighbours, I hope we shall frequently see each other, and I promise never to ask you a single question about your masquerading time. You must dismiss it from your thoughts."

"That will not be so easy. I should like to explain——"

"But I always detested explanations. What interests me at present is that you should take a com-

fortable chair and rest yourself: you are weak from loss
of blood. You are trembling : take my arm."

In truth Egon was giddy for a moment, and involuntarily availed himself of the hand she extended to him.
Wangen came forward to assist his wife, and conducted
Egon to a luxurious chair on the balcony, where Bertha
flitted about him, placing the cushions comfortably beneath his head, silently lavishing upon him a hundred
little kindnesses, which scarcely contributed to dispel
a certain embarrassment which began to possess him.
Wangen was unwontedly silent; in truth his thoughts,
like those of his wife and his guest, were busy with the
past. Although hardly of a jealous temperament, his
sense of his wife's intellectual superiority was always
present to prompt him to self-depreciation, and he had
remembered more than once during the morning the
many brilliant qualities which he had long since heard
attributed to Egon von Ernau,—the same man who, mar-
vellously enough, had played the part of the Candidate
at Castle Osternau. As he marked his wife's eager attention to their guest it occurred to him to wonder—it
was but a passing thought—whether Bertha had not
once been more interested in the tutor than she would
have cared to admit. He felt ashamed of himself on
the instant that such an idea should have found entrance in his mind, and yet he could not quite forget it.

His wife's influence, however, was so great over his
moods that she soon conquered his taciturnity, and
Egon was both interested and charmed by the lively
talk that occupied the next hour. Bertha passed in
review for her guest's entertainment and information
all the principal persons in the neighborhood. True,
her wit was sometimes far from kindly, but her tact
was great, and she was quick to mark and to obliterate

any adverse impression with regard to herself which she might produce. He therefore resigned himself to the spell of the moment, and had quite forgotten the unfortunate cause of his presence in Linau, when Inspector Kämpf made his appearance to announce to Wangen that the conveyance was about to start for Station R——· with the body of the unfortunate driver. This recalled Egon to a sense of reality, the spell of the moment was broken; he begged the inspector to inform himself as to the poor man's family, for whose future he should care, and then, turning to Wangen, asked that he would kindly allow him the use of a vehicle in which to drive immediately to Plagnitz.

"Impossible! Indeed you cannot, you must not leave us, Herr von Ernau," Bertha exclaimed, in answer to his request. "You must stay in Linau until your wound is healed. We cannot let you go until you are perfectly strong."

Wangen added his entreaties to his wife's, although not with the same urgency, but Egon was firm. He declared that it was a matter of necessity that he should be in Plagnitz before evening, that he was quite strong enough to undertake the short journey thither, and that, with many thanks for the kind hospitality extended to him at Linau, he was resolved not to trespass upon it further. Neither Wangen nor Bertha could turn him from his purpose, and the former therefore yielded to his request, and directed Inspector Kämpf to have a light wagon made ready for Herr von Ernau's use.

CHAPTER XXV.

AT HOME.

THE old administrator, Sieveking, at Plagnitz, had at last actually taken to his bed, and the whole responsibility of the management of the estate devolved upon Storting. He was quite equal to it, but just at present he was rather anxious; a few days previously a magnificent grand piano, with several large cases of books, had arrived from Berlin, addressed to Herr Egon von Ernau, Plagnitz, and it was evident that the proprietor of the estate was shortly to arrive and establish himself in his home.

There were many matters not yet ordered as Storting could have wished. Herr Sieveking belonged to the old school of agriculture; he was an old man, and had been ailing for some time; abuses had crept into his management which Storting had not been able to reform in the short time that had elapsed since his installation as inspector.

Thus the honest fellow was anticipating the arrival of the unknown proprietor with a degree of trepidation of which he was quite conscious, when, upon returning at noon from some distant fields, he became aware of a light carriage rolling along the road that led to the manor-house.

The gentleman leaning back in it must, of course, be Herr von Ernau; but no, it was not he. Storting's keen gaze recognized an old acquaintance, in spite of the distance and of the bandage beneath his hat. The

pale face in the rapidly-approaching wagon was that
of the Candidate Pigglewitch!

The inspector overtook the vehicle as it was turning
into the court-yard. "Welcome, Herr Pigglewitch!" he
cried, jumping on the step of the light conveyance,
and extending his hand to its occupant. "How odd!
Yesterday I met Wangen, and to-day you arrive at
Plagnitz. This is an unexpected pleasure; you are
cordially welcome."

Egon grasped the hand extended to him. "Your
hearty greeting shows me that you at least bear me no
grudge, Storting," he said, with some emotion. "I
trust you will think none the worse of me when I tell
you that I have no claim to the name by which you
knew me. I am called Egon von Ernau."

Storting's surprise was so unfeigned, and his stare
one of such blank amazement, that Egon burst into a
laugh. "Why, what's the matter, Storting? Were you
so attached to the Candidate with the charming name
that his sudden disappearance fills you with dismay?
I assure you that Egon von Ernau is excessively like
him, except that just at present he is rather shaky from
a fall over the Dombrowker Pass, and will thank you to
lend him an arm, that he may enter his home with becoming dignity."

The carriage stopped before the principal entrance.
Storting opened the door, silently offered his arm to
Egon, and conducted him up the steps and into a lux-
uriously-furnished room.

In truth the lord of Plagnitz had, in his impatience
to be really at home, rather overrated his strength. He
begged to be left to himself for a while, and throwing
himself upon a lounge, fell almost immediately into the
profound sleep of exhaustion, from which he did not

awake until after several hours. The housekeeper answered his bell, and upon his declaring himself positively famished hurried away to see that dinner was instantly served for the master so anxiously expected. To this Egon did ample justice, and when Storting again made his appearance, just as dessert was placed upon the table, he was eagerly welcomed. Egon told him of the accident of the previous evening, which made it unwise for him to attempt as yet any inspection of his fields and meadows. He regretted this all the more as he was anxious to show Herr Storting that he was now really capable of appreciating his valuable services. "And we should have grown very confidential, Storting, tramping around together. You know, I owe you an explanation of the sudden transformation of your old acquaintance Pigglewitch into Egon von Ernau, and this you shall have, even if I am tied to the house for a day or two. Sit down, take a glass of wine, make yourself comfortable, and we will each unfold the tale of the years that have passed since we last saw each other."

Storting readily complied, and eagerly awaited the solution of the riddle that had frequently occupied him during the past four years. He had, of course, suspected that there was a story attached to the tutor who rode so wonderfully, played billiards with such skill, was so admirable a musician, spoke French, English, and Italian fluently, and was rich enough, although he had as yet received no salary from Herr von Osternau, to remit, after his departure from the castle, the amount of a debt which he had contracted, but it had never entered the inspector's head that the Herr von Ernau, who had been so often and so severely

26

criticised at Osternau, and the Candidate tutor were one and the same.

Egon leaned back in his arm-chair, and after a few moments' pause began his story, and, just as he had done long ago to the wretched Candidate on the shore of the little lake, told of his unhappy childhood and youth, and of his weariness of life. From this he went on to his sudden resolve to purchase the name and papers of the unfortunate Candidate. He condemned in sharp terms his useless, misspent existence before going to Castle Osternau, and spoke with reverential admiration of Herr von Osternau and his family, gratefully acknowledging the influence which the life at the castle had exercised upon his entire manner of thought. He told of his determination to turn his energies to some account, and of his pursuit of the study of agriculture during the past four years. He frankly confessed his faults and failings, and extenuated none of his follies. Upon one point alone he was silent: to no human being could he accord a glimpse of the inner sanctuary of his heart.

"And here you have me," he said, at the end of his story, "with a broken head, to be sure, but perfectly sound in limb, having escaped the death which befell my ill-fated driver, and all ready to begin my life as a country gentleman, in which I rely, Storting, upon your advice and assistance. I have been thus frank with you, because it seemed to me an absolute necessity that you, who once befriended me so unselfishly, should know me as I am. In fact, I should now like, if possible, to obliterate your memory of that aimless, idle, good-for-nothing fellow who came as tutor to Castle Osternau. He had but one good quality: he was not vain, and when he got among really capable, intelligent people he recognized his own worthlessness. He did not deserve such friends, but the ambition to be worthy of them arose within him, giving a new interest to existence. Yes, I learned from you, Storting, and especially from that admirable old Herr von Osternau, how there could be no weariness in a life of constant occupation directed towards worthy aims. I had to begin at the beginning; I attempted no royal road to the knowledge which was to shape my future career. I obtained a subordinate position on an estate in Saxony, and worked my way up. Now I am ready to reap the benefit of these years of hard work,— work that has been a positive blessing to me. And now, enough of myself and my doings, tell me of yourself, and of those among whom I was so happy for a while that I could scarcely carry out my plan of not returning to them. Tell me of Herr von Osternau, Storting, and why you resigned your position with him."

Storting looked in amazement at Egon as he thus calmly asked for news of the Osternau family. "Is it possible, Herr von Ernau," said he, "that you know nothing, positively nothing, of what happened at Castle Osternau scarcely three months after you left it?"

"Such is the case," Egon replied. "When I resolved to begin a new life I rigorously broke with all old associations, and although I could not drive Castle Osternau from my memory, I strictly refrained from informing myself with regard to its inmates. But my finding Wangen and his wife yesterday and seeing you to-day have called up old associations so vividly that I beg you to tell me minutely of every one of the Osternau circle,—of Herr and Frau von Osternau, of Fräulein Lieschen, of my pupil Fritz,

even of Lieutenant Albrecht, if you will.   I am eager
for it all."

Storting gazed sadly at his companion.   "Your eagerness to hear, Herr von Ernau, makes it even harder to
tell you of the terrible misfortunes that have befallen
Castle Osternau and its inmates."

"You amaze and distress me.   Is Herr von Osternau
not living then?"

"He has been at rest in the graveyard at Osternau
for almost four years.   I have a sad story to tell you,
Herr von Ernau.   It all happened in the night of the
18th of November.   I had been to Breslau on that day
to draw the money to be paid for the Wernewitz and Rudersdorf farms, which Herr von Osternau had bought.
I was tired out with travelling in the cold November weather, and of course slept more soundly than
usual.   In the middle of the night I was wakened by a
bright light shining into my face, and I sprang out of
bed to find the flames leaping up to my window from
the story below.   You remember my room was directly
above that of Herr and Frau von Osternau.   I threw on
my clothes and opened my door; the passages were filled
with stifling smoke.   The fire must have broken out
in Herr von Osternau's study adjoining his bedroom,
and the lives of himself and his wife were in danger.
The staircase was already in flames.   My only course
was to climb from one of my windows down into the
court-yard, which I accomplished successfully, shouting
the while at the top of my voice to arouse the servants
and labourers from the various farm-buildings.   Two
grooms, who had rooms in one of the barns, were the
first to appear, when suddenly Lieutenant Albrecht
stood beside me; whence he had come I could not tell,
but he must have been aware of the fire for some time,

for he was entirely dressed. The instant I looked
at him a terrible suspicion occurred to me. 'Good
heavens! what a misfortune!' he said. His face was
ghastly pale, and his eyes avoided mine. I made no
reply, the urgency was too pressing. Every minute
the flames were gaining ground. They had caught the
curtains of the open window of my room, and as yet
Herr and Frau von Osternau gave no sign of being
awakened by them. Had the fire reached their room,
or were they already smothered? I rushed to the side-
entrance, forgetting that it was always locked at night
from within. I found it, however, unfastened, and
as I flung it wide open a huge tongue of flame burst
from the open door of the study. There was no reaching Herr von Osternau's bedroom by this way, neither
could either of its occupants have penetrated through
the smoke and flames of the study to gain safety. The
only possible way to reach them was from the garden,
upon which their bedroom windows opened. Meanwhile all the farm-people were thronging the court-yard;
the fire-engine had been dragged from its shed, but
there was no one to take the lead there, for Lieutenant Albrecht seemed paralyzed, and I was intent upon
saving my good old employers. In the garden I found
one window of their bedroom open, and the smoke
pouring from it in volumes. I called Herr von Osternau
loudly, but there was no reply. Two stout labourers
lifted me upon their shoulders, and I leaped thence into
the room. Near the window on the floor I found both
of those whom I sought, unconscious from the effect of
the stifling smoke. I can hardly tell you how we contrived with the help of the gardener's ladder, luckily
left leaning against the wall of the house, to lift the
unconscious master and mistress of the house through

the window into the open air. We carried them immediately to the parsonage in the village, and left
them in the care of the pastor and his good wife, while
I returned to the burning castle. Here I found the
wildest confusion; the peasantry from the neighbouring hamlets had flocked to the scene, women were
shrieking, children crying, and through it all the crack-
ling and roaring of the flames made night terrible
indeed. The engine had been found useless, and when
the men turned to the Lieutenant for counsel he had
none to give. He was as one dazed. When I appeared
among the terrified people they rushed to me for orders.
What could I do? The fire had made terrible headway
during my brief absence, there could be no hope of ex-
tinguishing it. The wing in which Fräulein Lieschen
and Fritz slept was the only part which was as yet
untouched by the flames, but they were already stretch-
ing hungry tongues towards it.

"'Where are Fräulein Lieschen and Herr Fritzchen?'

"No one answered my question; the men looked at
one another in mute horror. All the servants who
lodged in the castle had contrived to escape from their
rooms unhurt. Some had leaped from the windows,
and even old Hildebrandt was in safety, and had gone
to the village to do what he could for his beloved master
and mistress. Fräulein Lieschen and Fritz were alone
missing. 'They are still sleeping, they are lost!' one
of the servants wailed. The Lieutenant did not speak,
but watched with horror the creeping flames that had
already reached the roof of the wing.

"It was high time indeed to try some means of
rescue. To enter the castle was impossible, but at my
command a dozen willing hands brought two of the
long ladders from the engine-house, and just as they

were placed against the wall of the house, beneath Fräulein Lieschen's window, the young girl herself, with Fritz by her side, opened it and stood for an instant looking out upon the dreadful scene. The shout that went up from the crowd at sight of her I never shall forget. Two stout men had mounted the ladders in an instant; the young girl opened wide the window, lifted her little brother in her strong young arms, and delivered him to one of her rescuers, then easily climbing on the window-sill she stepped out upon the topmost round of the other ladder, and descended to the ground as lightly as she had been used to do when as a child she had climbed about the barns and granaries.

"All were saved then, but the dear old castle was gone beyond hope of rescue. In the early morning, when I left it again to go to the parsonage, it was a heap of smoking ruins, and but for the direction of the wind, which blew the flames towards the garden, the barns and storehouses would have shared its fate.

"At the parsonage sorrowful tidings awaited me. Frau von Osternau had indeed quickly recovered consciousness; she was now sitting with Lieschen at the bedside of her husband, who was in a most critical condition. The physician gave no hopes of his recovery. He was perfectly conscious, but n inflammation of the lungs had set in, which, in the precarious state of his usual health, could not but be fatal.

"When I entered the darkened room Fräulein Lieschen arose, and coming towards me spoke two or three kind words in acknowledgment of what she called my devotion; she was quite calm and collected, but her eyes were brimming with tears, and she was evidently controlling herself by an effort marvellous in one so young.

"Herr von Osternau was no sooner aware of my presence than he begged to be left alone with me for a few minutes. His poor wife burst into tears as she tried to speak to me, and Fräulein Lieschen gently led her from the room.

"I sat down beside the bed where lay the man who had been so true a friend to me, and pressed the hand which he feebly extended.

"'It will soon be all over,' he whispered, 'I have but a few hours to live, but I cannot go without confiding to you, my faithful friend, the terrible suspicion which makes these few hours miserable for me. To you alone, Storting, can I tell this: the fire last night was the work of a robber, who used this means to prevent the discovery of his theft, and this wretched incendiary is my cousin Albrecht.'

"I was horrified to have my own vague suspicion of the past night thus confirmed, and by a dying man. Herr von Osternau signed to me to bend down over him that he need use no unnecessary exertion, saying,—

"'I must have strength enough to deliver over to your special protection my little Fritz. A man who is a thief and an incendiary would scarcely hesitate to commit any crime; therefore I do solemnly commit my boy to your care, asking you to be as faithful a friend to him as you have always been to me.'

"I was naturally greatly moved, and willingly gave him the promise he asked for. Then, after a short pause, he went on in his failing voice to tell me how he had suspected, some weeks before, that a sum of money which had been taken from his secretary had been stolen by the Lieutenant, and that he had the lock replaced by one of most intricate construction to guard against any further loss. On the previous evening he had, before going to bed, arranged the notes I had brought him from Breslau, and had carefully put them into his strong-box and locked it up in his secretary, placing the keys on a little table beside his bed. When roused from his first deep sleep by the stifling smoke he had first called his wife, and then, remembering the money in the next room, which represented his daughter's portion, he looked for his keys to possess himself of it. They were gone from the table! In an instant it was all clear to him : his keys had been stolen! He rushed to the door which separated his room from the study, it was locked on the other side. Through the crack of it he could see the flames. He called to his wife to come and help him, and received no reply. He succeeded in opening the window, but knew no more until he recovered consciousness at the pastor's. He went on to say that no one save myself and Albrecht knew of the sum brought that day from Breslau, no one else could have taken the keys from his table while he slept. Then, when the theft was committed, he had locked the door leading into the next room, and set fire to the scene of his crime, that all chance of discovery might be destroyed in the flames. His end had been answered, the secretary was destroyed; how baseless must be any charge of theft or of incendiarism brought forward now! It would be worse than useless to stain with such an accusation an ancient and noble name, which he had taken pride in keeping untainted. The thief must be left to enjoy the result of his crime, but again he adjured me to watch over his boy. Then, utterly exhausted, he bade me farewell, and asked for his wife and daughter.

"They came again to his bedside, and I left the room
and the house, encountering Lieutenant von Osternau
as I did so. 'I hope my cousin is doing well,' he said,
but he did not look me in the face as he spoke. I
longed to strike him to the earth, but I controlled myself. Of course I shared Herr von Osternau's conviction, but all proof in the matter was wanting. I managed to tell him with tolerable composure that Herr
von Osternau was so ill that there were fears for his
life. I fancied I saw a gleam of triumph in his eye
that belied his hypocritical words of regret, as he declared that under such sad circumstances he would not
disturb his cousin's wife and daughter. As superintendent, it was his duty instantly to communicate with
the insurance companies,—he must start immediately
for Breslau.

"Convinced as I was of his guilt, I then committed
an act of unwarrantable rashness. As he talked on so
smoothly of going to Breslau in his cousin's interests,
I made up my mind that it was to deposit his booty
in a place of security that he was departing so soon,
and the wild idea seized me that Fräulein Lieschen's
portion might be recovered by a bold stroke. He most
probably—nay, certainly—had it a¹ at him. I lost my
head, and seeing two of my farm-hands who I knew
were devoted to me coming down the street, I shouted
to them, 'Seize Lieutenant von Osternau! he is the incendiary!' It was all wrong. I had no right to resort
to such means, but, as I tell you, Herr von Ernau, I lost
my head. The two men hesitated but for an instant,
and then, with an 'Ah! we thought so!' fell upon the
Lieutenant. He defended himself against them, and
struck out wildly both at them and at me when I approached him, but of course he was quickly over-

powered and bound. The noise of the struggle brought
various labourers and villagers from their houses. No
one took part with the Lieutenant, who had evidently
aroused their suspicions by his strange conduct during
the fire. For fear of disturbing Herr von Osternau, we
did not carry the fellow into the parsonage, but into a
cottage near at hand, where I searched him thoroughly,
but found no trace of the money. If he had taken it,
he had already made it secure elsewhere. I saw how
rash I had been, what a terrible error I had committed,
and I stood before him overwhelmed with shame. I
ordered the men, who had stood by curiously while the
search was going on, to release him, declaring myself in
the wrong and my suspicions unfounded. They obeyed
me with reluctance, and left me with the Lieutenant,
who up to this moment had not uttered a single word,
either during the search or while he was being un-
bound. When we were at last alone he confronted me
with folded arms and an evil look.

" ' You are only the servile tool of my cousin, or of his
wife, who always hated me, and in whose brain was
conceived the infamous suspicion of which I have been
the victim.'

" I would have interrupted him to tell him that he was
mistaken, but he exclaimed, 'Hush! I will listen to
no excuse from you. If you were my equal in rank I
should require from you the satisfaction of a gentleman;
as it is, you cannot insult me. Tell Frau von Osternau
that every tie of kindred is broken between us forever.'

" 'Frau von Osternau knows nothing——' I began.

" 'Spare me all falsehood,' he interrupted me. 'I do
not believe you. I know that Frau von Osternau and
Lieschen are my mortal enemies, and I shall not forget
that they are so.'

"He turned on his heel and went out of the house, leaving me in a state of mortification and depression quite indescribable. I gathered myself together, however, and went again to the parsonage, feeling it my duty to confess what I had done to Herr von Osternau. This, however, I could not do: Herr von Osternau had died a few minutes after our interview had ended.

"I cannot describe to you, Herr von Ernau, the utter wretchedness of his poor wife. She had loved her husband with her whole heart; in her eyes he was the wisest and best of men, and at first she could find no consolation even in her children.

"Indeed, she was an object of compassion in every respect, for after Herr von Osternau's death his affairs were found to be in by no means so prosperous a condition as had been supposed. In former years he had devoted all his surplus income to the improvement of his estate, and when he began to save, in order to leave his wife and daughter independent, his own generous, kindly nature, which led him to pay Lieutenant Albrecht's debts repeatedly, and into other similar acts, was a bar to the fulfilment of his purpose. Only very lately had he succeeded in accumulating the sixty thousand thalers which was to purchase Wernewitz and Rudersdorf for Fräulein Lieschen, and this money— the only independent fortune which he had to bequeath —was either destroyed in the fire, or the prey of a scoundrel. There was no solution of this last question, for nothing came to light to confirm the suspicion which Herr von Osternau had confided to me.

"The Lieutenant had gone to Berlin immediately after being treated in the disgraceful way of which I told you, and did not return to Osternau, for, as he explained in a letter to Frau von Osternau, not even his cousin's death could obliterate from his mind the insult offered him, which must henceforth estrange him from his kindred. He lived in Berlin, as he had done formerly,—not more expensively, but on a scale of such luxury as to make a certain income indispensable. I was quite sure that I knew its source, but my conviction was useless in the matter. Popular opinion in the country round regarded the Lieutenant as the incendiary, but no proof of his guilt was forthcoming. Since, however, it was the common talk of the country, the courts took the matter up, and there was an investigation of the cause of the fire. It was without result, however; the only suspicious circumstance with regard to it being the state in which the fire-engine was found, after having been thoroughly examined and pronounced in good order a few days previously by the Lieutenant at Herr von Osternau's request.

"I thought it my duty to acquaint Herr von Sastrow, Fritzchen's guardian, with what the boy's father had confided to me, but I could not gainsay the good old man when he advised me to dismiss from my mind such apparently groundless suspicions.

"Frau von Osternau, after her husband's death, could not bring herself to leave the place which she so dearly loved. Herr von Sastrow tried to persuade her to remove to Berlin, where it would be much easier to educate Fritzchen; but she preferred to remain, for a while at least, in a modest little cottage which she rented in the village of Osternau. The allowance made her from the estate for the education of its heir sufficed amply for her wants. Herr von Sastrow confided the management of Osternau to me, and this rendered it possible for me to fulfil the promise made to his father to keep watch over Fritzchen.

"Three sad months passed after Herr von Osternau's death, and then the widow was called upon to sustain another terrible blow, in the loss of her prop and stay, her darling Fritz."

Egon had listened hitherto without a word to Storting's sad tale; he had been profoundly moved by the account of the burning of the castle, and of the death of its master, but at Storting's last words he started forward, exclaiming, "Fritzchen dead! What a terrible trial! Was his father's dying foreboding——"

"No, no, Herr von Ernau," Storting interrupted him. "Whatever crimes Lieutenant von Osternau may have committed, he is guiltless of Fritz's death: the boy died of scarlet fever. Fräulein Lieschen tended him night and day with a devotion which I have never seen equalled. She would not leave his bedside for an hour, although the physician tried to induce her to resign the care of him to some one else, since she had never had the fever herself. She was his only nurse, for her mother was ill in another room,—too ill even to see her darling, who breathed his last in his sister's arms.

"After Fritz's death the Lieutenant was the heir of Osternau; his cousin's wife and daughter could lay no claim to anything save the late proprietor's private property, and this had been destroyed on the night of the fire.

"A week after the boy's death the new master came to Osternau. He had told the pastor of his coming, and had asked him to rent a couple of rooms for him in some farm-house, which he could occupy until the rebuilding of the castle was complete.

"Immediately after his arrival he sent for me. I could not but obey his summons, for he was the lord of Osternau, and I was obliged to hand in to him my accounts for the management of the estate since Herr von Osternau's death.

"I went to him with a heavy heart, fully expecting that he would make use of the power now in his hands to revenge himself for the insult I had once offered him, and as fully resolved to requite scorn with scorn.

"He was sitting in a bare little room, the best the pastor could procure for him, at a table covered with papers. As I entered he rose and came towards me. He was greatly changed. The last few months had made him many years older. His eyes had an uncertain, flickering brilliancy; his face was haggard and very pale. The erect military carriage that had formerly characterized him was gone: he had grown old.

"He offered me his hand, and addressed me in a tone of hypocritical friendliness that disgusted me, as after one fleeting glance of keen scrutiny his eyes fell before mine.

"'We were hardly friends when we parted, Storting,' he said. 'You offended me, and I used harsh words towards you. We were both in a state of unnatural agitation, induced by the events of the night and my cousin's danger. You meant to act for the best, as the friend and servant of my dear departed relative. When I was cooler I perceived this, and therefore, I assure you, I bear you not the faintest grudge. Here is my hand. I trust you will take it in the spirit in which it is offered.'

"I could not refuse to take his hand, although my whole nature rose in revolt against any fellowship with the man. I had to sit down and take a cigar, while he talked to me as one would to some dear old friend, without a trace of the arrogance which had formerly

made him so disliked by me. He asked, with every
appearance of sympathy, after Frau von Osternau and
Fräulein Lieschen. I had to inform him of the particulars of Fritz's death, and of Fräulein Lieschen's devotion; he showed the keenest interest in the welfare
of his relatives, and postponed all business details, remarking that the management of the estate could not
be in better hands than mine, and that he would discuss
business with me when his relations with Frau von Osternau and Lieschen should be arranged. That they
might become so, he begged me to assist him.

"'I assure you, Storting,' he said, 'that I am profoundly distressed by the terrible trials that have fallen
to the lot of my dear relatives. For Frau von Osternau I entertain a greater regard than words can express, and Lieschen, whom I have known from her early
childhood, has always been my ideal of feminine loveliness. My cousin Fritz formerly frequently expressed
the wish that a nearer tie might some time exist between his daughter and myself,—the dear child was in
a measure brought up for me. This thought has often
solaced me in hours of depression. I always regarded
her as my future wife, even in the midst of our trifling
disputes. Unfortunately, by my own fault, the relations
between my relatives and myself have not of late years
been so harmonious as they once were, and I fear that
Lieschen may not think favourably of her father's former
promises, the fulfilment of which forms the chief—I may
say, the only—hope of my existence. My heart would
lead me to declare this myself to Frau von Osternau
and her daughter, but my head tells me to entreat your
mediation, Storting; no rash word uttered by Lieschen in
the excitement of the moment must be allowed to place
a barrier between us. I ask of you a favour, Storting,

which will make me your debtor for life: tell Frau von Osternau what I have just told you. She is a woman of practical sense and discernment, she will not be led astray by the mood of the moment, but will perceive that a union between Lieschen and myself is the most natural and harmonious solution of the present unhappy state of affairs, for which the law of entail is to blame. As my wife, Lieschen will be mistress of the Osternau estate. Surely Frau von Osternau will use her influence with her daughter to induce her to encourage my hopes.'

"My blood ran cold at the idea of Fräulein Lieschen's becoming this man's wife, but I could not refuse to carry his proposal to Frau von Osternau. What had the future in store for them save a life of poverty and care? By the terms of the Osternau entail, the widow of a former proprietor was entitled to but three hundred thalers yearly from the revenues of the estate; the daughters were entirely unprovided for. Under these circumstances was not a marriage with the Lieutenant to all appearances Fräulein von Osternau's only resource? Was there not a degree of generosity in the offer just made? I could not but make it known to the mother and daughter.

"It was a hard task. When I presented myself in their lodgings, I found them already informed of the Lieutenant's arrival. I reported to them the conversation I had just had with him, and strove, to the best of my ability, to do so in an entirely impartial manner. I must have succeeded in this, for my words evidently produced an impression upon Frau von Osternau.

"'We have done Cousin Albrecht injustice,' she said, gently. 'He may be thoughtless and imprudent, but he cannot be bad, or he would not so soon forget the

insult lately offered him in Osternau. His offer is magnanimous at least. You never treated him well, Lieschen, you often offended him, and yet he loves you,
and would make you mistress of Osternau.'

" Fräulein Lieschen gazed at her mother with an expression of positive horror. 'You cannot think for an
instant that I could accept his terrible proposal?' she
asked, and her voice trembled.

" 'Do not judge your cousin so harshly, my child,'
said Frau von Osternau. 'He hopes, as you have
heard, that you will not decide hastily; he knows your
impetuous temperament, and dreads your saying to
him in a personal interview words which could neither
be forgiven nor forgotten. What you have just said
proves him right. Therefore he has asked our good
Herr Storting to be his messenger, conscious also that
you are my dear, unselfish child, and that you may be
brought to overcome your momentary impulse of aversion to this marriage when you consider that your
'no' would drive us both away from our dear Osternau,—from the graves of your father and Fritz,—out
into the world, to struggle with poverty and want, while
your 'yes' would make you mistress of Osternau, and
allow me to live here, where I have been so happy, and
where, in the midst of memorials of the past, I never
can be quite unhappy. I feel sure that, after due reflection, you will decide for the best, and, therefore, I beg
you not to decide at once.'

" Fräulein Lieschen wept bitterly while her mother
was speaking, but when she paused, and, taking her
daughter's hand, drew her towards her, the young
girl embraced her tenderly, and, controlling herself,
said, calmly and firmly, 'It would be wicked to
postpone my decision for an hour. I will sacrifice

everything for you, mother dear, except my soul's salvation, and that would be imperilled by false vows. How can I promise to revere and love a man whom I despise? I cannot sell myself to him, mother, even for your sake. To require this of me would be to doom your only child to death.'

"'Lieschen!' cried her mother, 'do not blaspheme.'

"'No,' she rejoined, 'I do not blaspheme. I should not lay hands upon my own life, mother, but the sense of my degradation would kill me. But you will not compel me to such a fate? you will not be faithless to the memory of my father, who never would have permitted it? I will gladly share poverty with you, gladly work for you, dearest mother, but marry that thief——"

"'Hush, Lieschen, hush!' her mother interrupted her.

"'It was my father's word, whispered in my ear in his last moments," the girl went on. "'Watch over Fritz,' he said; 'protect him from the thief and incendiary.' Go back to Herr von Osternau, Herr Storting, and tell him what you have heard; tell him the mere thought of him inspires me with aversion, and that I would rather die in misery than sell myself to him. You have carried his message faithfully, do the same by mine.'

"You know, Herr von Ernau, that I was never at any time able to resist Fräulein Lieschen's requests, and I did not fail her in this the darkest hour of her life. I promised to report her decision to the Lieutenant. She thanked me with a look, and Frau von Osternau said, with a sigh, 'I must submit. Lieschen has inherited her father's strength of will in matters of conscience. The foolish child is destroying her future; it is sad, but I cannot prevent it. I must yield to her resolve. Since it must be so, it is, perhaps, better not to postpone acquainting Albrecht with her decision.'

"I left them with a far lighter heart than I brought to them. The commission with which I was charged could hardly be considered an agreeable one, especially as Fräulein Lieschen begged me to repeat to the Lieutenant everything that she had said concerning him; but the sense of relief in knowing that she was in no wise to belong to that villain outweighed every other consideration in my mind.

"The Lieutenant had probably foreseen the answer he should receive. He calmly listened while I repeated, as far as I could recall it, all that Frau von Osternau and her daughter had said, only omitting to mention that Fräulein Lieschen had called him thief and incendiary. An evil smile played about his lips, but he only glanced at my face from time to time, seeming unwilling to meet my eye.

"'I meant well,' he declared, when I had finished, and then he went on to explain his regret that his relatives should be so limited as to means, that he would gladly have shared his wealth with them, and that, in view of Lieschen's youth and inexperience, he should continue to hope that with time she might be brought to regard his suit favourably. Meanwhile, he offered Frau von Osternau and her daughter a home in the castle so soon as it should be rebuilt. If they refused to avail themselves of this offer, he should, of course, confine himself to the payment to the widow of the yearly sum allowed her by law. It would weary you, Herr von Ernau, to recount to you all the details of our conversation. I thanked God when it was ended.

"Of course Frau von Osternau refused to live beneath his roof, dependent upon his bounty. There was no need of Fräulein Lieschen's indignant rejection of any such idea to influence her mother's decision. The two went to Berlin, where it was easier than in any country town to find some employment wherewith to eke out their scanty income. They left the village of Osternau two weeks after the Lieutenant's arrival, without having seen him, and on the day of their departure I too bade farewell to the place where I had spent such happy years.

"Herr von Osternau offered me a large salary if I would continue to occupy my position as superintendent of the estate, but I could not bring myself to serve the man who could never be to me anything save a thief and an incendiary. I procured another situation not nearly so profitable in a pecuniary point of view.

"I corresponded at first very frequently with Frau von Osternau, and although of late our letters have been fewer, I have never lost sight of her. She has had a weary, anxious time of it. Too proud to ask help from her wealthy relatives, she had no resources save her paltry yearly pittance of three hundred thalers and the untiring industry of Fräulein Lieschen, who furnished embroidery for one of the large Berlin firms. Frau von Osternau wrote with positive enthusiasm of her daughter, who, in spite of her constant labour at her embroidery, found time to study and to complete her defective education, so that last spring she passed a brilliant examination as governess. My last letter was received from Frau von Osternau between three and four months ago, when this examination was just passed; and while the mother spoke of it with pardonable pride, she mourned over the probability of a coming separation from her daughter, who was about to accept a situation as governess, thereby greatly increasing her

v

mother's means of support. Of Cousin Albrecht she had heard only through Herr von Sastrow. He lived for a short time the life of a hermit in his gorgeous new-built castle, avoided by all families of his own rank in the neighbourhood; for the report that he had set fire to the castle was rife in the country around, and he was virtually sent to Coventry. He therefore spent most of the year in Berlin, where he associated with needy members of the aristocracy and doubtful characters whose good will he could purchase with his money. The doors of the first people in society were closed against him. His large income he wasted in all sorts of extravagant dissipation, and it was reported in Berlin that he had contracted enormous debts.

"For herself Frau von Osternau wrote that, if her daughter accepted a situation as governess away from Berlin, she too should leave the city and go to some Silesian village, where her small income would suffice for her modest wants."

CHAPTER XXVI.

A CONSPIRACY.

What a story was this! To Egon, Storting's narrative seemed like some wild romance. Herr von Osternau and Fritzchen, the bright, intelligent little fellow, dead, Frau von Osternau the victim of a scoundrel's crime, and Lieschen forced to work hard to stave off destitution! He could hardly trust his ears, and it needed the sight of Storting's sad, earnest face, as he spoke, to confirm his words.

Egon's mind was filled with the eager desire to aid those to whom during the past few years his heart had so often turned,—those who, as he was now painfully aware, had formed part of every vision of his future life. He had resisted all impulse to revisit Castle Osternau; only when his new existence was fairly and honestly begun at Plagnitz could he hope to find there the pardon for which he thirsted for the deceit practised upon its inmates. And now this could never be, and the thought that he was possessed of superfluous wealth, while those dear to him were working for their daily bread, was positively intolerable. He sprang up, but the instant and intense pain in his head reminded him that the physician had forbidden all exertion for some days, and that he could not hasten as he longed to Lieschen's side, to shield her from all further distress. He sank back wearily in his arm-chair.

"Confound that miserable accident!" he said, angrily. "It keeps me a prisoner here when every moment is precious. Frau von Osternau must not live a day longer in such unsuitable circumstances. Storting, you must do me a favour to-morrow,—no, to-day. By the night-train you must go to Berlin. I cannot go myself, as you see, and perhaps it is better that you, Frau von Osternau's old friend, should act for me. I will give you an order on our bank. You must draw any sum necessary to provide handsomely for Frau von Osternau, and to prevent Fräulein Lieschen from taking the place of a hired servant. I will not allow it; it shall not be. Make haste, Storting! I will write to our cashier and get the order ready for you while you are preparing to set off. You must be in Berlin to-morrow."

Storting smiled, but shook his head.

"Your kind and generous intention does you honour, Herr von Ernau," he said, cordially, "but I fear it will be of no avail. My journey to Berlin, where, according to her last letter, I should no longer find Frau von Osternau, would be of no use even were the lady still there. She would thank you for your generosity, but would refuse to accept your money, as she has already refused the offers of help made her by Herr von Sastrow and others of her relatives. 'As long as I can work, we are not objects of charity,' I myself heard Fräulein Lieschen say, while her head was held as haughtily and her eyes sparkled as brightly as in the dear old times. She will work to the last, but she never will suffer her mother to receive aid from outsiders."

What had Egon been thinking of to propose to offer money to Frau von Osternau? Storting's words convinced him that Lieschen would indeed refuse such a gift. It was well that his wound had prevented his immediate departure for Berlin. How mortified he should have been to have his thoughtless gift rejected with fitting pride! And yet he could not endure the thought of Lieschen—in his heart he almost said *his* Lieschen—forced to labour for her daily bread, to resign her freedom and place herself at the beck and call of strangers. Oh, it was intolerable! What could he do? A happy idea suddenly suggested itself.

"Did you not once tell me, Storting," he asked, "that old Herr von Osternau had lost large sums of money through his careless generosity? was there not some story of a manufacturer in Breslau whose factory burned down, and to whom Herr von Osternau loaned a very considerable amount of money without sufficient security, and lost it all by the man's absconding?"

"Yes, that did really happen. The swindler was a paper-manufacturer by the name of Simon; he ran off to America ten years ago, and Herr von Osternau lost every penny of the twenty thousand thalers he loaned him."

"Now, perhaps the poor fellow was no swindler at all. Probably only extreme need drove him to America, and so soon as he is aware of the circumstances in which Frau von Osternau and her daughter are placed he feels it his duty to restore, both principal and interest, the loan so generously made him. As he does not know Frau von Osternau's present place of abode, he naturally makes application to Herr Storting, whom he knew formerly as the admirable Osternau inspector, and to him he sends the owing money, commissioning him to hand it over to the heirs of the late Herr von Osternau. Of course Herr Simon will require from these heirs a receipt for the sum handed them, and a quittance of all further claims. You must not be surprised, Storting, to receive a communication from Herr Simon this very evening, with an order upon the firm of A. C. Ernau & Co., in Berlin, for the sum in question; and of course I shall give you leave of absence for some time that you may arrange the matter satisfactorily. I am sure you will not refuse to undertake the affair, Storting."

"What can I say, Herr von Ernau," cried the delighted Storting, "except that I am honoured in being the instrument of such generosity?"

"After all, there is really not much honour, my dear fellow, in being made accomplice in a forgery. But we must contrive to answer all that to our consciences. Go now and get ready to start. In an hour you shall receive Herr Simon's letter. You will be obliged to

28

suppress the envelope, which may not bear the correct stamp."

"No need even of that, for I received a letter from New Orleans yesterday, and its envelope will serve your purpose admirably. It followed me to Plagnitz from my former place of abode, and will explain my desire to leave here as soon as possible: of course I am in a hurry to hand over her property to Frau von Osternau."

"Bravo! and now to business."

Two hours later Storting was on his way to the nearest railway-station, with a letter from Carl Johann Simon, New Orleans, Louisiana, U. S. A., and an order upon the banking-house of A. C. Ernau & Co., Berlin, in his pocket.

CHAPTER XXVII.

A MISCHIEVOUS COQUETTE.

THE morning after Storting's departure, Egon received a visit from the vivacious little Ostrowko doctor, who declared that he could not be responsible for the consequences if his patient persisted in neglecting his instructions. "I distinctly told you, my dear Herr von Ernau, that rest was all that you required, that rest you must have, and what has been your course? Instead of remaining where you certainly were very well off, and with a charming *châtelaine* to attend to your every wish, you jolt off over here, along an infernal road, a few hours after I leave you, and, I make no doubt, purpose to inspect your estate to-day. Not at all, not at all, my dear Herr von Ernau. You have had a shock to your system. Great as was your escape, 'tis no joke falling from the Dombrowker Pass, and you must be quiet. You've a fine library here, and a magnificent grand piano: sit still, read some trashy romance, and play Offenbach for the next week, and leave your estate in the hands of your admirable inspector,—Storting is his name? What! he has gone to Berlin for a time? Well, the younger fellow—I forget his name—is quite competent, with old Sieveking to direct. I am going to see that, now we have got you here at Plagnitz, we keep you from any ill effects of your accident, or you'll be saying that the climate does not agree with you, and you'll be running off to Berlin. Aha! I know you young fellows. I was young myself not a hundred years ago."

And he rattled on, until he had indeed fully convinced his patient that rest was an admirable remedy for many ailments.

Egon was doomed, then, to a time of inaction, and this just when he was most eager to enter upon the supervision of his affairs. Still, there might be much to interest him in these first days at home, and he resigned himself with the best grace that he could to refrain from riding, driving, or any long walks for a while, according to the doctor's orders.

The degree of order and method which prevailed everywhere at Plagnitz delighted him, and no less was he pleased, when he sauntered through the fields in the immediate vicinity of the manor-house, with the kindly courtesy of those of his people whom he met, and who greeted the master without a trace of that slavish servility so frequently to be found in the Polish-German provinces, and so odious to Egon. Day-labourers and

grooms took off their hats to him, but did not, half
kneeling, offer to kiss his hand, as is the invariable custom elsewhere; nor were they at all embarrassed in the
intelligent replies which they made to his inquiries concerning their various occupations. To the master's
great satisfaction, he perceived that there pervaded
Plagnitz an air of freshness and freedom beyond what
was enjoyed upon most other large estates of the
province; the people were treated like human beings,
not like slaves, and, in consequence, manifested an
interest and vivacity almost unknown to the ordinary
imbruted Polish labourer. Here old Sieveking's influence had been admirable, and all that Egon had
thought lacking upon his previous visit to Plagnitz
had been largely supplied by Storting's diligence and
experience.

A young man presented himself as the bailiff, Hensel, and modestly asked permission to show Herr von
Ernau through the farm-buildings and to give him any
desired information concerning them. When Egon
accepted his offer, he showed himself so intelligent and
well informed in all matters pertaining to his special
province, that the master of Plagnitz was even more
than ever impressed with the faithful care taken of
his estate during his absence by old Sieveking, who,
although he could not entirely fulfil the requirements
of a disciple of the modern school of agriculture, had
yet prepared an excellent foundation for the new
methods which Egon hoped to introduce with Storting's assistance.

Even the slight inspection which he thus made, on
the first day of his residence in his home, was condemned by the little doctor on his next visit. He declared that for a week at least nothing in the way of

out-of-door exercise must be attempted. "As much fresh air as you please, my dear Herr von Ernau, but taken by an open window, or seated on your terrace, whence the prospect should surely content you for a while."

This enforced repose was particularly irritating to Egon just at the present time. The delicious weather lured him into the open air; he was feverishly desirous of beginning the work for which he had been preparing for four long years, and to sit quietly gazing abroad over his fields and meadows, at the groups of labourers, among whom he longed to be, was almost intolerable.

If Storting had only been at home he could have conversed with him. But he was entirely alone; old Sieveking was too ill and feeble to be disturbed, and young Hensel, although excellent in his way, was entirely unavailable for purposes of conversation that did not bear upon his vocation.

His only consolation during these wearisome days was the fine grand piano which he had had sent to Plagnitz from Berlin. During his years of study he had rather neglected his music, and he now found in it all the delight it had formerly given him. His feverish restlessness was soothed by giving it musical expression; as of old, he was able to forget himself in the world of harmony.

He was seated thus at his instrument, on the fourth afternoon after his arrival at Plagnitz; the last chords of a wild rhapsody had just died away, and his fingers were wandering over the keys in a dreamy fantasia, half memory, half hope. Lost in his fancies, he did not hear a footman announce an arrival, or the sound of footsteps in the room behind him. He suddenly seemed aware of a soft sigh near him; he turned hastily and

28*

gazed into a pair of dark eyes. At first he saw Bertha only; but she was not alone, behind her stood Wangen and Clara.

"If the mountain will not come to us, we must come to the mountain," Wangen said, with a laugh, holding out his hand. "You must not think us too eager to thrust ourselves upon you, Herr von Ernau, in coming thus soon to see how the patient is faring, since the doctor tells us that he may receive visits, although he can pay none."

Involuntarily Egon passed his hand across his eyes, as if to banish the vision of the moment. Yes, this was reality. Here was no Bertha von Massenburg, but Frau von Wangen, with her husband, and the charming child with whom he had exchanged a few words at Linau; and he was the lord of Plagnitz, whose duty it was to welcome his guests and pray pardon for having at first been unaware of their entrance.

Hugo von Wangen laughed in his good-humoured way. "We stood behind you listening for a minute," he said. "I do not think anything short of an earth-quake would have aroused you when we first came in, you were so absorbed. We ought to ask pardon for disturbing you. My wife would not let me come alone, as I thought of doing. She was too anxious, she said, to see how the patient was getting on."

What was there for Egon to do but to express his gratitude to madame, and to kiss the fair hand extended to him, while declaring his pleasure in welcoming beneath his roof both Frau and Fräulein von Wangen?

These formalities concluded, the visitors took seats, and a very lively talk ensued. Bertha was positively charming; she dwelt just long enough upon her anxiety lest the drive from Linau should have proved too much for Herr von Ernau, and was so easy and cordial that she banished all feeling of restraint from the conversation, which soon turned to Herr von Wangen's favourite theme, agriculture. All the party regretted Egon's inability to act as their guide in an inspection of so famous an estate as Plagnitz, which Wangen had never before visited. In especial was he desirous to see a certain wonderful breed of sheep. Of course, Egon proposed that his bailiff, Herr Hensel, should act as his guest's cicerone in default of his own companionship, and Wangen eagerly accepted the proposal, after consulting his wife by a glance.

Herr Hensel was summoned, and was much honoured by the office intrusted to him. He asked whether the ladies also might not perhaps be interested in the sheep-stalls, which were constructed upon an entirely new plan. Frau von Wangen declined to accompany her husband, but Clara gladly arose to go with her brother and Herr Hensel: she took all a country girl's interest in sheep and cows.

Wangen seemed a little disconcerted by this arrangement; he was in his heart reluctant to leave his wife alone to the fascinations of her old admirer. He could not possibly let this be known, however,—Bertha would have laughed at his foolish jealousy. Nevertheless, he felt far from comfortable when Bertha added her approval of Clara's intention, saying, "Do go, my dear Clara, and take note of all the improvements, which we may be able to introduce at Linau." He could not, without making himself ridiculous, insist upon Clara's staying behind; she was already hanging upon his arm, and he quietly followed Herr Hensel.

For the first time in his life Egon was alone with Bertha. Even at Castle Osternau they had never met except in the presence of some member of the family, and there was a vague sense in his mind of wrong done to his ideal by this *tête-à-tête*, although he had done nothing to bring it about; it was purely accidental. In fact, the young man's mind had been, during the past four days, so continually filled with thoughts of Lieschen, he had so constantly recalled her every look and word of former years, the restlessness that possessed him had been so largely caused by his anxiety to hear from Storting, and had been so much more keenly felt since he was forbidden to allay it by physical exertion or hard mental effort, that he was not as open as it was his wont to be to the impression of the moment; it cost him some pains to prevent his imagination from driving present realities from his mind. Therefore, for some time after they were thus left alone, the conversation was of a quite indifferent character; and yet how exquisitely lovely she was as she sat opposite him, with a gentle smile hovering upon her charming mouth! How sweet and tender was her voice as, at last, after a pause, she leaned towards him, her eyes seeking and holding his, and asked, softly, "Herr von Ernau, are you still angry with me?"

Honestly, Egon did not understand why she should ever have thought him angry, and honestly he rejoined, "Why should I be angry with you, madame?"

She blushed slightly as she said, sadly, "Ah, yes, I see you are still angry. You persist in dwelling upon the past, although I begged you to forget it: Yet can we forget? I cannot practise what I would enjoin upon you. The consciousness of the wrong I did you has robbed me of rest since I last saw you. I long to hear you say that you forgive me. I came to-day with Herr von Wangen, hoping for this opportunity, which accident has given me, to entreat you not to add to all that is hard and cruel in my lot by withholding your forgiveness for the past. Believe me, I have suffered in listening to the dictates of prudence, rather than to the voice of my heart."

She would have gone on, quite charmed with her own eloquence, absolutely fancying herself thrown away upon her idolizing husband, playing a part which had presented itself as most attractive to the shallow imaginings of her idle hours, but that something in Egon's face arrested the words upon her lips; she paused and waited for his reply.

In truth, while she had been speaking, Egon's thoughts had been hardly such as it would have pleased her to divine. Yes, she was incomparably lovely; he saw it all,—the dark, pleading glance, the wonderful grace of every movement; but how, he was asking himself, had he ever thought it possible to find his other self in this woman? How well he had known her kind in days gone by! Fate had been only too good to her in bringing her the devotion of so honest and single-hearted a man as Hugo von Wangen. He had surrounded her life with luxury and affection, and she had neither the heart to return his love, nor the mind to appreciate it. How false, how shallow she was! And his memory conjured up another face and another voice. 'There is nothing which I so detest as false words and false seeming.' His mind wandered from the present for an instant; but Bertha was silent, he must answer her, and, little fitted as he felt himself to play the part of a moralist, the thought of Wangen, so cordial in his kindness to his new neighbour, lent an additional coolness to his words:

"I assure you, madame, that I never imagined that

I had the smallest right to feel myself in any way ag
grieved by your conduct. All who know Hugo von
Wangen can well understand how happy a woman she
must be upon whom he bestows the treasure of his
devotion. Let me repeat your kind advice to me when
first I met you at Linau: Forget the past; we have to
do with the present and the future."

The expression of Bertha's face as he spoke was not
pleasant to see; the pathetic lines about her mouth
vanished, her eyes lost their gentle, pleading look. The
change was so sudden that it rather disconcerted Egon,
who was immensely relieved by hearing footsteps in
the corridor and by the rather hurried entrance of
Clara, eager to tell her sister-in-law of all she had lost
in not joining Hugo and herself. The girl was followed
immediately by her brother, whose first glance, always
for his wife, took note of her embarrassment, and then
sought Egon's face, where also, he thought, he discerned signs of confusion. All his jealous suspicions,
vague as they were, and therefore all the more tor-
menting, sprang to life. He tried his best to follow the
lead of his host and talk with interest of the Plagnitz
cattle and the various improvements in stalls and
stables. It was of no use; conversation would no
longer run in easy grooves, and all were rather glad
than otherwise when the time for the departure of
the guests arrived.

When their carriage was announced, Egon would
have escorted them to it, but this Wangen would in no
wise permit. The doctor had expressly told him, he
said, that Herr von Ernau must avoid all exertion for
a while and keep his room. Bertha added her words
to his to prevent their host's accompanying them down
into the hall, and even Clara sagely observed that if

Herr von Ernau were not careful he never would be able to come to Linau shortly as he had promised.

Egon went to the window to wave a farewell to his guests, when he observed the young girl, who had taken her place on the back seat of the barouche, suddenly spring out of it again. "I have forgotten my parasol!" she called up to Egon.

The footman, who had been helping the visitors to get into their carriage, would have gone back for it, but with a "Never mind, I will get it myself," she ran into the house and up the stairs. The next instant she stood, with flushed cheeks and sparkling eyes, beside Egon, and said hurriedly, in a low voice, "I left it on purpose, because I wanted to say something to you, Herr von Ernau. The doctor, I know, told Hugo yesterday that you could not drive to Linau before Monday, but you must come before. You are perfectly well, promise me to come on Saturday at the farthest,— to-day is Monday. Oh, you can easily come before, or on, Saturday, if you drive slowly."

"Why must I promise you to come 'before, or on, Saturday,' little Clara?"

"Oh, because I want you to come so much that I can hardly wait for the time to pass."

"Oh, I am not vain enough to believe that."

The girl laughed merrily.

"Indeed! Well, there is somebody, at all events, who does want to see you, I know, and I must not tell you who it is, because I promised not to. But I did not promise not to beg you to come before Sunday. Oh, you must, or it will be too late. Adieu, Herr von Ernau! Here is my parasol; they are waiting for me. Remember, before Sunday!"

She hurried away, and waved her hand, flourishing

her parasol, from the carriage, as it drove out of the court-yard.

Egon stood a long while at the window, gazing after the carriage as it disappeared. What had he just heard? Had Bertha made that innocent child her messenger, her tool, in the idle flirtation with which she would fain employ her empty hours? Yes, she was indeed false and shallow; and good, kindly Wangen deserved a better fate. What had become of the magical charm which Bertha von Massenburg's beauty had exercised over the Egon of former days? He thought of her almost with aversion. Nevertheless, he must return the visit that had been paid him; kindly relations with Linau must be preserved.

CHAPTER XXVIII.

CLARA TO THE RESCUE.

THE afternoon was delightful, the setting sun glorious in the crimson splendour of the west, but the elder members of the party driving home to Linau through the warm summer air were scarcely in the mood to enjoy it. Wangen was annoyed at what he declared to himself were groundless suspicions of his beautiful wife; he tried to atone for them by redoubled tenderness in his manner when he addressed her, and this very tenderness irritated Bertha, in her consciousness of failure in her first attempt to vary the monotony of her existence by what she assured herself should be but an innocent flirtation,—merely a piece of feminine vengeance upon the man who had so insulted her vanity in years gone by. Clara, indeed, rattled away about the various delights of Plagnitz, winding up her eulogium of its lord, however, with a heavy sigh.

"If my darling Elise could but have been with us!" she exclaimed. "And now she may never see it! Oh, Bertha, how could you be so unkind to her? I know that it is all because of your bitter speeches that she is going to leave us on Sunday. Why do you not love her? Why can we not all be happy together?"

To this question Bertha deigned no reply, and Hugo said, rather sadly,—

"I too, dearest Bertha, should have been glad to have kept Fräulein Elise with us. But perhaps she is right. You two are like fire and water, and since she has so advantageous an offer, and can be so near her poor mother, I have nothing to say, only I am greatly mistaken if you do not wish for her many a time after she has left us."

"You know, Hugo, I cannot agree with you in your estimate of Elise. She has always disliked me, and of course I see her from my point of view. Before she came, everything that I did was right in your eyes; her presence irritates me, and leads you to criticise and object to what I do and say; in short, I cannot be sorry that she leaves us on Sunday."

The sun was just disappearing as Linau was reached. Hugo and Bertha betook themselves to the balcony, and Clara went in search of her dear Elise, guessing correctly where she should find her. At the farthest end of the extensive garden at the back of the old manor-house of Linau, just where it was separated from the road that divided it from the meadows beyond by an old-fashioned picket-fence, there stood, concealed among the luxuriant shrubbery, a shady arbour, which was reached by a narrow pathway among the tall bushes bounding the garden on one side. This arbour had formerly been a favourite retreat of old Herr von Wangen; from it he could see far over his meadows and fields; here he was wont to sit with his pipe and book through the long summer hours, overlooking his people at work; and hence it had come to be called 'the master's arbour.' After his death the shrubs and bushes about it were allowed to grow more rankly, so as almost entirely to conceal it, for his son did not like to sit here; he preferred to ride out over his estate, to visit his labourers; and his young wife would have thought it excessively tiresome to spend any time on a wooden bench in this lonely spot, when she might be lounging in a luxurious chair on her favourite balcony.

But for Elise this arbour was a delightful retreat, —she liked to teach Clara here, sure of freedom from all interruption,—and here Clara found her after the wonderful visit to Plagnitz. She was in the midst of writing a long letter, and the child's presence might have been more welcome at another time, but she responded affectionately to her pupil's enthusiastic caress; not for the world would she have grieved, by any show of a desire to be alone, the girl whom she had grown to love dearly.

Clara's talkative gaiety, however, seemed to have exhausted itself upon the homeward drive. She sat down beside her governess, and gazed thoughtfully from the leafy opening of the window in the little arbour abroad over the fields and meadows in the direction where in the unseen distance lay Castle Plagnitz. She was silent for a long while, and then, suddenly turning to Elise, she exclaimed,—

" You do not know how dearly I love you ! "

" Oh, yes, I do, dear child ; I know your warm little heart very well."

" But indeed you cannot dream how much I care for you. I did not know it myself. And how can I bear to have you leave us forever on Sunday ? "

" I must go, Clara."

" I suppose you must, for Bertha does not love you ; she does not know you. But, oh ! Elise, why would you not. let me tell Herr von Ernau that you are here, and that you are going away on Sunday ? "

" Clara ! "

" Yes, Elise ; it grieves me to the very heart that you have no confidence in me. I am not such a child that I do not see and understand a great deal more than you think I do. You might confide in me."

" What could I confide in you, Clara ? "

" You might have told me how much you cared for Herr von Ernau."

Elise blushed crimson and uttered another indignant " Clara ! " but the girl threw her arms around her, and, undeterred, continued, "Oh, your blush betrays you ! You need tell me nothing ; I knew it all before. I love you so much that I saw it in your dear, beautiful face,— in your eyes. I knew it when you recognized him as he lay, pale and bleeding, in the hall. I saw it in your happy look when Hugo told us that his wound was not dangerous. And then I asked Hugo, and begged him to tell me when he and you had known Herr von Ernau, and he told me all about how he had been in disguise at Castle Osternau, and had given you music-lessons. Oh, I know it all, and a great deal more ! "

" Much more than it is right that you should," Elise said, gravely.

"No, just enough to let me show you that I am not such a child as you think me, and that, at all events, I am old enough to have plans and schemes of my own. I was very glad to go to Plagnitz to-day, and I enjoyed my visit there very much."

"Clara, you did not forget——"

"No, you need not be anxious. I promised you that I would not even mention your name, and I shall keep my promise, although I cannot see why you made me give it. But I shall find some way to let Herr von Ernau know that you are here without breaking my word. My mind is made up, and I tell you so, because I never mean to deceive you."

"Clara, promise me, if you love me, to do nothing."

"Oh, it is just because I love you that I will make you no more promises. I have learned wisdom."

From the manor-house came the clear tones of the bell ringing for the evening meal.

"There goes the bell!" Clara exclaimed. "We must hurry to be in time. I am glad we can stay here no longer, for I do not wish to say another word. My mind is made up, and I feel much pleased with myself."

With a laugh she left the arbour and tripped along the path towards the house. Elise slowly followed her; she needed a few moments of solitude to evoke some order in the wild confusion of thought caused by Clara's words. She trembled as she reflected upon the possibility of seeing again him upon whom her mind had dwelt for four long years, and who had occupied her thoughts ceaselessly during these last days and nights. How she dreaded meeting him! and yet, in thinking of such a meeting, a strange, sweet hope stirred within her which she herself refused to recognize.

CHAPTER XXIX.

CLARA DEA EX MACHINÂ.

NEVER during the past four years had Egon been so lonely, never had he felt so deserted, so miserable and dissatisfied, as during the first ten days of his residence at Plagnitz. Everything combined to make his mood of the gloomiest. He was not ill, and yet he was not perfectly well. The doctor now permitted him to take short walks, but had exacted from him a promise that he would curb his impatience to take more exercise until the next week. There was nothing for him to do, after walking through a field or two, but to return to his room and take up a book or sit down at the piano.

Could he only have given entire attention to his book, or have become absorbed in his music,—but this was impossible. After he had determinedly read a page or two his rebellious thoughts would wander back to old times at Castle Osternau, or fly after Storting in his travels, or try to peer into the future. And it was just the same when he sat down at his piano: before long his hands would drop listlessly from the keys, and he would resign himself to profitless and cheerless musings.

After the visit of the Wangens he was, if possible, more uncomfortable than before; he was annoyed to feel any restraint in his intercourse with Linau. Bertha's presence, too, had made old memories more vivid than ever. Where, where was Lieschen? He had received only one brief letter from Storting, in Berlin.

29*

Frau von Osternau had left the capital a couple of weeks previously; the mistress of the house where she had lodged could not tell him whither she had gone, and Herr von Sastrow and his wife were unfortunately absent, travelling. Storting could do nothing save go to Osternau, where he hoped that the pastor might tell him what he wished to know; if this hope were disappointed, he was resolved to apply directly to Herr Albrecht von Osternau, who would certainly know the address to which the quarterly payment of the widow's legal income was to be sent.

After this letter, which had been dispatched immediately before Storting's departure for Osternau, no further news had been received from him. His silence filled Egon with restless anxiety; he sent a mounted messenger to the post-office three times every day, but on Friday evening he had not yet heard that Frau von Osternau had been found.

At last, on Saturday morning, Egon's eager expectations were gratified,—the post-bag contained a letter addressed in Storting's handwriting. Egon tore it open with a hand trembling with anxiety, and read,—

"MY DEAR HERR VON ERNAU,—Your admirable plan has been successfully carried out, as I am most glad to inform you. I did well in going to Osternau, where I learned from the pastor that Frau von Osternau had established herself at Hirschberg. I instantly travelled thither, and found the dear lady in excellent health. She was no less pleased than amazed to see me, and when I told her the story of Herr Carl Johann Simon and showed her his letter, she was at first quite speechless with surprise, and then burst into tears of joy and gratitude. Evidently it never occurred to her to doubt

my account. She blessed her husband's memory, remembered his lending the money perfectly, and that
she had remonstrated with him for his ready confidence in every one's honesty. And then she broke
forth in exclamations of delight at knowing that she
could now bring her daughter home to live with her,
and that Fräulein Lieschen need no longer sacrifice
herself for her mother's sake. I only wish that you
could have witnessed the joy of which you were the
source.

"Frau von Osternau is to go with me to Berlin to
take possession of her property and have the receipt
for the same duly made out and signed. This we do
to-morrow; the result of our expedition I shall tell you
by word of mouth, but I write to-day to let you know of
my success, and of a fact which you ought to know immediately. Fräulein Lieschen is at present your neighbour; you have, without knowing it, passed a night in
the same house with her. Herr von Wangen engaged
her as governess for his young sister. In order, however, to be near her mother, she has accepted another
situation in the vicinity of Hirschberg, and is to leave
Linau next Sunday. Fortunately, there is now no need
of her accepting any situation whatever, as her mother
joyfully declared. It seems rather odd—does it not?
—that you should neither have seen Fräulein Lieschen
nor heard of her presence in Linau when you were
there; but then your accident probably chased everything else from the minds of your hosts. I thought it
my duty to let you know immediately that Fräulein
Lieschen leaves Linau on Sunday, thinking that you
may be able to drive over and see her on Saturday
afternoon, if this reaches you, as it should do, on the
morning of that day."

Egon dropped the letter; he could not read further; the last lines danced before his eyes. Lieschen was in Linau! for only one day longer, it is true, but this day was his own. What did he care for the physician's prohibition? He must drive to Linau; every moment of delay was an opportunity lost.

Lieschen in Linau! She had been his nurse that night; it was her lovely face of which he had been aware in his semi-consciousness; her cool, gentle hand had been laid upon his forehead; she had leaned over him in anxious hope for his return to life. His dream had been no dream, after all.

And he had supposed that Bertha had cared for him so kindly! He rejoiced that he owed nothing to her nursing. He could not think of her save with a sensation akin to dislike. Her charm was utterly gone. Why had she concealed from him that Lieschen was beneath her roof? No one had even hinted at her presence there. But yes, Clara! Egon suddenly comprehended the child's parting words to him, words which he had understood falsely: 'There's somebody, at all events, who does want to see you.' She had flown back to say this to him unheard by her sister-in-law.

Oh, he understood it all,—the *ennui* of the woman trained to live in the whirl of society and stranded in her quiet home, knowing 'so ill to deal with time' as to turn for excitement to an idle flirtation with the first man available, and dreading lest another should interfere with her schemes. But it was not too late to baffle them.

To Linau then! He went himself to the stables to order the horses put to a light hunting-wagon. The coachman could not obey his orders quickly enough.

Anton shook his head over his master's impatience,
while to Egon every moment that passed seemed an
irreparable loss.

At last he found himself seated behind his spirited
horses; but Anton did not drive fast enough; his master
took the reins from him, and urged the pair to their
quickest speed. To him they seemed to travel at a
snail's pace. On they flew; not until Anton ventured to call his attention to their condition did he be-
think himself that there really was no need for such
urgent haste. The servant's words recalled his resolve
to exercise self-control, to curb the impulse of the
moment, and he gave back the reins to his coachman's
hands.

The way seemed to stretch out infinitely, but at last
Linau appeared, half hidden in trees, on the summit of a
gentle incline. A quarter of an hour would bring them
to its court-yard, but Egon was forced to curb his impatience and to order the coachman to rein in his
horses. This he did in obedience to the flutter of a
white kerchief waved by a graceful horsewoman who
came galloping across-country towards him. It was
Clara, who had seen him from a distance and thus sig-
nalled him to await her approach. The high-road was
separated from the meadows bounding it on one side
by a tolerably wide and deep ditch, but this was no
obstacle for Clara; her pretty little mare took it at a
leap, and in a minute its rider drew up beside the light
wagon. With sparkling eyes she greeted Egon, saying,
with a confidential nod, "You have come at last, Herr
von Ernau! I expected you yesterday and the day
before, as poor old Jost knows to his cost," and she
pointed with her riding-whip to the old groom, who
had followed her and was riding about on the other

side of the ditch, looking for a narrow place at which to cross it.

"You expected me, Fräulein Clara?"

"Of course. I considered that you promised me to come before Sunday, and therefore on the day before yesterday and yesterday I rode about the fields here at the time when I thought you would appear, looking out for you. If you had not come now, I was going to send my old Jost to Plagnitz to remind you to keep your promise this afternoon, and, if the worst came to the worst, I should have gone and brought you over myself, for I was determined that come you must to-day."

"If I am right in my conjecture," Egon said, very gravely, "you wished me to come to Linau to-day because Fräulein von Osternau leaves it to-morrow."

Clara dropped her bridle and clapped her hands. "Oh, this is delightful!" she exclaimed. "You know that Elise is here! I have never told you, and now my silly promise not to tell you binds me no longer."

"To whom did you make this promise?"

"Why, to Elise, of course. But you need not look so cast down, Herr von Ernau. I'm sure she felt sorry that she allowed herself to be so influenced by Bertha's ill-natured words as to make me promise. I was determined that you should know that my darling Elise is here, for if you knew her long ago at Castle Osternau, I am sure you must want to see her again."

"Does Fräulein von Osternau know that you expect me?"

"Of course not. That would have spoiled it all. I took good care not to tell her. It is all a little plan of my own. Elise never tells me anything; she thinks me nothing but a child, but I can see in her eyes how glad she would be to see Herr von Ernau again. But indeed there is no time to go on talking. Tell me, honestly and frankly, Herr von Ernau, do you come to Linau to-day to see Elise?"

"Honestly and frankly then, my dear little Clara, yes."

"And for that only?"

"Yes."

"And would you like to see her now, just when she is alone and expecting nobody?"

"That is just what I desire beyond all else."

"Then you must not drive on to Linau, but follow me on foot. We will let your carriage wait, lest it should betray us. Get out, Herr von Ernau, and I will show your coachman a spot where he can wait for you without exciting any one's attention. Let him drive along that path that skirts the fields, and he will find a cool, shady place on the edge of the forest, where the horses will not tire of standing."

Egon did as he was bidden; and, while his coachman obeyed the young girl's directions, his master walked beside Clara's horse as she slowly rode along the highway towards Linau. Old Jost, who had managed to cross the ditch, followed at a respectful distance.

Clara was in the gayest mood, enchanted that her charming plan, which she had contrived entirely by herself, was on the eve of being so successfully carried out, without any necessity on her part of breaking the promise made to Elise. She never asked what happy chance had informed Egon of Elise's presence at Linau; it was enough for her that he knew of it, and that she had not been forced to reveal it herself. There was no longer any secret to keep, and she ran on with a long description of how Elise had taken such care of Herr von Ernau on the dreadful night of the accident, and how her eyes had filled with tears of joy when she heard the next morning that his wound was not dangerous. Nor did she fail to dwell upon her own insight in making sure from Elise's face, without hearing one word from her lips, that nothing would please her more than to renew her acquaintance with Herr von Ernau. It was so sad, too, that Bertha did not seem to care for Elise, and that made it easier for her, Clara, to part with her. Did Herr von Ernau know that Elise had found another situation near her mother? For her part, Clara wished that Frau von Osternau lived near Linau, and then, perhaps, if Bertha would only be as sweet and kind as she was sometimes, Elise might be persuaded to stay with them. Did not Herr von Ernau think it a real misfortune to lose so charming a person from the neighbourhood?

In truth, Egon's mind and heart were in such a turmoil of hope and fear that he heard but vaguely his young guide's talk. He was absolutely conscious of but one fact, that along this road, led by this charming child, he was on his way to see once again the fairy of Castle Osternau, the girl who had held him captive all these years, whose influence, established in a few short weeks, had transformed him from an idle, weary, useless creature to a man who felt that he had a part to play in the world, and who meant to play it to the best of his ability. And yet, if she should refuse to stand by his side to aid him in this new life, how dark the future looked! Could she ever pardon the falsehood he had practised upon her and those dear to her? Clara was obliged, to her dismay, to repeat her question before Herr von Ernau heeded it and looked up with, " The greatest misfortune that could befall us, my little Clara."

The warmth of the reply when it came soothed Clara's fears lest Herr von Ernau did not fully appreciate her services in thus procuring him an interview with her adored Elise. She went on to tell him that at this hour on Saturday Elise was sure to be in the 'master's arbour,' which he might now see, half hidden among the trees on their left. "And there is a gate in the picket-fence," she added, "always kept locked; no one goes out of the garden by it now that poor papa is dead. He always went to the meadows that way, but I knew perfectly well where the key was kept, and I have had it in my pocket since the day before yesterday, all ready for just this moment. Here we are, Herr von Ernau, and here is the key," she said, handing it down to him. "Let it stay in the lock. I will go off with Jost for a ride, and then, after about half an hour, when you have talked enough with Elise, I will come back and take you to the house. I want to see how surprised they'll be when they know that you have found Elise. Good-by, Herr von Ernau! Do not miss the path,—the one on the left leads directly to the house, and the one on the right to 'the master's arbour.' Good-by! I shall see you again in half an hour."

With a merry laugh and a wave of the hand she was off at a pace at which old Jost found it hard to follow her.

Egon unlocked the little gate, and with a beating heart struck into the winding right-hand path. The moment that was to decide his future was at hand; he was to see Lieschen again. Had she really, as Clara would have given him to understand, cherished his memory kindly? Was it not more likely that the child's insight had been utterly at fault, and that his image had long since been banished from the mind and heart of one so pure, so true, to whom all deceit, all disguise was hateful?

And now the little arbour, about which the vines hung heavily, making the closing of its rustic door quite impossible, was just before him. How quiet it all was! Suppose Clara was wrong, and that upon pushing wide that door he should find nothing but solitude. He paused for a moment, half afraid to go on, and as he did so there fell on his ear the low tones of the voice which he knew so well, singing softly the words of the old Folksong,—

"In Oden forest stands a tree."

It was the first he had ever sung at Castle Osternau. He saw it all again,—the good old Herr in his arm-chair, the sweet face of his wife as she sat beside him knitting, and Lieschen's eyes gazing in rapture at the singer. For an instant memory wellnigh unmanned him, but that she should be singing just that song gave him more encouragement than he was himself aware of; he gently pushed open the door. Yes, it was she. She sat half turned from him, her hands resting in her lap upon the embroidery with which she had been occupied, her gaze fixed upon the distant landscape, visible through an opening in the vines and shrubbery. The door had swung noiselessly, she did not look towards it. "Lieschen!" It was all. She started and turned towards him a face from which all colour departed, only to return in an instant and mantle neck, cheeks, and brow in crimson. "Herr von Ernau!—I—" Then, burying her face in her hands, she burst into an uncontrollable fit of weeping. In an instant Egon was beside her, at her feet, pouring forth protestations, vows, entreaties for pardon.

"My love, my darling, can you ever forgive me for deceiving you as I did? I have no right to ask it, still less to hope that you can, and yet I do hope. Your memory has been the light of my life since I left Berlin, four years ago; the thought of you and of your words spurred me on to begin a new existence, it gave me strength in all my struggles with self, and, oh! Lieschen, take pity upon me. The future will be so cheerless without you. Complete your work, dear. Try to make me of some use in the world. You have suffered, my darling; I know it all. Let me shield you in future, at least from suffering alone. Can you forgive me and heed my pleadings, for the sake of the love I bear you, which will always be yours, and yours only, whatever may be your answer to me now?"

Elise did not speak, but her sobs ceased; she let her lover wipe away her tears, and read her answer in her eyes.

CHAPTER XXX.

CONCLUSION.

MEANWHILE, on this particular day, Hugo von Wangen had been taking a long ride to a distant part of his estate. He had asked Clara to accompany him, quite despairing of inducing Bertha to leave her luxurious balcony and mount a horse, but, to his surprise, his young sister had declared that she was far too busy, and that a short ride across the fields with Jost was all she should allow herself. His expedition had been a successful one. The improvements which he had set on foot in the way of draina,re of outlying meadows answered his expectations fully, and it was in a very satisfied and peaceful frame of mind that he dismounted at a short distance from his home, and, ordering the groom who had accompanied him to ride to the stables with his horse, undertook a short ramble on foot through the fields bounding his garden. The sun was hot overhead, and he gladly sought the cool shade of the strip of forest on the hither side of these fields, where, throwing himself on the soft moss, he resigned himself to reflection, which ended in a pleasant noon-day nap. He was wakened by what seemed to him the stamping of horses. Yes, his ears did not deceive him, that was an unmistakable neigh; there must be horses near, but how they came here he was at a loss to divine. There was but a narrow driving road along the edge of this bit of woodland, and it led abroad into the fields in one direction and in the other—yes, in the other out on the road to Plagnitz.

Why should he think of Plagnitz? The road was a highway, and led to other estates likewise, but the fact was that the jealousy lately born of his self-deprecia-tion, and of his immense appreciation of his wife's personal charms and intellectual capacity, was never quite at rest in his mind.

He arose and walked in the direction whence the sound proceeded. Sure enough, on the edge of the forest, drawn up in the shade beside the narrow road-way, stood a light, elegant vehicle, and harnessed to it were two fine horses, which he well remembered to have seen in the Plagnitz stalls. The coachman, too, who had made himself as comfortable as possible on his high seat, was the same fellow whom he remembered to have noticed about the stables at Plagnitz.

But where was the master of this equipage? and why had Herr von Ernau transgressed the physician's orders by this early visit? The answer to the latter question was plain: Herr von Ernau had never forgotten his former love for Bertha von Massenburg, and he was willing to run all risks to enjoy the society of Frau von Wangen. Poor Hugo! his jealousy was no melodramatic passion, but a very uncomfortable, uneasy sensation that quite poisoned his morning's enjoyment. He had entire confidence in his wife's honour, but was not so sure of her discretion; at all events, it 'was confoundedly irritating to think of Von Ernau spending his idle time at Linau, singing his songs and discussing with my wife all the books, in which I never could take the smallest interest. We were very happy before the fellow came.' These were Von Wangen's thoughts as he tried to find some reason for Egon's leaving his equipage at this point, if he had really come to pay a visit at Linau. He walked on to the road, and was about to jump the picket-fence at the bottom of the garden, when he perceived that the key was in the lock of the little gate. It puzzled him to know how it came there. Had it anything to do with Ernau's visit? He opened the gate, and then remembered the winding path to 'the master's arbour.' Surely the lord of Plagnitz was not being received there by the fair lady of Linau. The idea was ridiculous, and yet, instead of taking the left-hand path leading to the house, he walked slowly along that on the right, at the end of which stood the rustic structure. As he approached it, the door, which had partly closed again after Egon's entrance, prevented any view of the interior, but surely those were the tones of a man's voice that struck upon his ear; he advanced more quickly, his steps quite inaudible on the soft moss of the path, when, just as he was about to enter the half-closed door, the same voice, which he had continued to hear, said, in a tone of fervent affection, "Lieschen, dearest Lieschen——" Wangen turned and positively fled, quite dazzled and confused by the light that suddenly dawned upon him, and yet filled with a sense of relief for which he could hardly have accounted to himself. But what would Bertha say? She must have been mistaken in that idea of hers with regard to Ernau's affection for herself; yes, entirely mistaken. And affairs at Osternau must have gone further between the Candidate and his pupil than any one suspected. Now he came to think of it, all the evidence of Ernau's sudden passion for Bertha had been given by Werner von Mässenburg, whose word, as his son-in-law had had frequent opportunities of discovering, was not always to be received with implicit faith. Really this was a delightful ending of affairs, for, as for Bertha's opinion of Fräulein Lieschen, it was all the consequence of those old Osternau misunderstandings. Never could he, Hugo von Wangen, believe that the daughter of his kind old friend was any other than she seemed,—a dear, gentle, unselfish girl. Oh, Bertha would see it all now, and she could not but rejoice, for the sake of Clara, for whom she certainly was beginning to care as a sister should, that Fräulein Lieschen was to be their neighbour at Plagnitz.

Filled with these thoughts, he reached his home, and sought his wife where he was sure to find her,—not however, so much bored as usual, for she was engaged in reading a long letter from her father, which contained an enclosure for her husband, the contents of which Hugo was at no loss to divine.

"What have you to tell me, Hugo? your smile is positively beatific. Has your last purchase of cattle turned out a wonderful bargain, or is the wheat crop on the east meadow twice as heavy as you supposed it would be?"

Hugo laughed good-humouredly; he cared nothing for the pin-pricks of his wife's ridicule. "Oh, better than all that, my darling, although both your suppositions are correct. Circe has gained possession of her victim."

"What do you mean? Nothing short of insanity, Hugo, can drive you to mythology."

"I'm only quoting you, Bertha; when I wish to be convincing I always do so. Herr von Ernau has found his way over here in spite of the doctor, and I played eavesdropper involuntarily just now at the door of 'the master's arbour,' and can assure you that Fräulein Lieschen will not go very far away from Linau. For my part I am delighted, and so will you be, dear child, when you get over the remembrance of old times and your fancied dislike of Fräulein Lieschen. Think what an advantage it is to have such neighbours at Plagnitz! Clara will, I am afraid, spend half her time there."

Bertha had listened in bewildered dismay to her husband's words. How had this result, against which she had schemed, been brought about? How could she endure to have the Lieschen whom she had always detested carry off the prize which she had failed to win? It was scarcely to be hoped that a daughter of Werner von Massenburg's should submit with a good grace to be thus foiled. And yet she was not all worthless. We must leave her, in hopes that Lieschen's unconscious influence may in time assert itself here, as it had so often done elsewhere. Frau von Wangen was assuredly shrewd enough and self-controlled enough, as we have seen, to be outwardly all that could be desired and quite equal to the occasion.

What need to tell of the happiness that reigned in future years at Plagnitz? In Lieschen's joys and in Lieschen's children Frau von Osternau lived over again her own peaceful existence at Osternau. Egon had found that for which he had so thirsted; the discontent and folly of his early time seemed to him like some evil dream, the very memory of which was dispelled by the clear light of love and truth shining in his wife's eyes.

THE END.

CPSIA information can be obtained
at www.ICGtesting.com
Printed in the USA
BVHW05s1321120418
513190BV00010B/239/P